This is an exciting new book. Written largely by emerging researchers from several countries and disciplines, the volume treads a careful and principled line between reflecting on the ways in which young people, especially young women, face a hostile world and highlighting ways in which young people are agents for positive change.

Professor Simon McGrath PhD FAcSS FRSA, *University of Nottingham,*
UNESCO Chair in the Political Economy of Education,
Associate Head of School, UK

For those who want to feel inspired by the possibilities for young people everywhere to live flourishing lives, this is essential reading. Case studies from all over the world show the potential of thinking about youth, gender and social justice through the prism of expanding freedom and opportunities to make life choices.

Monica McLean, *Professor of Education, School of Education,*
University of Nottingham, UK

This is a timely volume which explores how education becomes both an individual and a public good that benefits communities and nations. The editors have done a wonderful job in drawing together the gendered experiences of young people from across the globe. The book is a necessary reference point for those interested in the potential of education in delivering global development.

Parvati Raghuram, *Professor of Geography and Migration*
at the Open University, UK

Youth, Gender and the Capabilities Approach to Development

Youth, Gender and the Capabilities Approach to Development investigates to what extent young people have access to fair opportunities, the factors influencing their aspirations, and how able they are to pursue these aspirations and to carry out their life plans. The book positions itself in the intersection between capabilities, youth and gender, in recognition of the fact that without gender equality, capabilities cannot be universal and development strategies are likely to fail to achieve their full objectives.

Within the framework of the human development and the capabilities approach, *Youth, Gender and the Capabilities Approach to Development* focuses on examples in the areas of education, political spaces, and social practices that confront inequality and injustice head on, by seeking to advance young people's capabilities and their agency to make valuable life plans. The book focuses on how youth policies and issues can be approached globally from a capabilities-friendly perspective; arguing for the promotion of freedoms and opportunities both in educational and political spheres, with the aim of developing a more just world. With a range of studies from multiple and diverse national contexts, including Russia, Spain, South Africa, Tanzania, Morocco, Turkey, Syria, Colombia and India, this important multidisciplinary collection will be of interest to researchers within youth studies, gender studies and development studies, as well as to policy-makers and NGOs.

Aurora Lopez-Fogues is a teacher in a Vocational Education and Training college, researcher in INGENIO (CSIC-UPV) and an Associate Professor at the Universitat Politècnica de València, Spain.

Firdevs Melis Cin is a Postdoctoral Research Associate in the Department of Geography at the Open University, UK.

Routledge Explorations in Development Studies

This Development Studies series features innovative and original research at the regional and global scale. It promotes interdisciplinary scholarly works drawing on a wide spectrum of subject areas, in particular politics, health, economics, rural and urban studies, sociology, environment, anthropology, and conflict studies.

Topics of particular interest are globalisation; emerging powers; children and youth; cities; education; media and communication; technology development; and climate change.

In terms of theory and method, rather than basing itself on any orthodoxy, the series draws broadly on the tool kit of the social sciences in general, emphasizing comparison, the analysis of the structure and processes, and the application of qualitative and quantitative methods.

Youth, Gender and the Capabilities Approach to Development

Rethinking Opportunities and Agency from a Human Development Perspective

Edited by
Aurora Lopez-Fogues and
Firdevs Melis Cin

Routledge
Taylor & Francis Group

LONDON AND NEW YORK

First published 2018 by Routledge

2 Park Square, Milton Park, Abingdon, Oxfordshire OX14 4RN
52 Vanderbilt Avenue, New York, NY 10017

Routledge is an imprint of the Taylor & Francis Group, an informa business

First issued in paperback 2019

British Library Cataloguing in Publication Data
A catalogue record for this book is available from the British Library

Library of Congress Cataloging in Publication Data
A catalog record for this book has been requested

ISBN: 978-1-138-23468-0 (hbk)
ISBN: 978-0-367-26309-6 (pbk)

Typeset in Times New Roman
by Wearset Ltd, Boldon, Tyne and Wear

Dedicated to Martin, Braulio, Belgin and Mesut

Life should not deprive us of childhood without first giving us a good place in youth.

(Miguelito—character in Mafalda, by Quino)

Contents

Figures

Tables

Contributors

Zeynep Balcioglu is a PhD student at the Political Science Department at North-eastern University (Boston, MA). She holds an MA degree in Ethics from King's College London, and a BA degree in Political Science from Bogazici University (Turkey). Her specialisation lies in comparative politics and public policy. Her research interests are migration, social capital, and social and public policies.

Alejandra Boni Aristizábal, Associate Professor at the Universitat Politécnica de València (Spain), Deputy Director of the INGENIO Research Institute (CSIC-UPV), Honorary Professor of the University of the Free State (South Africa), co-convenor of the thematic Education Group of the Human Development and Capability Association and Vice-president of the International Development Ethics Association. Her research interests are human development, higher education, collective social innovation, development education and communication for social change.

Talita Calitz is a lecturer in Education Management and Policy Studies at the University of Pretoria. She holds a PhD from the University of the Free State, South Africa. She works on equality, human development and social justice in higher education.

Firdevs Melis Cin is a Postdoctoral Research Associate in the Department of Geography at the Open University, UK. She holds a PhD from University of Nottingham and a Master's in Education from the University of Dublin, Trinity College. Her research interests include gender, education, development, feminist research and equality and justice in education. She is the author of the book *Gender Justice, Education and Equality: Creating Capabilities for Girls' and Women's Development*.

Gynna Millán Franco is an architect, urban designer and PhD candidate at Queen Mary University of London. She holds an MSc in Building and Urban Design in Development from the Bartlett's Development Planning Unit, University College London (DPU-UCL). She has international experience using video for documentation and inclusive development planning in India, Brazil, Haiti and Bosnia and Herzegovina. Gynna's PhD research focuses on the potential of digital technologies in enhancing and amplifying citizens' participation in the process of decision-making within urban planning.

Leonardo Jiménez García is co-founder of *Corporación para la Comunicación Ciudad Comuna* (Corporation for Communication Ciudad Comuna) (2009), Medellín, Colombia. He is a researcher in the lines of Memory, Territories, Communication for Mobilisation and Social Change and is a Master's student of Education and Human Rights, Universidad Autónoma Latinoamericana. Leonardo has directed participatory social documentaries and is a member of the research group Education and Human Rights from the Universidad Autónoma Latinoamericana.

Natalia Karmaeva is an Associate Professor at the Institute of Education, National Research University, Higher School of Economics (Moscow, Russia). She holds a PhD in Human Development from Bielefeld University (Germany). Her research interests are in the sociology of education, labour market, professionalism, agency, social inequality, and the capability approach.

El-Mahdi Khouaja is a PhD candidate in economics at Aix-Marseille University (France) and a member of the Institute of Labour Economics and Industrial Sociology (LEST). He is also the coordinator and a technical advisor for the public programme against school drop-out in the Aix-Marseille academic district (France). His research interests are in education economics, youth, vocational training, evaluation of public economics, inequalities.

Sonja Loots, at the time of publication, was a researcher at the Centre for Research on Higher Education and Development (CRHED) where her research focused on gender inequalities, equity and social justice in higher education. Currently she is a researcher at the Centre for Teaching and Learning at the University of the Free State, where she focuses on promoting student success through a student engagement lens. She has been the recipient of a CICOPS scholarship from the University of Pavia, Italy and has been involved in several research, academic and student development programmes. She holds a PhD in psychology.

Aurora Lopez-Fogues is a Vocational Education and Training teacher, research fellow at INGENIO (CSIC-UPV) and an Associate Professor at the Universitat Politècnica de València (Spain). She holds a PhD in Education from the University of Nottingham. Her research interests are in the field of education, social justice, youth, learning methodologies and the capability approach.

Sergio Belda-Miquel is a researcher at INGENIO Research Institute (CSIC-UPV) and lecturer at the Universitat Politècnica de València. He holds a PhD in Local Development and International Cooperation. His interests are knowledge, learning and innovation in grassroots organisations; politics and power in international development management.

Ángela Garcés Montoya is an Associate Professor for the Faculty of Communication from the Universidad de Medellín and researcher in the line of Communication and Youth Cultures from the research group Communication. Ángela holds a PhD in Communication from the Universidad Nacional de La Plata and has research experience in the fields of youth cultures, youth collectives of communication and youth's political participation.

Noémie Olympio is an Assistant Professor at the Aix-Marseille University (School of Teaching and Education) and a member of the laboratory ADEF (Learning, Didactic, Education and Training). She completed a PhD in Education Economics at Aix-Marseille University (France) and a postdoctoral fellowship at Laval University (Quebec, Canada) on the operationalisation of the capability approach to an international comparison of education systems. Her interests are in the fields of social justice, the capability approach, education, international comparison, school choice, quantitative and qualitative analysis.

Mari-Anne Okkolin is a sociologist and educationalist, whose research interests focus on gender, education and development, teacher education and teaching profession, human capabilities, and qualitative research methodology. She holds a Master's degree in social sciences and a PhD in education. She's currently a lecturer at the Department of Education, University of Jyväskylä, Finland, and research fellow at the Institute for Reconciliation and Social Justice, University of the Free State, South Africa. Her recent publications include a book entitled *Education, Gender and Development—A Capabilities Perspective.*

Bhavani Ramamoorthi is a Master's degree student in Educational Leadership at the University of Jyväskylä, Finland. She holds a Master's Degree in Home Economics from Bangalore University, India. In addition, she is a certified special educator for children with cerebral palsy. Her work experience includes co-teaching for multi-age classrooms, curriculum development, teacher training and school reforms. Her interests are in the field of educational leadership, teacher development, access to education in the Global South and educational policy.

Gwendoline Promsopha is an associate member at Aix-Marseille University (France) and a member of the Institute for Labour Economics and Industrial Sociology (LEST). She holds a PhD in economics from University of Paris West Nanterre La Defense and a Master's Degree from Sciences-po Paris. Her research interests are in the field of development economics, inequalities, poverty, human development, natural resources and property rights.

Pinar Uyan-Semerci is the Director of the Centre for Migration Research and the head of the International Relations Department at Istanbul Bilgi University. Her research interests lie at the crossroads between political philosophy, social policy and methodology in social sciences. She has coordinated numerous projects and published on topics universalism, justice, rights, participation, citizenship, human development, capability approach, poverty, migration; collective identity formation and well-being of children.

Laksh Venkataraman is an academic with wide range of experience in research, teaching and consultancy works in Development Studies. His publications can be seen in *Development in Practice*; *Indian Journal of Human Development*; *Economic and Political Weekly* among others. He is closely associated with various academic leaders and actively delivers lectures and project presentations both in India and other countries. He has a DPhil from the Universitat Bielefeld in Germany and a Postdoctorate from the University of the Free State in South Africa.

Melanie Walker holds a South African research chair in higher education and human development at the University of the Free State. Her research focuses on the contributions of higher education to reducing inequalities and poverty.

Acknowledgements

The origins of the book trace back almost to the first time we met. We were formally presented to each other by our thesis supervisor Melanie Walker at the University of Nottingham, to whom we dedicate our first and most sincere acknowledgement. We are grateful to Melanie and Monica McLean for being sources of inspiration and for their constant support, guidance and belief in us. Their enthusiasm, commitment and work on human development to make the world—and academia—a better place has, over the years, been an admirable example for both of us.

However, the genesis of the book was not the university, but rather Harrington Drive, NG7 1JJ, where we met as neighbours. It was on that street that we spent three years living next door to each other. There we had the opportunity to get to know each other and share many moments of uncertainty that walks along the canal, homemade meals and wine, made it possible to overcome. From these two neighbouring houses, we went to university every day. Harrington Drive was where we packed suitcases to go to conferences, and to where we returned with our heads buzzing with exciting debates about development, social justice, gender equality or operationalisation. It became our intellectual base camp, where we exchanged these experiences and our friendship. Nevertheless, we were not alone in this camp. We would like to thank all our friends: Julia Long, Earl Kehoe, Tham Nguyen, Ecem Karlıdağ, Monica Gestal and Jon Gurr, for their intellectual debates and friendship, and for contributing to our learning.

As always, an edited book is the combination of many authors. For this reason, we would especially like to acknowledge all the contributing authors, most of whom we have met via the Human Development and Capability Association community, and to whom we are thankful for being a continuous source of stimulating debate.

During the life of the writing and editing of this book we have been very fortunate to enjoy supportive colleagues and mentors in our own locations. Aurora, at the Universitat Politècnica de València and INGENIO (CSIC-UPV) has enjoyed superb working conditions and the invaluable support of Alejandra Boni (Sandra), whose mentorship and care extends beyond the professional arena. This acknowledgement is extended to the big 'INGENIO' family that helped her to think and laugh at the same time. People such as: Victoria Pellicer-Sifres, Sergio Belda-Miquel, Begoña Arias, Teresa de la Fuente, Alvaro Fernández-Baldor, Carola Calabuig, Jose Felix Lozano, Monique Leivas, Maria Ten and Gynna Millan Franco, to mention a few, are responsible for this. Additional thanks go to Simon McGrath and Veronica Crossbie for their constant support. Melis would like to thank her colleagues in Istanbul: Koza Çiftçi Gizem Cesur, Ela Arı, Gökhan Malkoç, Aydın Karaçanta, Ertan Kardeş, Sevda Deneçli, Ceyda Deneçli, Deniz Akçay, Tuba Yağcı Herrera, Rahime Süleymanoğlu-Kürüm, Elvan Şentürk, Bedri Mermutlu, Necmettin Dogan, and Görkem Altınörs, whose emotional and intellectual support were important in finalising this project. Melis owes special thanks—and would like to express her gratefulness—to Dimitrios Anagnostakis, whose endless support in times of despair and disappointment has been so valuable for her to achieve her goals in every aspect of her life. Also, our students both in Valencia and Istanbul, who shared ideas, classes, seminars and discussions and made us aware of the heterogeneity of youth and the need to understand it as a multifaceted variable.

Thanks also to James Hunt, who provided meticulous editorial support by polishing the English of all the contributors, and Leila Walker from Routledge who has been very encouraging towards the project from the outset.

We would also like to acknowledge our respective partners, families and friends. Melis owes her greatest debt to Belgin Cin, her mother, Mesut Cin, her father, Mehmet Melih Cin, her brother, Yelda Baba and Fevzi Baba, her aunt and uncle. Aurora would like to express her gratitude to those of you who supported her during the extra hours of work with help (Braulio M. Lopez and Ana Ferrer), food (Mari Carmen Ramos) or welcoming distractions (sisters, friends, nephews and extended family), and especially to Martin Walter, her husband, and Ingrid, her daughter, for making her smile every day. You make it all worthwhile.

Abbreviations

CA	Capabilities approach
CCE	Caste, class and education
CGE	Commission for Gender Equality
DHET	Department of Higher Education and Training
EUY	Educated unemployed youth
GEAHE	Gender, empowerment, agency and higher education
GER	Gross enrolment rate
GPI	Gender parity index
HCA	Human capital approach
MDG	Millennium development goal
MENA	Middle East and North African
MHYS	Morocco Household and Youth Survey
NER	Net enrolment rate
NYP	National Youth Policy
OBC	Other backward class
OCEMO	Office of Economic Cooperation for the Mediterranean and Middle East
ONDH	National Observatory for Human Development
PAR	Participatory action research
PSD	Participatory social documentary
PV	Participatory video
RFFI	Russian Fund for Fundamental Research
RNF	Russian Scientific Fund
SA	Identifier for data from South African study
SARChI	South African Research Chairs Initiative
SC	Scheduled caste
SDG	Sustainable development goal
SWB	Subjective well-being
TDHS	Tanzania Demographic and Health Survey
TRT	Turkish Radio and Television Corporation
Tz	Identifier for data from Tanzanian study
UN	United Nations

UNDP   United Nations Development Programme
UNFPA   United Nations Population Fund, formerly the United Nations Fund
         for Population Activities
VAK   All-Russian Attestation Commission

Introduction

Aurora Lopez-Fogues and Firdevs Melis Cin

The publication of this book on youth, gender and capabilities aims to signal that there is a large enough cohort of researchers to instigate a change to the perspective under which youth and gender have been traditionally explored. Having said that, youth, gender and the meaning of what a valuable life constitutes, are all contested terms; therefore, the book's first task is to engage researchers who, in different areas, investigate, develop or even put into practice the capability approach as the theoretical umbrella that makes that engagement possible. Thus, the book is concerned with the experiences of youth, and in particular the ways in which gender may play a role on how young people are able to pursue a valuable life, and explores how the capability approach can be applied as a normative framework of analysis to understand multiple gender-related issues surrounding youth, with a particular focus on the public/political platform and education. In so doing, it provides the voices of young people across the world and conceptualises the issues grounded in political life and education from human development and social/gender justice perspectives.

So far, research has not connected young people's challenges to the educational sphere and to social and political constructions, to the contextual level and to personal development. It is often forgotten that education as a fundamental capability leads to debate and public reasoning and establishes a culture of tolerance in which women, especially young women, have an equal say with men and can develop powerful voices to challenge norms and practices that undermine their well-being. However, we need to be aware that some practices and cultures created and perpetuated within educational systems have the potential to thwart capability expansion when institutional regulations and practices do not value everyone equally (Unterhalter, 2007). Hence, there is a need for qualitative research into the aspirations, experiences and perceptions of young people. It is also important to note that the connection between the education one receives and the extent to which one can be a full member of political and social life is significant, as a high-quality education flourishes and nourishes individuals' participation in the public and political spheres, with dignity as citizens, and with agency by being part of collective movements to bring about change (Cin, 2017). Thus, focusing on these two public spheres of young people's lives, we link human development values (e.g. equality, participation, inclusiveness, democratic process and sustainability) and core ideas of the capabilities approach (e.g. well-being, agency, capabilities, functioning, conversion factors, adaptive preferences) to youth issues.

From a methodological aspect, whilst there is no universal definition of 'youth', this book broadly concerns the young people that fall within the United Nations (UN) definition, where 'youth' comprises those aged 15–24 years, but expands it to 30 years old. The chapters here presented offer a reason for the enlargement. They compile stories across the world that evidence the shortcomings of that definition based upon chronological age. The ability for a young person to achieve different status in transition to full adulthood is not based on a chronological age but rather is circumscriptive to conversion factors such as individual traits, social norms and procedures and environmental circumstances (Robeyns, 2003a). Based on the concern with the ability of young people to carry out their life plans and pursue their aspirations, the book places the second focus of attention on the aspect of gender, especially on how this individual trait, at the same time, configures one's genuine opportunities to engage in political practices, such as the effective guaranteeing and protection of freedom of thought, cultural practices and educational achievements, and hence, determines social structures, social institutions, public goods, social norms, traditions or habits.

With a strong emphasis on the issue of equity at the individual and collective-institutional level, the book acknowledges the economic factors that impede the realisation of youth aspirations such as unemployment, level of education, or political changes, but goes beyond this in order to explore the factors that influence the formation of these aspirations, the non-economic factors that shape one's life plans and ultimately the effect that all these have on the realisation of one's well-being, regardless of gender. Without neglecting economic factors, the book centres on the '*doers*' and the conception of inequality and agency—that is, the question of whether all young people have fair opportunities and see themselves as making contributions to fairer societies. Furthermore, in relation to this, the chapters raise interesting questions such as: What role does gender play in the formation of these genuine opportunities? These deeply interwoven issues are critical in the twenty-first century, given that young people, a rich source of dynamism in our societies, globally face a situation marked by high rates of inactivity, mobility, and environmental and societal challenges.

The book stands under the principles that only a culture that is seen and lived by all the members involved in it can create capabilities for everyone in the society, particularly girls and women, to voice injustices in political and social life. Thus, we propose an examination of the aspects of youth related with gender, using the framework of human development and the expansion of human capabilities as cornerstones. This is because gender and gender equality are central to development and we argue that without gender equality, any attempts and strategies of development are likely to fail. Across the world, regardless of location, be it Western Europe, the Global South or North, gender continues to influence and dominate the way inequalities are reproduced and resources and opportunities are distributed. As long as the differences marked by gender exist, development approaches and theories (particularly those in welfare economics and ethics) are less likely to ensure a sustainable understanding of 'human' in thinking about human development (Frediani *et al.*, 2014). Therefore, using a theoretical framework drawn from the human development and the capabilities approach of Amartya Sen (1999, 2009) and Martha Nussbaum (2000, 2011), the book offers a contribution to scholarship and future research on gender and youth by engaging with the capability approach critically and outlining how the core tenet of the approach can guide us to understand the issues around youth empirically.

I The core tenets of the capability approach

What is the capability approach?

The traditional human development approaches have remained at a macro perspective throughout the years, where they have been concerned with measuring economic growth as an important indication for assessing development. Such a perspective was very much influenced by the United Nations Development Programme's (UNDP) institutional role of supporting national governments by ignoring the policies that could provide micro-dimensional analysis, addressing the political space and civil society (Comim and Nussbaum, 2014). However, the aim of broadening welfarist policies based on utilitarian principles in traditional human development approaches requires a freedom perspective, as they cannot provide us with the necessary lenses to think in broader terms about social justice and human development. This can be best informed by the capability approach.

The capability approach, as developed by Nobel Laureate Amartya Sen and Martha Nussbaum, assesses well-being in terms of people's ability to function and whether they are provided with the real opportunities—the capabilities—to function in ways that matter to them, so that they can choose the lives they have reason to value. Functionings are the beings and doings of a person—such as working, resting, or being healthy. Capabilities are the combinations of functionings that a person holds the possibility of achieving (Sen, 1993: 31)—such as having the conditions for freedom of speech, having the conditions (hospital, healthcare workers) to recover from an illness. So, capabilities are opportunities or freedoms to achieve what an individual reflectively considers valuable. Thus, within the remit of this book, the capability approach would ask to what extent a young person is able to construct his or her 'capability space', which in turn would require a broader informational base than traditional performance measurements, which are solely based on level of education, background or economic context. This is because the evaluation of equality should focus on the freedom in opportunities and choices. Both Sen (1999) and Nussbaum (2000) stress the importance of looking into capabilities because one may have the functionings, but may not necessarily have the resources or social and political context to turn the capabilities into functionings. So, the approach makes interpersonal comparisons and scrutinises whether the circumstances in which people make choices are just, and pays attention to resources, economic growth, social cohesion, social institutions, and the availability of commodities and legal entitlements, stressing that these are means to well-being. Therefore, it is crucial to question to what extent people have genuine access rather than mere preferences to operationalise their capabilities.

The issue of preferences takes us to the concepts of choice and adaptive preferences. Unequal circumstances can lead to unequal capacities to choose, because the choices we make are shaped by the opportunities available to us and the context we are situated in (Nussbaum, 2000). For instance, a girl may think she does not need an education because her main duties are domestic duties and childcare. This means the girl adapts what is valuable to herself according to the norms and conditions in which she lives and her preference for not receiving an education is formed without her control or awareness of opportunities and the existence of other options, by a causal mechanism that is not of her own choice (Nussbaum, 2000). Such preferences can limit not only choices and capabilities, but also aspirations for the future.

Additionally, the concept of conversion factors that enable, influence and constrain the beings and doings also require elucidation to understand how capabilities work. Sen (2009: 255) identifies four factors that affect one's choices and conversion of capabilities: personal heterogeneities (age, gender, disability, proneness to illness), physical environment (environmental conditions, including climatic circumstances, such as temperature ranges or flooding), social climate (social conditions, public healthcare, community resources, policies and practices, public educational arrangements), and relational perspectives (patterns of behaviour in a community that can affect one's choices and capabilities). Each individual may vary greatly in their needs for resources or abilities to achieve their valued capabilities (Nussbaum, 2000: 68). Therefore, the approach takes each human being as an end, and rests on the idea of ethical individualism, which takes every individual as a subject of their own lives and 'primary objects of moral concern' (Brighouse and Swift, 2003: 258) and evaluates the actions according to their effects on individuals. In this sense, the approach is sensitive to human diversity and argues that people can reflect on what they value not only for themselves, but also for others. The approach regards individuals as an extension of their social environment where, as an agent, they are socially embedded and connected to others. It is primarily based upon ethical individualism but it is not ontologically individualistic. Thus, it accounts for social and environmental factors, discriminatory practices, social relations, constraints and structures that impact on individuals' choices and capabilities (Robeyns, 2003a: 64). Social structures and institutions are the means of capability sets, not the ends.

Although Sen and Nussbaum collaboratively developed the approach as a means to scrutinise, question and assess human development, they also have a different take on the capability approach; Sen's work is grounded in economic reasoning, poverty, and participatory human development, whereas Nussbaum's work focuses on moral, legal and political philosophy, arguing for the political principles that should underlie a constitution to secure the rights of citizens. Nussbaum's approach engages with narratives and texts to better understand people's lives (Robeyns, 2005) and advocates that each person has the right to live their life as they choose and is responsible for their own determined values. Therefore, Nussbaum's approach pays more attention to people's actions, aspirations and desires, which makes it more individualistic and humanistic than Sen's approach. Sen's approach, on the other hand, makes a significant contribution by advocating that capabilities should be the space of comparison if we are to think about theories of social and gender justice, and that utilitarian, resource-focused or preference-based analyses are inadequate in addressing human development. Yet, Nussbaum's conceptualisation of the capabilities approach has an Aristotelian philosophical perspective, largely based on 'a good political arrangement' and 'capabilities to have a fully flourishing life' (Nussbaum, 2000: xiii), which directed her to work on a number of non-commensurable lists of capabilities needed for a life with dignity.

Inspired by Rawls' list of primary goods,[1] she argues for a list of ten central human capabilities[2] based on the idea of social justice. She argues that her list is not rigid and definite, but 'open-ended and humble' and 'can always be contested and remade' (Nussbaum, 2000: 77) or adjusted to different legislatures and courts. It can be adopted according to cultural needs, which makes it sensitive to cultural differences and pluralism and it is a consensus of cross-cultural discussions and debates on the international platform about how a life with full human dignity can be maintained, and it is free of any metaphysical, religious, political or ethical views. This is the point where we see a divergence in the understanding of Sen and Nussbaum. According to Sen, the list closes the way for any deliberation or dialogical democratic process or discussion and offers a paternalistic approach on what capabilities are best. Instead, he argues that those who are affected by any policy or practice should be the ones to decide on what will count as valuable capabilities. Yet, as can be seen in the stories and lives of young people in this book, the danger of bias is a central concern in societies where cultural practices or political system subordinate and exclude certain segments of the society. Therefore, not all freedoms are good and of equal worth—some freedoms can have bad dimensions and some freedoms can limit others (Nussbaum, 2000)—and a concrete non-commensurable list of capabilities to protect the vulnerable and the disadvantaged individuals and groups in the society may be desirable. Although Sen offers a vague stand on which capabilities matter in our ethical judgement, his take on the concept of agency in the capability approach offers us a robust ground to talk about genuine human freedoms and well-being.

Agency

Agency is a key concept that intertwines with the development paradigm taken in the book and articulates it synchronically with youth and gender studies, where this concept may adopt the form of empowerment, being a leader or a doer, amongst others. Asking people which capabilities are valuable or how well they are doing is not sufficient for assessing or advancing well-being, it is essential to look at the agency of individuals to see whether they decide on what matters to them. People need to be understood as 'active participants in change rather than ... passive and docile recipients of instruction or of dispensed assistance' (Sen, 1999: 281). Thus, an agent is an individual who is willing to have a shared responsibility for building a process that ensures everyone's capabilities to decide, to self-determine and to bring about change in the world (Crocker, 2008). Concretely, capabilities can be generated through individual efforts and collective processes and, similarly, agency can be individual as well as collective (Ibrahim, 2006). Here, the collective agency means individuals responsible for the development and empowerment of their own community and country (Crocker, 2008).

Accordingly, Sen (1985, 2009) distinguishes between well-being achievement and agency achievement, and well-being freedom and agency freedom. Well-being achievement is related to a person's 'wellness' or 'personal welfare'. Well-being freedom is concerned with whether people have the freedom to choose to fulfil their own well-being—namely, to possess capabilities. Well-being, regardless of whether it is a functioning or a capability, is often part of a person's objectives. It does not stand for their valued objectives or goals. Agency includes all the goals that a person has reason to adopt, including goals other than his or her own well-being. A person's agency achievement refers to the realisation of goals and values she has reason to pursue, whether or not they are connected with her own well-being. Agency freedom is more general and related to what the person is free to do and achieving the goals s/he regards as important.

Robeyns (2003b) exemplifies the distinction between agency and well-being and between freedom and achievement:

Suppose two sisters, Anna and Becca, live in a peaceful village in England and have the same achieved well-being levels. Both of them believe that the power of global corporations is undermining democracy, and that governments should prioritize global justice and the fight against poverty in the South instead of taking care of the interests of global corporations. Anna decides to travel to an Italian town to demonstrate against the G8 meetings, while Becca stays home. At that moment Anna is using her agency freedom to voice some of her political concerns. However, the Italian police do not like the protesters and violate Anna's civil and political rights by beating her up in prison. Obviously Anna's achieved well-being has lowered considerably (as has her standard of living). Anna is offered the opportunity to sign a piece of paper declaring that she committed violence organised by an extreme-left organisation (which will give her a criminal record and ban her from any further G8 demonstrations). If she does not sign, she will be kept in prison for a further unspecified time. At that moment, Anna has a (highly constrained) option to trade off her agency freedom for higher achieved well-being, which our heroine refuses. Becca had the same agency freedom to voice her concerns and protest against either the G8 itself or against the way the Italian police officers abused their power, but chose not to do so. She is concerned about the hollowing of democracy, the protection of human rights and the fascist tendencies among some police officers, but does not want to sacrifice her well-being to achieve these agency goals.

(Robeyns, 2003b: 16)

This example shows that humans can possess altruistic goals and risk their own well-being for that of others, or in pursuing what they value. Becca sacrificed agency freedom for well-being achievement, whereas Anna was driven into a situation where agency freedom meant more to her than well-being achievement. This example also shows that humans are not only led by their egoism or animal instincts to fulfil their own self-interests and needs, but may also devote themselves to causes beyond their own welfare, such as improving the opportunities of others or creating change in society (Sen, 1990). Therefore, agency can have both self-regarding and other-regarding motivation. This means that individuals are not only driven by their self-interest or to achieve the goals that matter only to them, but also engage in goals for community good and social change. 'The agent' is someone who not only pursues their interest goals, but also cares for others, and can sacrifice their health or life for valued objectives.

Agency, used throughout the book, is taken to mean that each person has a dignity and responsibility and shapes his or her own life in accordance with what they value, rather than simply being shaped or instructed how to think (Walker and Unterhalter, 2007). One's life matters beyond being healthy, voting, working or studying and without the agency concept, capabilities and functionings cannot explain everything about human life. Therefore, we need the concept of agency to contemplate young people's individual or collective actions, desires and motivations that lead them to act beyond their self-interests. The chapters of this book span different contexts and show us how the concept of agency for the sake of well-being is strongly emphasised and expressed as a form of resistance, an indicator of maintaining livelihoods and initiating a change.

Why the capability approach?

Capability as a measure of equality, offers a method for evaluating a policy, or a society, on the basis of the freedom that it gives individuals to reflectively develop plans and choose how to act to achieve them. The capabilities approach is useful as far as its advocates see it as an approach rather than a well-defined theory (Deneulin and Shahani, 2009; Sen, 2009; Nussbaum, 2003; Alkire, 2005). Robeyns (2003a: 8) offers three ways of using this framework, as outlined:

- As a framework of thought for the evaluation of individual opportunities and recommendations for social arrangements.

- As a critique of other approaches (mainly commodities, primary goods, or basic needs) as appropriate to the evaluation of well-being and justice.
- As a formula to make interpersonal comparisons of welfare or well-being into a well-defined theory.

Throughout the book, different uses of the capabilities approach can be seen. However, a central aspect is the use of the capabilities approach as a theoretical contribution of centring the debate on people, which is a key aspect to examine whether there is a gender-specific manifestation of agency.

By considering every individual as an able being who is willing to participate in every sphere of life, barriers such as social norms, personal abilities or environmental conditions move from being an individual issue, to a shared responsibility for building a process that ensures everyone's capabilities to decide, to self-determine and to bring about change in the world (Crocker, 2008). The concept of agents as individuals who decide and act but who also have the real freedom to bring about change, defines individuals as social beings interested in goals beyond individual well-being, but who, in their daily actions, can constrain or impede other people's agencies. Concretely, the approach acknowledges that capabilities can be generated through individual efforts and collective processes and, similarly, agency can be individual as well as collective (Evans, 2002; Kabeer, 2003; Ibrahim, 2006). The capabilities and level of agency development achieved through the collectivity is, as argued by Ibrahim (2006), something that the individual alone would neither have, nor be able to achieve. In conclusion, attention would need to be given to the diversities of people, range of aspirations, and formal and informal structures and conditions that act as enhancers or barriers to one's freedoms and agency. While the focus is on individual well-being, this lens would also focus attention upon collective well-being and collective capabilities and agency, in relationship with how interactions, values and societal norms and practices interact with one's confidence, knowledge, values and perceptions of what they ought to be and do. Therefore, the approach, in configuring a diverse lens on youth and gender, has considerable potential in relation to justice; yet it is still undeveloped in this respect. Consequently, our conceptual framework combines an analysis of social institutions with attention to structural and relational factors that demonstrate how development, or lack of capability development, has an impact on the lives of young people and the enactment of their agencies. The main capability domains analysed here are: (1) restricted opportunities for the development of capabilities through education or in education; (2) limitations on political and civil liberties, agency, gender justice; and (3) gender inequalities within the lives of youth. Although these make up the core capability domains, we also use the capabilities approach as an 'umbrella gender-justice' approach to offer a normative and global framework that is concerned with widening opportunities and freedoms. In this framework, education is a fundamental capability, given that it allows individuals to develop critical reflection and cultivate their minds, and as such is crucial to development and creating active agents of social change.

II Conceptualising youth, gender and capabilities

Whilst research using the capability approach is well-established, especially in the area of education (Walker and Unterhalter, 2007; Walker and McLean, 2013; Boni and Walker, 2016), the specific contribution of this book lies in it going beyond an area of study and focusing on the qualities of the subjects: youth and gender. Regardless of global concern, research on youth has not been theorised in an integrated manner to evidence the complex challenges at the intersection of aspirations, inequality, inclusive development, gender discrepancies and the political space. Research may address one of these dimensions, but fails to coherently address and integrate them in the way that this collection of research, conducted in various parts of the world, does successfully. Within the perspective of the capability approach, deprivation in young people's capabilities goes beyond the lack of income that impedes some core capabilities, such as lack of education, health, and the channels to participate in economic life and in decision-making (Fukuda-Parr, 1999; Wolff and de-Shalit, 2007). It rather provides an alternative framework to resourcist or instrumental approaches by focusing on the individual rather than on pre-established and normative outcomes.

A dominant theme in Sen's writings is the promotion of human well-being and development, understood as agency or the enhancement of one's capabilities. From this perspective, a young person needs to be analysed within the space of capabilities, understood as the genuine opportunities that they have in order to lead a meaningful life. Capability scholars have put emphasis on the barriers and difficulties that children and young people have in accessing educational opportunities for fostering core capabilities such as critical thinking, self-reflection or awareness (Unterhalter and Brighouse, 2007; Walker, 2005; Nussbaum, 1999). Within this field, there is a special concern for young people living in the developing world (McGrath, 2010; Tikly and Barrett, 2011), where in many cases the educational systems are being built, but in many countries, it is still with the purpose of producing and reproducing the privileged elites (Katusiime, 2014). Special attention is also paid to the conditions that make young people vulnerable, these being individual traits in the areas of: disabilities (Biggeri *et al.*, 2011; Terzi, 2005; Mitra, 2006); gender (Cin, 2017); and with much less intensity, the study of race (Lezama, 2009; Marovah, 2015). Another area that has attracted the attention of capability scholars is the study of socio-economic factors such as the labour situation (Egdell and Graham, 2016; Egdell and McQuaid, 2014; Kjeldsen and Bonvin, 2015), livelihood conditions (Oughton and Wheelock, 2003; Bebbington, 1999, Scoones, 1998). Essentially, the literature written in the light of the capabilities approach describes and explains the conditions and possibilities of human development in terms of what Robeyns (2005) coined 'conversion factors'. Based on individual traits such as mental ability, health, ethnic origin, and social conditions—understood as the laws, norms and costumes or institutional support that the person may or may not receive and the environmental conditions that foster or impede the development of concrete actions—each young person would be able to frame a determined number of options. Research pointing at the use of the capability approach as an evaluative tool for determining the political space is intertwined with the theoretical literature of the area (Alkire, 2005; Gasper, 2007; Deneulin and McGregor, 2010) but it has not been concerned with experiences of youth in educational and political spheres.

Under the capability lenses, youth is understood different ways. Here, youth is a social construct and a product of historical circumstances rather than a physical category. It has a normative description and elements, such as the characteristics attributed to young people of different sex, how they are treated and how society values them (Ansell, 2016). Our understanding of youth rests on defining them as potential threatening political actors that can change and challenge society but, at the same time, that are in need of a political remedy to provide them with empowerment and development. Much of the youth literature deals with particular groups, such as those based on gender, ethnicity, class and religion; and specific problems, such as exclusion, abuse, school dropout or oppression, which concern government and development issues (Rumberger, 2001; Ginwright and Cammarota, 2002). We take on that literature and expand it by applying the capability and gender lenses to the analysis of youth. Whilst there is no universal definition of what counts as youth, for instance, the UN defines it as individuals aged between 15 and 24 although it also uses different terms for young people of different ages, such as adolescent, teenager or young adult. Yet, there are some common experiences of youth across the world, such as participation, age-based discrimination, gender-based discrimination, health care and education needs, and their role in public and political space. These experiences are more important than the specific age concerned (Boyden and Ennew, 1997). Therefore, this book extends the age range proposed by the UN and broadly concerns all young people that are aged between 15 and 30 years. However, what unites the young people researched in this book is woven through the particular issues of education and political participation marked by gender and gender inequalities and affected by development in different ways.

The interdisciplinary and international character of this volume aims at assessing the situation of youth from an interlinked perspective that contributes by joining the gender perspective with the educational one, with a particular focus on political structures.

The volume argues through a wide arrange of case studies that youth deprivation in terms of individual traits, education or social conditions is not only a burden for individuals, as well as societies from an utilitarian and economic point of view, but also that it diminishes individual well-being and future prospects for the young people to fully become agents in terms of raising their voices for democratic participation, opportunities for self-realisation and contribution to a less unjust world. Consequently, the starting point of the volume is to address the question of youth from the observation that a high number of young people are disaffiliated in social life, leading to the question as to what extent an analysis from a capability perspective can re-direct the analysis and, hence, the particular policies targeting that.

The questions of gender and gender inequality pervade the lives of young people. The book provides an examination of the aspects of youth related with gender, using the framework of human development and the expansion of human capabilities as cornerstones. Amartya Sen's work on the capability approach has been critical to understand the gender aspect and has led to the development of gender analysis. The capability approach offers a space to compare justice-related issues, including gender justice, and examines the underlying gender order and related asymmetries. To illuminate this, the authors tackle a wide range of gender issues in young people's lives including, religion, social justice, child care, political participation, poverty, gender-based division of labour or misrepresentation. To elucidate gender, we, as editors, challenge the understanding that equality depends on numbers. Our understanding of gender in this book extends beyond numerical terms and looks into political, social, cultural and traditional structures, relationships with society, family relations, poverty, and political and cultural contexts as they all influence the opportunities that one person, regardless of their gender, has to lead a valuable life. We address gender from a relational and comparative account and represent it as an analytical and normative idea in order to open meanings of gender. This means we acknowledge that studying young women's and girls' lives is not necessarily an equivalent of researching gender; however, we also look into young men's and boys' lives to draw relational comparisons and offer a 'voice-centred' perspective on the human development and capabilities perspective. At the same time, we go beyond taking gender as a category or vis-à-vis comparison of men and women, or boys and girls and unravel the meanings of gender by looking into gendered relations of power, distribution of resources, issues of representation and participation in public and education settings, and gender fluid and changing identities, performance and actions in different contexts. We address different patterns of behaviour and social categorisations that differ according to gender, such as gender roles, masculinities and femininities, identities of young men and women, and focus on the explanation of gendered practices of social power, status, organisation and relations. This is because power structures and categorisations and identities related to gender differ across different cultures and societies are embedded within cultural and historical discursive practices. Gender, as much as a sociological construct, is also a historical and an economical construct. It contests history, politics and ideas and power, and provides historically located analyses of women, girls and relations and the changing space in its movement between times, spaces and discursive forms. It is implicated and reproduced in economic relations, particularly in the commodification of education, labour force, and wage relations and care and domestic labour (Unterhalter, 2014), which positions women and young people to a comparatively disadvantaged status, 'cheap labour force' or a 'precariat' in todays' capitalist setting, economy and societies. To address concerns of gender, getting girls into school, increasing women's participation in the labour force, making more women visible in the political, public or decision-making platform may be read as the significant indicators of development; but if they occlude discussions of socio-economic relations, livelihoods, what is thought at school or relationships associated with discrimination, inequality, sexism and the politics of who represents what to whom (Koffman and Gill, 2013), then challenging gender remains at a rhetorical level.

Thus, gender operates at levels of material, social, ethical, historical and representational relationships and helps us capture interconnections and multidimensionality. Therefore, when combining gender with capabilities literature and research, we tease out the hegemony and traditional notions that place women and men in different positions in society, determine the extent to which social, political and economic opportunities that are available to both genders qualify the freedom of agency they can have. In this sense, gender offers us a transcultural and complex analytical tool to understand the structural conditions that directly affect one's genuine abilities, aspirations and opportunities and to look into the improvement of the quality of young women's and men's lives and what stands in the way of their enactment of agency and freedoms that could lead to structural transformation and development.

This edited book is, therefore, located at the intersection of youth, gender and capabilities studies. The chapters focus on the agency and capabilities of young people, considering how youth and gender dimensions have a role upon their reflection, lives and desires. Yet it should be noted that whilst the central focus is on young people's lives and experiences, the dimensions of gender and youth may not be always the dominant concepts in the chapters, and that being young might matter more in some contexts whereas being a woman or the issue of gender can be less or more determinant on one's agency and capability sets. This does not mean that these chapters or the young lives across the world have little to say about gender or being young. On the contrary, within this fluctuation, the concepts of gender and youth are collaboratively woven and threaded throughout the chapters as they focus on examples in the areas of education, political spaces, and social practices that go against the current and confront inequality and injustice head on, by seeking to advance young people's capabilities and functionings and their agency to make valuable life plans. The book presents and touches upon the lives of diverse young people who are students, migrants, refugees, conservatives, professionals and activists. Rather than only seeking to critique and evidence gender disparities and how the structures or spaces mentioned above impede the advancement of social justice, here our focus also strengthens cases that advance social justice and gender equity. As such, the book creates a platform for the analysis of cases and the sharing of good practices to enhance participation and inclusion amongst diverse young people. It brings together 19 authors working in the field and located in various countries, with a range of specialisations in terms of research and practice. The examples, taken from across the world, offer helpful starting points for ongoing dialogue and action on the way that youth is portrayed. Rather than a homogenous group of people, young people represent an array of diversity in which the gender and capability lenses are helpful in interrogating and analysing how relationships are constructed and developed.

III Organisation of the book

The chapters consider gender, youth and capabilities dynamics in the two most important contexts for young people: the educational and political spheres. Inside the educational arena, aspects of pedagogy, participation, migration, and educational transitions and labour paths are investigated. Regarding the political and social sphere, collective action, political freedoms, political participation and well-being are the primary focuses. Throughout the chapters, the aspect of gender is transversal in its multiple forms; it is explored across multiple and diverse national contexts, including Russia, Spain, South Africa, Tanzania, Morocco, Turkey, Syria, Colombia and India.

Our central aim in selecting the chapters has first been to identify rich examples of practices, situations and factors in which gender and youth were constant variables able to offer the diverse array of reasons behind one's ability to imagine and develop life plans. Thus, from the area of education and the socio-political sphere, together the chapters tell a holistic story about social justice. In addition, we have sought to ensure that a range of national contexts and methods (qualitative and quantitative analysis are provided) are included in order to demonstrate the potential of a capability and gender perspective to analyse youth globally. This range of contributors locates the global relevance and interest of the book within the rich contexts of local specificities to which educational and political authorities and professionals must also respond. It is also important to note that the book provides a methodologically rich approach and draws from qualitative paradigm of ethnographic research, participatory methods and quantitative methods and thus discovers experiences and lives of the young through different arrays of epistemic production.

We have organised the book into two parts. Part I: Aspirations and agency: issues of gender and justice in the educational programmes and spheres; and Part II: Political and public space: development and enactment of agency and capabilities for change and justice.

Part I is comprised of five chapters that tackle a range of contexts and look into challenges of access, participation, recognition and voice in education, which are closely related with the issues of youth participation, recognition and representation in the political and public domains. The failure of the former often leads to the exclusion of youth in the latter. In dealing with education and the educational sphere, we are not only interested in the challenges young people face or the extent to which education is liberating, empowering or distributing justice to their lives, but we also look into how young people work in the educational sphere, to see whether they have the agency and opportunities to challenge the inequalities within the system or how they are articulated within the current inequalities by limited resources and freedoms.

The chapter by Melanie Walker and Sonja Loots examines how gender equality is discussed in national and university education policies and sets out to understand gender inequalities in higher education in the South African context. The chapter presents capability sets that both male and female students value regarding gender equality and which opportunities these women and men find important for their personal development and—directly and indirectly—for gender equality, which provides a guidance for policy-makers for advancing well-being, agency and gender justice in policy and everyday practices.

Mari-Anne Okkolin and Bhavani Ramamoorthi's chapter draws on the experiences of young adults in Tanzania and South Africa and looks at female and male students who have reached higher education, with a focus of analysis on the critical issues that enabled them to reach higher education, understood as their well-being freedoms. It presents narrative accounts considering their school environments and familial contexts and focuses on the intersectionalities of race *and* class *and* gender to provide a better understanding of the multidimensional nature of educational well-being in Tanzania and South Africa, which can manifest and actualise in the planning and implementation of youth policies.

Talita Calitz offers an innovative method of a longitudinal participatory research to investigate the freedoms of female young black university students from working-class backgrounds in South Africa and argues that the socio-economic vulnerability and academic marginality they face navigate an intersecting range of structural barriers at university. She also foregrounds agency by demonstrating how these young women negotiated these barriers to resist a deficit view of their ability to participate in higher education. Her contribution touches upon the intersectionality of poverty, gender, socio-economic class and race of first-generation university students in the Global South.

Natalia Karmaeva touches upon young people's experiences as professionals in higher education and looks into structures working towards the marginalisation of the positions of young female academics in Russia. She discusses gender inequality from the perspective of the 'practical reason'. It is defined as a capability that represents 'being able to form a conception of the good and to engage in critical reflection about the planning of one's life' (Nussbaum, 2000), in universities located in the biggest cities and in the smaller regional centres in Russia, and teases out how gendered framings of academic roles or insufficient funding and lack of access to research grants make young female academics dependent on the support of their families. Her work enhances our understanding on the precarious conditions that young academics and professionals face in the neo-liberal world and settings.

Laksh Venkataraman deconstructs the intersectional complexities of caste, class and gender dynamics. Drawing from extensive ethnographic research, he underlines the intricacies of employability in south India. He analyses the human agency of the educated un/under-employed youths, and argues that, as opposed to the belief that education is an automatic solution for all development-ills, class, gender and caste still comprise a significant catalyst for the well-being and agency of young people.

All these chapters contribute to the understanding of how public policies, power relations and social structures influence the achievement of young people's basic capability of education, and how gender works as a primary frame of inequalities within education or caused by education. Thus, this part provides a generative account for thinking about and transforming education for gender equality so that it can lead to the formation of democratic citizens and enhance the necessary capabilities of the political effectiveness of youth, which are necessary for development.

In Part II, six chapters, each written from a different national context, show the challenges and lack of freedoms experienced by youth in accessing or creating change in public and political space. In the political dimension, the chapters take public space as an avenue for reaching political consensus, allowing dialogue and stimulating sociability. The chapters identify how gender acts with discriminatory social institutions, norms and practices that deny young women the ability to reach their full potential, and seeks to understand how this potential is both constructed and limited.

The chapter by Ángela Garcés Montoya and Leonardo Jiménez García shows how participatory and digital technologies can socially empower young people by giving voice to marginalised communities outlining personal barriers such as gender, status or geographical location. They underline the importance of media in young people's lives and how it can be used to generate bonds of unity among the inhabitants of the territory and generate collective youth agency among Columbian Youth.

Likewise, Aurora Lopez-Fogues, Alejandra Boni Aristizábal, Gynna Millán Franco and Sergio Belda-Miquel use participatory video (PV) to promote community empowerment and to enable young people living in urban Spain in—apparently—developed scenarios, to articulate their own perceptions on decisions that directly affect their daily realities overcoming structural barriers. Through giving voice to the young people, they provide an intersectional analysis where gender and level of education are variables to take into account, and flesh out the themes of participation, quality employment or education as demands to be taken into account when designing and implementing future youth policies.

El-Mahdi Khouaja, Noémie Olympio and Gwendoline Promsopha investigate how gender shapes youth's aspirations, subjective well-being (SWB) and capabilities in Morocco by operationalising capabilities through mixed methods (quantitative and qualitative) based on an innovative dataset collected by the Office of Economic Cooperation for Mediterranean and Middle East (OCEMO), among young Moroccan individuals living in rural and urban areas of the Marrakesh region and qualitative data collected in Morocco. They reveal the striking significance of adaptive preferences among rural young women; as well as the frustrations among young educated men resulting from an inability to fulfil a chosen lifestyle.

Zeynep Balcıoğlu unpacks the social relations among young Syrian women immigrants and refugees in Turkey and argues how social capital shapes information channels, patterns of inclusion and exclusion and trust networks of refugees and how they maintain their livelihoods. She scrutinises the way these women use the capability of social capital to overcome daily constraints along with the forced migration they face.

Pinar Uyan-Semerci and Firdevs Melis Cin provide an interesting—and one of the earliest and most recent—analysis of women's participation in resisting the July 2016 attempted coup d'état in Turkey. Drawing from the interviews, they argue that the women appearing on the streets on the night of the attempt were mostly from conservative backgrounds—who would not be usually seen in a public platform for political resistance—and explore the motivations of these women in relation to collective capabilities.

So, Part II offers experiences of how youth participate in the public sphere and how gender acts in a way that (dis)empowers young people from obtaining roles in the public sphere.

The book, in this sense, shows that the ability to plan a valuable life or the formation of capabilities is closely connected with realising what role is foreseen for young women and men in societies from different geographical locations, but what they all share is that they are strongly divided along gendered lines of doing, labour and behaviour. The book not only aims to highlight this intersectionality, but also offers support and evidence regarding the everyday difficulties and struggles faced by youth.

Notes

1 Rawls' listed primary goods are: basic rights and liberties; freedom of movement and free choice of occupation against a background of diverse opportunities; powers and prerogatives of offices and positions of responsibility in the political and economic institutions of the basic structure; income and wealth; the social bases of self-respect (Rawls, 2013: 181).
2 Nussbaum's list has ten central human capabilities: life; bodily health; bodily integrity; senses, imagination and thought; emotions; practical reason; affiliation; other species; play; control over one's environment (Nussbaum, 2000: 78–80).

References

Alkire, S. (2005). Why the capability approach? *Journal of human development*, 6(1), 115–135.
Ansell, N. (2016). *Children, youth and development*. London: Routledge.
Bebbington, A. (1999). Capitals and capabilities: a framework for analyzing peasant viability, rural livelihoods and poverty. *World development*, 27(12), 2021–2044.
Biggeri, M., Bellanca, N., Bonfanti, S. and Tanzj, L. (2011). Rethinking policies for persons with disabilities through the capability approach: the case of the Tuscany Region. *ALTER-European journal of disability research/revue Européenne de recherche sur le handicap*, 5(3), 177–191.
Boni, A. and Walker, M. (2016). *Universities and global human development: theoretical and empirical insights for social change*. London: Routledge.
Boyden, J. and Ennew, J. (1997). *Children in focus: a manual for participatory research with children*. Stockholm: RäddaBarnen.

Brighouse, H. and Swift, A. (2003). Defending liberalism in education theory. *Journal of education policy*, 18(4), 355–373.

Cin, F. M. (2017). *Gender justice, education and equality: creating capabilities for girls' and women's development*. Cham: Palgrave.

Comim, Flavio and Nussbaum, Martha C. (2014). *Capabilities, gender, equality*. Cambridge, UK: Cambridge University Press.

Crocker, D. A. (2008). *Ethics of global development: agency, capability, and deliberative democracy*. Cambridge: Cambridge University Press.

Deneulin, S. and McGregor, J. A. (2010). The capability approach and the politics of a social conception of wellbeing. *European journal of social theory*, 13(4), 501–519.

Deneulin, S. and Shahani, L. (2009). *An introduction to the human development and capability approach: freedom and agency*. IDRC. Ottawa: Earthscan.

Egdell, V. and Graham, H. (2016). A capability approach to unemployed young people's voice and agency in the development and implementation of employment activation policies. *Social policy and administration*. DOI: 10.1111/spol.12262.

Egdell, V. and McQuaid, R. (2016). Supporting disadvantaged young people into work: insights from the capability approach. *Social policy and administration*, 50(1), 99–118.

Evans, P. (2002). Collective capabilities, culture, and Amartya Sen's development as freedom. *Studies in comparative international development*, 37(2), 54–60.

Frediani, A., Boni, A. and Gasper, D. (2014). Approaching development projects from a human development and capability perspective. *Journal of human development and capabilities*, 15(1), 1–12.

Fukuda-Parr, S. (1999). What does feminization of poverty mean? It isn't just lack of income. *Feminist economics*, 5(2), 99–103.

Gasper, D. (2007). What is the capability approach? Its core, rationale, partners and dangers. *Journal of socio-economics*, 36(3), 335–359.

Ginwright, S. and Cammarota, J. (2002). New terrain in youth development: the promise of a social justice approach. *Social justice*, 29(4), 82–95.

Ibrahim, S. S. (2006). From individual to collective capabilities: the capability approach as a conceptual framework for self-help. *Journal of human development*, 7(3), 397–416.

Kabeer, N. (2003). Making rights work for the poor: Nijera Kori and the construction of 'collective capabilities' in rural Bangladesh. Brighton: Institute of Development Studies.

Katusiime, D. (2014). An enhanced human development capability approach to education: implications for technical vocational education and training policy in Uganda (Doctoral dissertation, Kent State University).

Kjeldsen, C. C. and Bonvin, J. M. (2015). The capability approach, education and the labour market. In: *Facing trajectories from school to work* (pp. 19–34). Switzerland: Springer International Publishing.

Koffman, O. and Gill, R. (2013). The revolution will be led by a 12-year-old girl: 1 girl power and global biopolitics. *Feminist review*, 105(1), 83–102.

Lezama, P. (2009). Afro-Colombian welfare: an application of Amartya Sen's capability approach using multiple indicators multiple causes modelling—MIMIC. Graduate Theses and Dissertations. University of South Florida. Scholar Commons.

McGrath, S. (2010). The role of education in development: an educationalist's response to some recent work in development economics. *Comparative education*, 46(2), 237–253.

Marovah, T. (2015). Using the capability approach to conceptualise African identity(ies). *Phronimon*, 16(2), 42–57.

Mitra, S. (2006). The capability approach and disability. *Journal of disability policy studies*, 16(4), 236–247.

Nussbaum, M. (2000). *Women and human development: the capabilities approach*. Cambridge: Cambridge University Press.

Nussbaum, M. (2011). *Creating capabilities: the human development approach*. Cambridge: Harvard University Press.

Oughton, E. and Wheelock, J. (2003). A capabilities approach to sustainable household livelihoods. With thanks to the Economic and Social Research Council for funding 'Enterprising livelihoods in rural households: new and old ways of working'. Award number R000238213 on which the empirical work is based. *Review of social economy*, 61(1), 122.

Robeyns, I. (2003a). Sen's capability approach and gender inequality: selecting relevant capabilities. *Feminist economics*, 9, 61–92.

Robeyns, I. (2003b). *The capability approach: an interdisciplinary introduction*. Amsterdam: University of Amsterdam, Department of Political Science and Amsterdam School of Social Sciences Research.

Robeyns, I. (2005). The capability approach: a theoretical survey. *Journal of human development*, 6, 93–114.

Rumberger, R. W. (2001). Who drops out of school and why. *Understanding Dropouts: Statistics, Strategies, and High-Stakes Testing*. Washington: National Research Council.

Saito, M. (2003). Amartya Sen's capability approach to education: a critical exploration. *Journal of philosophy of education*, 37(1), 1733.

Scoones, I. (1998). Sustainable rural livelihoods: a framework for analysis. IDS Working Paper 72.

Sen, A. (1985). Well-being agency and freedom: the Dewey Lectures. *Journal of philosophy*, 82, 169–221.

Sen, A. (1990). Individual freedom as a social commitment. *New York Review of Books*. 37, 10.

Sen, A. (1993). Capability and well being. In: Nussbaum, M. and Sen, A. (eds), *The quality of life* (pp. 30–53). Oxford: Clarendon Press.

Sen, A. (1999). *Development as freedom*. Oxford: Oxford University Press.

Sen, A. (2009). *The idea of justice*. London: Allen Lane and Harvard University Press.

Terzi, L. (2005). Beyond the dilemma of difference: the capability approach to disability and special educational needs. *Journal of philosophy of education*, 39(3), 443–459.

Tikly, L. and Barrett, A. M. (2011). Social justice, capabilities and the quality of education in low income countries. *International journal of educational development*, 31(1), 314.

Unterhalter, E. (2007). *Gender, schooling and global social justice*. Oxon: Routledge.

Unterhalter, E. (2014). Thinking about gender in comparative education. *Comparative education*, 50(1), 112–126.

Unterhalter, E. and Brighouse, H. (2007). Distribution of what for social justice in education? The case of education for all by 2015. In: *Amartya Sen's capability approach and social justice in education* (pp. 67–86). New York: Palgrave Macmillan.

Walker, M. (2005). Amartya Sen's capability approach and education. *Educational action research*, 13(1), 103–110.

Walker, M. and McLean, M. (2013). *Professional education, capabilities and the public good: the role of universities in promoting human development*. Oxon: Routledge.

Walker, M. and Unterhalter, E. (2007). *Amartya Sen's capability approach and social justice in education*. New York: Palgrave Macmillan.

Wolff, J. and De-Shalit, A. (2007). *Disadvantage*. Oxford: Oxford University Press on Demand.

Part I

Aspirations and agency

Issues of gender and justice in the educational programmes and spheres

1 Human capabilities and gender equality

What do higher education students have reason to value?

Melanie Walker and Sonja Loots

Taking South African higher education as our study site, we explore how gender equality is discussed in national and university education policies, and how the capabilities approach offers a more robust and multi-dimensional informational basis for advancing well-being, agency and gender justice in policy and everyday practices. We know that persistent gender norms and stereotypes continue to sustain gender inequalities in higher education institutions in many countries (e.g. Morley, 2006), while a recent in-depth exploration of gender equality in 20 countries (including South Africa) by the World Bank points to the resilience of gendered norms across societies, limiting men and women's agency development (Munoz Boudet *et al.*, 2013). Where gender parity has been achieved in universities, this is invariably measured numerically, ignoring the complexity of inequality beyond the numbers. Thus, while inequality can be envisaged in a macro perspective, e.g. with the objective to increase the numbers of women in higher education, the risk is that this focus on a single target may fail to take into account micro impacts in real lives (how diverse women and men are actually faring). To this end, the data on capabilities valued by diverse women and men at a South African university aims to shed light on lived experiences of gender in/equality. We conclude by arguing for the potential of applying the multi-dimensional capabilities approach in addressing complex issues such as gender inequalities, through linking theory and practice in developing gender equality policy goals that facilitate well-being freedoms (capabilities), strengthen agency and empower students.

With regard to our context, we note briefly that attention to gender can be found in South African legislation and policy. At a national level, the Women's Empowerment and Gender Equality Act (Republic of South Africa, 2013) has recently been approved; however, even though the Act includes more concrete descriptions of issues that should be addressed through the education system to empower women, the onus still rests on public and private bodies to draft and implement strategies. Furthermore, the Act focuses exclusively on women, with no regard for the influences of patriarchal roles on men's experiences and how this influences gendered relationships, nor does it include broader forms of discrimination related to gender, such as sexuality. Established as a national body to promote and monitor gender equality, the Commission for Gender Equality

(CGE) has the task of reviewing all national policies using a gendered lens; education is mentioned in the Act and forms part of the mandate. Moreover, there are significant concerns at the level of national policy with shockingly high levels of gender inequality and gender violence (e.g. Gender Links, 2012). Turning specifically to higher education, there is no national gender equality policy for higher education. Rather the focus is on redress for past injustices understood to be primarily race-based (see DHET, 2013); nonetheless, the Higher Education Act of 1997 also committed to values that, if implemented, would foster more gender equality, stating that "it is desirable to promote the values which underlie an open and democratic society based on human dignity, equality and freedom" (RSA, 1997: 2). The recent White Paper on post-school education and training also specifically acknowledges the grip patriarchal norms have in keeping women in subordinate positions in and beyond the education system (DHET, 2013). Moreover, the ministerial report on transformation (DOE, 2008: 20) noted that sexism and homophobia were widespread in universities, as well as the persistence of sexual harassment and "subtle and insidious" forms of gendered discrimination in higher education institutions, so that women were expected to study in conditions where the expectations, norms, values, traditions and ways of behaving are derived from masculinised conceptions of what is "normal". Even though women make up the majority of undergraduate students, gender equality in practice has slipped off the policy redress agenda.

For this chapter, the data from which we extrapolate valued functionings as a proxy for capabilities forms part of a mixed methods longitudinal project on gender, empowerment, agency and higher education (GEAHE) at a large, dual-medium (Afrikaans and English) South African university with a majority black student intake and slightly more women undergraduates than men. Our qualitative database consists of interview data from 39 female and 18 male, black and white, undergraduate and postgraduate student volunteers.[1] In the interviews, students were encouraged to reflect on their gendered experiences, biographically, socially and in higher education. Questions were also framed to include experiences within different university spaces, such as teaching and learning, on-campus student residences, sport, and other extra-curricular spaces.

Framing gender equality as human capabilities

From a capabilities perspective (Nussbaum, 2000; Sen, 1999), gender equality in higher education would extend beyond focusing only on equal numbers to include the expansion of capabilities—that is freedoms to choose valuable beings and doings—that advance gender well-being (for men and women) and that promote agency to act towards goals one values in life. The focus of the approach is on individual capabilities or freedoms, the choice of valued beings and doings (functionings) made possible by having the underlying capabilities, and the ability to convert capabilities into exercised functionings (Sen, 1999). Gender equality therefore does not only imply that equal opportunities should be available to people, but also takes into account the conversion of opportunities through decision-making and choice into achievements by diverse students. Furthermore, an intersectional approach is necessary because of the cumulative disadvantages individuals may experience because of race, gender and socio-economic status (e.g. Collins, 2000). Lived gendered experiences intersect with racial, cultural and social class issues and other differences. For example, Tebogo is a black student, she is also middle class, has attended a good state-funded school and lives in an urban area where patriarchal cultural traditions are somewhat diluted by metropolitan life. By contrast, Lerato is also black but comes from a poor rural area and has not attended a good school. In her region, there are strong cultural patterns of gender norms that limit the roles girls and women are supposed to play in the family and society. Both these young women are black, but their lives and opportunities differ considerably, and they enter higher education with differing amounts of financial and academic capital. All this in turn intersects with gender. We could derive similar kinds of examples of intersections of gender, race, class and culture for white women, white men and black men.

Thus, attention must also be paid to historical, social and economic (including income) arrangements and personal gendered biographies that may influence how each person is able to "convert" (Sen, 1999) her bundle of resources into valuable activities and states of being. Where conversion factors constrain the ability to pursue a dignified life in higher education, social change would be required through public policy and actions in universities. If we find inequalities when comparing women and men, or black women and white women, then social arrangements ought to be transformed to expand the freedoms and opportunities associated with development for students, and women in particular, to enable their active agency and empowerment. Information on capabilities and agency freedoms for diverse students would constitute the informational basis of justice (Sen, 1999) for evaluating the reach and responsiveness of gender equality.

Women's valued capabilities and functionings

From the interviews with women, we identified several functionings. We organised the functionings into four capability dimensions: (1) bodily integrity, (2) dignity and respect, (3) voice, and (4) having higher education and knowledge. These capabilities we suggest are normative for higher education, but the functionings may vary from context to context. With regard to the functionings of *not being subject to sexual harassment or violence, being safe,* safety for the women we spoke to extends from general campus safety from criminal acts such as theft or assault, to include having freedom of movement and self-expression on campus. In general, women feel safer on campus than off campus, as Buhle (UG Agricultural Science) stated: "for me, campus feels like I'm playing within my yard—that's how it's supposed to be, it's my protected space". Not all the women we spoke to agreed and some at least found moving around the campus less physically safe after dark. Moreover, safety ends at the campus gates and fences. An integral part of safety is also having bodily integrity (Nussbaum, 2000), which also means being free of sexual harassment and assault. Every woman we interviewed commented on experiences of sexual harassment, of which the predominant form was inappropriate or suggestive comments from men. Thumi (UG Accounting) explained the restrictions on expressing themselves that women experience:

> When you pass a group of guys, you're asking yourself, oh my goodness, what are they going to say this time? Are my jeans too tight? Is my cleavage showing? So sometimes you become so (self)conscious. And then, you know, when it's winter, you're so free, you're so comfortable, you're wearing your long coats and you're covered up.

Similarly, Buhle (UG Agricultural Science) recalled that the women in the residence she lived in would experience daily harassment from the men at an all-male residence that they would have to walk past to attend classes: "The comments we had to endure … some of the girls would leave the footpath and take the long way round because of the snide comments that they [male students] were making". The women viewed this form of harassment as "degrading" (Janine, PG Music), "demeaning" (Anne, PG Accounting) and "being viewed as objects" (Thumi, UG Accounting). The normative nature of such sexual harassment is evident in Thato's (UG Law) statement that "sexual harassment is something we don't even look twice at anymore", or Mary's (PG Accounting) statement: "that's how men are". One student had been sexually harassed by a male lecturer. Immediately after the incident she had phoned a friend and was asked by him, "What are you wearing that gave him the idea he could do that?" This response is consistent with the view that women are to blame for sexual harassment and assault, as well as the norm of restrictions on women's opportunities and choices for sexual satisfaction. For example, Elizabeth (PG, Economics) explained:

> When I ask my male friends, why is it that when you sleep around, your friends will be like: "Wow, you are this, you are that"; you applaud yourselves. But then once a girl does it, she gets called a slut or a whore or something. And then the response that I got was: "It's like having a lock. A key that can open many locks is very good and the lock that can be opened by many keys is useless".

In our examples, women students blamed for wearing "provocative" clothes or "initiating" a sexual response. However, much like other forms of gender-based violence, the act of sexually harassing someone is an act of power and dominance (Beiner, 2007), which relates directly to the gendered social norms in which we are socialised. While most of the women did not feel free from sexual harassment, it was also clear that they would value bodily integrity functionings if they were in a position to choose. For this reason, bodily integrity as a capability is presented as one of our core capabilities for gender equality.

Turning to our second functioning of *being treated as a dignified human being, and respected*, dignity and respect take the form of being recognised and treated as a human being, as well as applying the same principles to the treatment of others. All participating women valued equal treatment and receiving the same opportunities through higher education as men. As much as these women are able to participate in campus activities, assume leadership roles and enter male dominated fields of study, they still feel that they are treated like "the other". Sandra (UG Language Studies) stated: "it feels like the men they have this secret club, you know, and you're not invited". Similarly, Buhle (UG Agricultural Science) has experienced exclusion in her classes, "all my lecturers have been men and they tend to engage more with the males in the class—perhaps they reckon men know more about tractors than I would". Mary (PG Accounting) felt that women are generally "seen as inferior and weaker", and Thandi (PG Botany) did not want to be perceived as "vulnerable". While undertaking a law internship to complete her practical training, part of Lizelle's (PG Law) tasks had been to, "exchange my boss's wife's clothes" and "pick up his kids from school". When asked whether male students were allocated the same errands, she replied that the male students "were given real work; they were seeing clients, representing some of them in court, they were taught how to be lawyers".

Race also intersects with dignity and respect, where black women more often report that they are either discriminated against because of their gender, race, or both. Nthabiseng (UG Law) is a confident black woman, who had achieved a certain status on campus through being part of a highly selective study-abroad leadership development programme, as well as serving on the Law Society. She stated: "I get treated with dignity and respect there [in Law] all the time, but you find that in other departments, being a young black woman, you don't get treated with the proper dignity and respect that you deserve". Moreover, the type of respect accorded to women is often superficial in the sense that it reproduces women's "vulnerable status" through opening doors for them, giving up seats on buses, and not swearing in front of them. Glick and Fiske (1996: 491) define this type of behaviour as "benevolent sexism", where behaviours and perceptions toward women are stereotypical but are "subjectively positive in feeling tone (for the perceiver) and also tend to elicit behaviours typically categorised as prosocial (e.g. helping) or intimacy seeking (e.g. self-disclosure)". Faith (UG Accounting) recalled an example of this in a lecture:

> We had very small classrooms for a big group of people. So our lecturer would usually say that the boys should just let the girls sit first and then they can sit on the floor, I think it's the fact that we're just seen as so vulnerable and have to be protected.

This example also demonstrates normative gendered behaviour and attitudes being reproduced by university staff members as opposed to them providing an environment of inclusion. Benevolent sexism requires that women still acquiesce in what men have decided is the right way to act towards women, based on dominant norms of masculinity and femininity, rather than having a deeper acknowledgement or appreciation of the person beyond the gender. Yet many of the women we spoke to were not critical of this kind of behaviour, and accepted it as "natural".

Being treated with dignity and respect ought to correspond with Nussbaum's (2000: 79) central human capability of affiliation, which stresses the ability to "be treated as a dignified being whose worth is equal to that of others". From the students' experiences, deeply embedded gendered normative roles and attitudes which position women as lesser, accorded less dignity and less respect were evident. As Nthabiseng (UG Law) asserted: "the woman is perceived to be the softer person in society and she's undermined … she's not respected as much and her opinions aren't valued as much". Dignity and respect is thus our second core capability.

In order to have dignity and respect, we think, requires *having a voice and being heard;* to be treated with dignity and respect may not necessarily involve having freedoms to participate, to be taken seriously, to have one's opinions valued and to be heard. The capability for voice also includes the representation of women's voices through classroom practices and curricular content. Janine (PG Music Studies) commented on women's representation in her curriculum saying: "When you study composers, if I asked you to name five women composers, would you be able to? We should include some women composers. I think exposure would be nice". Thutu's (UG Architecture) explains how women, especially black women, are not taken seriously in all professional fields:

> The lecturer last year told me that men in the architectural industry do better than women do because they don't take everything too seriously. There is also a tendency for guys to do better than girls in terms of results, so it's usually the white males that are doing better and then it alternates between the white females and the black men with black females at the bottom of the group. In the first year class there is no black girl at all, in the second year class there is no black girl at all, there's just two black girls in my (third) year now.

Some women felt that engagement and participation in student activities, including social and sporting activities, was not always equal. Buhle (UG Agricultural Science) felt that women have, "limited access to, and [a limited] variety of sports" and less sports funding from the university. Jessica (PG Political Science) commented that women students are held back "hindering you from achieving anything that you want to". Furthermore, gendered norms influence whether women felt that they are being heard, as Jenny (PG Economics) commented:

> It's very difficult to have someone want to pay attention to you when you don't look a particular way, when you don't dress a particular way or speak a particular way. Men, even in my generation, listen to a woman based on

her appearance. Either way, there's no winning. Because if you're wearing very little, then you deserve very little respect. That's what they feel. And if you're wearing quite a bit and you're very covered up, then again, they feel that it's not necessary to listen to you because you're not that appealing to them.

Not being represented as women within university structures and disciplines also affects how women judge their own potential. Again, Jenny avowed:

When you come to a higher learning institution, the majority of lecturers are white and male. So it has a large impact on the way that you see society. And then you begin to think to yourself, especially if you move higher up, you find that women are found in the elementary phases of our education and later on it's just males—white men. It has a big impact on the way that we see ourselves, on the way that we view society and on the way that we learn as well. Because we are not too sure then, are we as capable as our male counterparts?

Molla and Cuthbert (2014) argue that to create an environment in which women's roles and contributions are recognised and properly represented in curricula, as well as freeing teaching and learning processes from stereotypes and misrepresentations, empowerment through voice and participation should be developed. However, as these examples show, having a voice, being heard and being able to participate extends beyond university classrooms, which implies a broader responsibility in creating a university environment in which all students feel free to participate and engage in various activities. *Voice* is thus our third core capability.

The functioning of *having a higher education, knowledge and gaining a degree* was highlighted unequivocally by all the participants. With graduate unemployment at under 6 per cent (Van der Berg and Van Broekhuizen, 2012), access to and success in higher education will make a significant difference to students' lives, opening up job opportunities, and enabling wider benefits of learning for themselves and their families and communities; higher education acts as a capability multiplier for choices regarding work, and life. Jenny (PG Economics) stated:

Education is empowering, it changes your mind-set. You find that women who find themselves at the bottom of the social ladder are less educated and because they are less educated they are less likely to pursue any kind of career or field independent from their male counterparts. Finding academic success or finding success in the working environment would mean to be liberated. It would mean to be free of having to have a spouse to provide for you.

Jenny's statement also testifies to the value women, and in particular black women from traditional cultures place on economic independence (which is not to say that they do not value some traditional values and draw strength from them). Thandi (PG Botany) agreed with the value of education and stated that having a career means "you can stand up for yourself now, you don't need to be dependent on other people". The intrinsic value of education was also highlighted by the interviewees, for example, Nadia (UG Language Studies) commented that, "since I've been at varsity I have to question everything, you can't just take anything as it is". Sune (UG Linguistics) remarked on the value to her of knowledge gained through higher education: "It broadens your knowledge, it really, really does. It's really a foundation for what you're going to do one day". Similarly, Anne (PG Accounting) explained:

> One of the best things at University is that I was taught to think for myself. To not accept everything at face value. To question as much as you can. And I had a professor who encouraged us to question everything he says in class. We should not accept it as what it is. And he told us, when you do an assignment, I want to hear what you think. Don't tell me what you think I want to hear. Otherwise you won't get good marks.

The potential of higher education to empower students includes, but extends beyond, gaining employment. Our fourth core capability is, thus, having a higher education and gaining knowledge.

What the male students said

The significance of persistent gendered norms and the impact of socialisation practices are evident in the differences between men's and women's perspectives on what they value. Even though the same four umbrella capabilities are valid for men to live the lives they value, they manifest in different ways and are accompanied with a sense of ambiguity related to gender roles, treatment and behaviours. To demonstrate this, we will also frame the men's valued functionings according to the capability themes. We should also bear in mind that the men who volunteered to be interviewed may be more gender aware than others on campus, hence the gaps in their gender equality understanding is of concern.

(1) *Bodily integrity*. For the men, as told to us, safety for them meant personal freedom on campus, freedom from rules and restrictions conducive to personal expression and development, for example:

> You cannot be an individual in schools, the system does not allow it, but I think at university you see people change completely and become who they really are. Because this is a safe area where you are allowed to be yourself.
>
> (David, PG Sociology)

However, the men also recognised that while safety means this for them, they were aware that it means something more for women. Two themes relating to women and safety were prominent in the interviews, physical safety on campus, and sexual harassment. The men had different viewpoints on both as compared to the women. For example, John (UG, Human Movement Science) felt that, "women feel unsafe on campus at night", while Sia (UG, LLB) stated:

> For most of the people coming here, they come from the worst situations. And this is sort of their escape and this is where, this is their chance. Where they come from, you know, women are getting raped. And now you come to a campus where there is a security guard who's sleeping outside of the door, protecting you and you can walk at 12 o'clock back to your residence without anyone harming you.

Regarding sexual harassment, most men felt strongly about not participating in such behaviour because they considered it disrespectful and degrading towards women, for example, as Eric (UG BEd) remarked, "I was taught not to treat women in that way, I was taught to respect women, not to whistle or to comment or to do anything like that. So, I don't do that", while Sia (UG LLB) said, "I know from my female friends who completely hate it and say it makes them feel cheap. It's really degrading". On the other hand, some admitted to taking part in harassing behaviour, claiming that it is simply a "natural" male reaction to women dressed in "revealing" clothes:

> I do it a lot. Women would be wearing short skirts and things that show a lot of cleavage. I normally say, "they like that attention, so I'm giving them attention". They like showing cleavage and wearing short skirts and after-wards guys are blamed and we are told that we give comments that are not OK. But, to be honest, if we see a lady who is dressed properly, we don't have such comments.

> (Manny, PG Plant Sciences)

Thus, men valued bodily integrity for themselves and for women but with significant omissions when it came to gender equality. It was not clear if all would have chosen full bodily integrity for all if they could have done so. On the other hand, they did not reflect on their own physical safety and did not raise it as an issue of concern to them, perhaps assuming that men are strong and capable of looking after themselves.

(2) *Dignity and respect.* For the women in this study, dignity related to being recognised as a human being, an equal member of society. For the black men we interviewed, the concept of dignity as it affected them manifested in intersectionalities between race and socio-economic status, with similar concerns to be treated as equal in society but also anger at the historical inequalities affecting black men. Thus, some felt it is "demoralising" knowing that black men cannot provide for their families because of the racial past. "Being a man in South Africa" then means providing for one's family, "being at the top of the food chain" with "the same privileges as white men" (Edward, UG BCom Accounting). Sia (UG, LLB) remarked on historical income inequalities based on race;

he asked, "count how many black students are driving cars compared to whites, you automatically feel how our history has affected us", and "as much as we don't want to be the angry blacks who complain about apartheid every day, its effects are real". Similarly, Adrian (UG, Agricultural Economics) affirmed that he grew up in a black township "and I could see the things that other people have that I don't have, or the people in the community do not have". He did not get a decent school education, commenting "those are the things that make me angry".

Another intersection particularly affecting black men with a more traditional upbringing, is balancing a cultural identity with a "university and Western" identity:

> In African communities we have this thing of being an African. And when you are an African you are an African in all aspects and all levels. It means you need to stay true to yourself. The moment you start behaving like me, you walk around with a pen in your hand with a Western influence, then that's a total betrayal to your culture. That's the kind of knowledge instilled by authorities in the townships. We grew up to know the Western culture as the culture that came and contaminated the African society. So if you are going to enter that society make sure that you uphold your African state. It puts a lot of pressure on you because you end up rejecting knowledge, because you move away from and start forgetting your culture.
>
> (Phil, PG Philosophy)

We found women also struggling to reconcile home and university culture and values but this was not raised in quite the same way, although the effect of being lesser in some way was similar for black men and black women. It was interesting that neither white women nor white men were especially critical of their patriarchal home cultures. This may have something to do with the nature of patriarchy in South Africa, which cuts across cultures in the emphasis on the father as the ruler of the family, transcending social class, and race differences. Thus, in 1998 the CGE (1998: 10) reported that "one of the few profoundly non-racial institutions in South Africa is patriarchy … to challenge [it is] … to be seen not as fighting against male privilege, but as attempting to destroy African tradition or to subvert Afrikaner ideas".

The idea of being treated with respect is therefore strongly influenced by accepted masculine norms, where family responsibilities were described as including being the head, the provider, being the disciplinarian, having authority, making the rules, taking care of the family, protecting them, being looked up to in the community, and having the final word on family matters. In general, the men were therefore ambivalent about women's changing roles, for example, Xander (UG BCom Tax) showed support for, and even attraction to empowered women, yet also expects a normative femininity:

> There was this one girl I was spending a bit of time with. She could challenge me and even maybe sometimes beat me in intellectual conversations.

I find it very attractive because I don't want a woman who's going to be submissive. In the corporate world you get women who run big businesses and men are under them. [But] for me specifically, I'd be disappointed in myself if my wife had more money than me. I feel that I'm supposed to provide for her and for my family, financially and in every other way. My wife must be soft. She must have a feminine side. She must be a woman. She mustn't be a man. She must be a lady. She must want to dress up, make up and wear heels and wear dresses.

The same sense of ambivalence was conveyed when talking about being a "gentleman", which we have suggested does not challenge gender norms:

I think being a gentleman isn't because a woman is weak. For me, that's the opposite. The status quo has always been that the woman is weaker. For me, opening a door for a woman is acknowledging her presence as a woman and acknowledging her as an important being. Not because she is weak, not because she is not strong enough to push a door or anything else. It's just because I feel like we need to make up for the last two thousand years where we did not appreciate women.

(TK, UG LLB)

We also found some anger towards women wanting both to be treated differently and as equals. Thus Eric (UG, BEd) complained that women expect them to give up their seats on the bus, yet "women scream equality, equality".

Thus, we found that men—and especially black men—value being treated with dignity and respect, although how they understand this is not always in the same way as women do, and aspects of their understanding may work to diminish the respect and dignity of women.

(3) *Voice*. Men valued voice but do not always feel they are heard in the university. They also mentioned cultural influences affecting their participation in classes:

One of the reasons why you would find that most males or Africans don't participate in class discussions is because of the values that were instilled within you. For example, in a black family when you speak to an elder you're not supposed to look at them in the eyes. When an elder says something to you and you don't agree with them you let it go, you don't argue. So we come here with those values and a lecturer is teaching you and you don't agree with that lecture, and you say, well it's fine, he's an elder, what can I say?

(Phil, PG Philosophy)

On the other hand, they value having a voice in being able to approach lecturers for advice and access to opportunities. Xander (UG BCom Tax) commented that his lecturers are interested in their careers and the choices that they make:

"they appreciate it so much when we go to them and we ask them, I'm facing these job opportunities, should I do this? Should I do that?" However, they had less to say about voice perhaps because they easily inhabit leadership roles (and this applies to black and white men).

(4) *Having higher education and knowledge*. The women's views of the value of higher education are echoed by the men, particularly the black men, as Xander (UG BCom Tax) noted:

> I'm not just a man. I'm a black man. And coming to University, obtaining a degree, its life changing. It changes a lot of things. For instance, my parents had to wait till they were way older than me to get any kind of tertiary education. I'm 21 years old and I already have a degree. So maybe in 15 years' time, I'll be far more advanced than my parents are and their parents were.

Other men mentioned the ability to form networks with lecturers and fellow students, learning to appreciate others' diversity, developing a broader view of the world, developing a social consciousness, and forming an identity. Manny (PG Plant Sciences) commented:

> You'll see that there are a lot of students who have changed courses. Not because they were struggling with the module, but because that's when they discovered or re-discovered themselves. Like, I was thinking that I'm a doctor or a scientist, whereas I'm actually an economist. It helps you to see who you are, to define yourself.

So, like the women, men unequivocally valued higher education and knowledge.

Gender equality: is capabilities on its own enough?

From the valued functionings identified under four capability dimensions we can see how gendered norms shape what students value. For the women in our study, inequalities are still very much part of their daily lives. They feel like they are not taken seriously, some are harassed, some feel that they are treated as being vulnerable and weak, and some experience intersectional discriminations. These inequalities shape what they value: to feel safe and not be sexually objectified; to be respected and live a dignified life; to have a voice, participate and be heard; and to benefit from the opportunities created through higher education. For men, who do not experience gender inequalities in the same way as women, the valued functionings within these four capability groups manifest differently. For the most part, the men in this study value the freedom and safety of the campus environment to form identities and express themselves without the restrictions of rules; they value respect and recognition as men (which is largely earned through being able to provide and take care of a family); the black men in particular value dignity and opportunities to rectify past injustices; and all of the men commented on the value of higher education, whether it contributed to personal development, relations with diverse others, networking, or just a sense of a better life. However, these capabilities are differently interpreted across men and women's lives, requiring that both are brought into a public conversation in which all perspectives can be heard and challenged critically, but also requiring—rather crucially—that feminist knowledge (Robeyns, 2003) and knowledge about gender equality are brought to bear in the capabilities approach. These capability dimensions—which look the same—hold different meanings for men and women, and these diverse meanings may work to hold inequalities in place.

What is then worrying is the ambivalence the men show towards women's empowerment and progress. Furthermore, the women's and men's perceptions that sexual harassment behaviours are attributable to how women dress, as well as the uncritical attitudes about being a "gentleman" are also concerning. From our data, women feel they have to fight to be treated as equals, pointing to the strength of gendered norms, as well as the failure of higher education to challenge these. Where black men struggle to be treated as equals by others (whites), this is embedded in particular views of masculinity which do not necessarily challenge norms that hold gender inequality for women in place, nor even question dominant norms of masculinity in South African society. Such gendered norms "stem from a society's ideal values of what it means to be a woman or a man" (Munoz Boudet *et al.*, 2013: 24). Together with cultural practices, these norms determine values and shape choices. Failure to conform to socio-cultural norms and practices could result in social rejection, since greater respect is awarded to those who conform.

Challenging values that hinder dignity and equality might expand certain freedoms, but might also create dissonance between individuals, their families and their communities, thereby diminishing well-being and requiring women in particular to negotiate their home culture and the aspects they value along with the university culture aspects, which they also value greatly. Moving to a more conscious and critical reflection of values requires alternative ways of "being and doing" that challenge normalised ways of doing things and a critical perspective that challenges gender inequalities. In this respect, higher education processes should develop this capacity to challenge and question prevailing gendered norms. The freedom of individual choice, agency and reasoning emphasised by the capabilities approach (e.g. Sen, 1999) suggests that policy and practices should focus on expanding capabilities for critical thinking, including self-reflection, practical reasoning and access to knowledge to increase the ability of students to make informed choices about their values.

We suggest that students' voices and gendered experiences—crucially, taken together with feminist ideas—can act as a starting point for discussions on higher education's role in disrupting the reproduction of inequalities in society and its citizens, which resonates with broader debates on higher education's responsibility towards human development. As Nussbaum (2000) has argued, education plays a significant role in either creating justice or recreating injustices for girls and women. However, the higher education experiences of the students in this study are ambiguous, both showing the expansion of opportunities afforded by higher education, but also its limits in addressing (or understanding) socially embedded gender norms and discriminatory behaviours. Without explicit counter-education that challenges conventional gender norms, students remain caught within dominant gender norms, thereby reproducing inequalities within and beyond higher education institutions. A second debate we hope to stimulate is what gender equality should look like within a higher education community and broader society. Through the process of identifying valued functionings and capabilities, implementation strategies could be developed around the capabilities that expand valuable functionings for diverse women. As we noted earlier, current South African higher education policies understandably have a strong race-based transformational focus. However, disadvantaged groups are then homogenised, and although promoting broad anti-discriminatory attitudes, policy does not take into consideration the variety of contexts and constraints that shape individual choices. Instead the capability approach considers individual circumstances and experiences and provides space for individuals to debate what they collectively value (Sen, 1999). At the same time, as Sen reminds us, where there are gaps and interpersonal differences we need to look at wider conditions—economic, social and political—and how these enable or constrain opportunities and achievements, acting as conversion factors for each person to convert the resources and commodities she has at her disposal into functionings.

In our view, higher education institutions ought to foster capabilities for women and men to enable them to choose the functionings they have reason to value for more gender-equal lives. In turn, women will be empowered and able to challenge gendered social structures and identities. Therefore, the identification of gender equality capabilities is of importance in the development and sustainability of gender justice. Other factors deserving attention are the social expectations women (and men) are subject to and institutional practices and cultures that often reinforce persistent gendered inequalities. These conversion factors have to be taken into account as they not only influence agency, but also impact on valued functionings. The sensitisation of lecturers and curricula to gender are also needed in promoting gender equality, as pedagogical and curricular content shapes (or hinders) critical thinking, values and ethical ideas of humanity.

The capabilities approach allied to feminist ideas could be an important instrument to foster more gender-just higher education and for changing gender norms in society. We have deliberately focused on an essential core of capabilities and reduced our original codes to capture a smaller number, which are likely to be regarded as more rather than less operational, and that can be expanded and added to in different contexts. Moreover, the four capabilities are not only essential for promoting gender equality in higher education, they also act as capability generators. For example, the freedom to be educated and have access to knowledge stimulates critical thinking, reflection and reasoning, which in turn empowers women to live the lives they value. It is also clear that policy and practices at the individual and university level aimed at gender equality cannot ignore intersecting influences and injustices regarding race, class, current cultural and social influences (which form and sustain adaptive preferences), as well as historic disadvantages, which still impact on students' experiences. Universities need to pay attention to gendered cultures and norms that are shaping identities perhaps in subtle and not well-recognised ways, but nonetheless laying down or reinforcing patterns of identity and acceptance, which may not serve women or men well in the future.

Acknowledgements

Our thanks to the NRF for funding under the (South African Research Chairs Initiative (SARChI) in higher education and human development, grant number 86540 for the funding that enabled this research.

Note

1 All names used are pseudonyms.

References

Beiner, T. M. (2007). Sexy Dressing Revisited: Does Target Dress Play a Part in Sexual Harassment Cases? *Duke Journal of Gender Law and Policy*, 14(125), 125–152.

Collins, P. H. (2000). *Black Feminist Thought: Knowledge, Consciousness, and the Politics of Empowerment* (2nd edition). New York: Routledge. Commission for Gender Equality (CGE). Online, available at: www.cge.org.za/.

Commission on Gender Equality (1998). *Annual Report of the Commission on Gender Equality*. Pretoria: Government Printer.

Department of Education (2008). *Report of the Ministerial Committee on Transformation and Social Cohesion and the Elimination of Discrimination in Public Higher Education Institutions*. Pretoria: DOE.

Department of Higher Education and Training (DHET) (2013). *White Paper on Post-School Education and Training: Building an Expanded, Integrated and Effective Post-School System*. Online, available at: www.fpmseta.org.za/userfiles/file/White%20Paper %20for%20post%20school%20education%20and%20training-final.pdf.

Gender Links (2012). *The War at Home: Findings of the Gender Based Violence Prevalence Study in Gauteng, Western Cape, Kwazulu Natal, and Limpopo Provinces of South Africa*. Online, available at: http://genderlinks.org.za/wp-content/uploads/ imported/articles/attachments/21537_the_war@home_4prov2014.pdf.

Glick, P. and Fiske, S. T. (1996). The Ambivalent Sexism Inventory: Differentiating Hostile and Benevolent Sexism. *Journal of Personality and Social Psychology*, 70(3), 491–512.

Molla, T. and Cuthbert, D. (2014). Qualitative Inequality: Experiences of Women in Ethiopian Higher Education. *Gender and Education*, 26(7), 759–775.

Morley, L. (2006). Hidden Transcripts: The Micropolitics of Gender in Commonwealth Universities. *Women's Studies International Forum*, 29, 543–551.

Munoz Boudet, A. M., Petesch, P., Turk, C. and Thumala, A. (2013). *On Norms and Agency: Conversations about Gender Equality with Women and Men in 20 Countries*. Washington, DC: World Bank.

Nussbaum, M. (2000). *Women and Human Development: The Capabilities Approach.* Cambridge: Cambridge University Press.

Republic of South Africa (RSA) (2013). *Women Empowerment and Gender Equality Bill.* Online, available at: https://jutalaw.co.za/media/filestore/2013/11/B50_2013.pdf.

Robeyns, I. (2003). Sen's Capability Approach and Gender Inequality: Selecting Relevant Capabilities. *Feminist Economics*, 9(2–3), 61–92.

Sen, A. (1999). *Development as Freedom.* Oxford: Oxford University Press.

Van der Berg, S. and Van Broekhuizen, H. (2012). Graduate Unemployment in South Africa: A Much Exaggerated Problem. *Stellenbosch Economic Working Papers*, 22(12), 1–53.

2 Well-being freedoms to construct one's educational career

Narratives from Tanzania and South Africa

Mari-Anne Okkolin and Bhavani Ramamoorthi

Introduction

Research of young adults in sub-Saharan Africa has made critical observations about the individualistic view of the understanding of youth. For instance, findings from the studies by Arnot, Chege and Wawire (2012) in Kenya; Arnot, Jeffery, Casely-Hayford and Noronha (2012) in Ghana and India; Helgesson (2006) in Mozambique and Tanzania; Posti-Ahokas and Okkolin (2015) in Tanzania; and Tranberg Hansen (2005) in Zambia, question the individualised view of young people's lives and aspirations, which subsumes individual autonomy as the major goal of the transition from the dependence of childhood to adulthood's independence. This refers to a period of transition from the childhood family to a family of one's own, on the one hand, and from (compulsory) education to employment, on the other. Critical accounts have also pointed out how the individualistic rhetoric does not adequately consider the socio-cultural ideas, expectations and assumptions that may especially govern women in the Global South into social and familial responsibilities and obligations; yet, research has shown the strong impact of social norms and familial relationships on young women's strategies in life and education, their individual aspirations and their realisation. As an example, pursuing and studying upper secondary and higher education often overlaps with working, getting married, becoming a parent and establishing a family (see Latvala 2006; Okkolin 2017; Posti-Ahokas 2014; Unterhalter 2016; Wilson-Strydom 2015). Evidently, for young people (female and male alike) to construct and decide upon one's educational career is not a characteristically autonomous project, but a complex social phenomenon par excellence.

As a response, there has been increasing attention in international educational research to recognise the various intersecting aspects of educational development, calling for a broadening of perspectives and a deeper understanding of what is perceived as evidence of change and human well-being. The need to eliminate the sharp distinction between sector-specific areas of social policy and gaps in coverage of narrowly focused targets has also been on the global agenda to redefine MDGs (millennium development goals) into SDGs (sustainable development goals). As an example, the interactions between education, poverty reduction, health, and gender *are* complex, and a more holistic approach could bring along particular synergies (see e.g. Unterhalter 2012; Waage *et al.*, 2010). Interestingly, this becomes evident in thinking of the planning and implementation of youth policies. The UN, for statistical consistency across regions, defines youth as those persons between the ages of 15–24 years. For activities at the national level, youth may be understood in a more flexible manner. For instance, Tanzania and South Africa, the two country cases represented in this chapter base their definition on that given in the African Youth Charter, where youth means every person between the ages of 15–35 years. Clearly, during such a long and critical period of life, young people's lives are embedded with complexities; with social relationships, norms, expectations, negotiations, and various aspects of human life that interrelate and intersect.

The research from the Global South is characteristically problem oriented and packed with challenges. In this chapter, drawing on two independent studies conducted in Tanzania and South Africa with female and male students who have beaten the odds of low national participation rates and reached higher education, the focus of analysis is on the issues that *enable* them to reach higher education. We are particularly examining social relations and aspects within school environments and family contexts (see Okkolin 2017; Wilson-Strydom and Okkolin 2016). We base our argument theoretically on the capabilities approach and understand the elements of (educational) well-being as equity of opportunity (well-being freedoms aka capabilities) and outcome (well-being freedoms aka functionings). Before entering into the empirical section of this chapter, that is, narrative accounts of opportunities/enablers for educational outcome/achievements (access to, participation in, and completion of education), an introduction of the two country contexts, and the two studies on which this chapter draws, is appropriate. We have selected particular indicators from both of the countries, which although they do not correspond with each other, are meant to provide a situational analysis and illustrate the realities in which young people live.

Tanzanian and South African country contexts and studies

Tanzania

As per the 2012 Population and Housing Census (NBS 2012), one third of Tanzanians belong to the official youth age group (15–35) and the median age in the country is 18. More than 60 per cent of the youth population lives in rural settings. The average household size is 4.7 members, but it is 7.3 when the household is female headed, in comparison with 3.5 in male headed households. More than half of the females but less than a third of males of the 20–24 age group are married: however, over 70 per cent of the population in the 30–34 age group are married. Interestingly, with regards to the indicator of 'type of usual activity', more or less the same amount of youth in the age group of 15–19 years were employed as those who were full time students; however, as per the age group of 25–29 there were no full-time female students reported; instead, their 'type of usual activity' was home maintenance, whereas 70 per cent of their male counterparts were employed and 19 per cent were full-time students (URT 2014).

Regardless of the positive trends in the expansion of secondary school enrolment since 2000, low transition rates from ordinary (forms 1–4; ages 7–13) to advanced (forms 5 and 6; ages 18–19) level continue to translate into low coverage of the secondary education. The proportion of both male and female students who are of official secondary school age in advanced secondary education remained under 3 per cent in 2013, implying that the majority of Tanzanians will not only have no access to tertiary education opportunities, but may also face limited employment options that may require skilled graduates with a secondary level of education (MoEVT 2014). The net enrolment rate (NER) in secondary education increased from as low as 6 per cent in 2002, to 29 per cent in 2013. In 2012, the gender parity index (GPI) in secondary education was 0.88. National demographic and health data also reveal that regional and wealth disparities have a bearing on access to secondary education. For example, the Tanzania Demographic and Health Survey (TDHS) reports secondary NER in the wealthiest households at 49 per cent, which was more than five times that in the poorest households (9 per cent). Moreover, secondary school-age youth in urban areas were more likely to attend secondary school than their counterparts in rural areas (44 per cent and 19 per cent, respectively) (URT 2011). In Tanzania, the enrolment in higher education grew significantly between 2005/2006 and 2011/2012—an increase of more than 200 per cent. However, in comparison to other sub-Saharan African countries (with similar kinds of economic status) the gross enrolment rate (GER) in higher education has remained very low: in 2009/2010 GER was 5.3 per cent, and reached 9.5 per cent in 2011/2012; yet, it dropped to 3.7 per cent in 2013, signalling that more needs to be done to address *transition* and *quality* at earlier stages of the education system to ensure a critical mass of the population attains tertiary qualifications. While the proportion of females in higher education has consistently increased at a faster pace than that of male students, the proportion of females was 2.5 per cent in comparison to 4.9 per cent of male students in 2013 (URT 2014).

South Africa

South Africa's National Youth Policy (NYP 2015–2020) defines youth as persons from 15–35 years old. As pointed out in the policy document, although much has changed for young people since the advent of democracy in 1994, the motivation for the age limit of 35 years has not yet changed because historical imbalances in the country are yet to be fully addressed (NYDA 2015: 11). Building on the first NYP, the current policy is also geared towards the needs of young people with respect to education, health and well-being, economic participation and social cohesion.

The population of South Africa is largely made up of young people: those who are below the age of 35 years constitute about 78 per cent of the total population; with over 50 million South Africans, 18.5 per cent are between the ages

10–19 and 24 per cent are aged 15–24. As summarised in the situational analysis by the United Nations Population Fund, formerly the United Nations Fund for Population Activities (UNFPA) (2013), improvements in the living conditions of South African youth have taken place, including access to formal housing, potable water, proper sanitation, electricity, and communication platforms, such as access to information and communication technologies. Furthermore, young people in South Africa are highly technological, with 88 per cent of those aged 15–34 living in dwellings with access to a landline, mobile phone or internet access. Yet, South African youth still face significant challenges, specifically with regards to high unemployment rates, high HIV infection rates, and an increase in youth-headed households for the ages 15–24 (ibid.). For instance, according to the South African June 2014 labour force survey, 36 per cent of young people between the ages of 15–35 are unemployed, which is almost double the 15.6 per cent of unemployed adults (aged between 35–64). The labour absorption rate for adults is 58 per cent; almost twice that of youth. Young women face even higher levels of unemployment—34.5 per cent of young women are neither employed nor at school, including further and higher education, compared to 30 per cent of young men (NYDA 2015). The data also shows that a significant proportion of youth in South Africa are heading households. About 6 per cent of youth between the ages of 15–14 years are heading households, and 1 in 5 or around 20 per cent of youth between the ages of 25–34 are heading households. On average, a quarter of the young people in South Africa are heading households (NYDA 2011).

Household income is a proxy for poverty. There seems to be some intersecting differences between age group, gender and population group and low-income households albeit generally speaking. African[1] youths are more likely to live in poor households than youths in the other population groups (coloured, Asian and white): for instance, in 2009 66.7 per cent of African females and 62.7 per cent of African males (in the age group of 15–24) were living in low-income households in comparison to 8.4 per cent and 7.9 per cent of white females and males, and to 33.3 per cent and 35.5 per cent of coloured females and males, respectively (NYDA 2011).

The 2010 labour force data indicate that the level of unemployment decreases with the level of education and age (NYDA 2011). Young people with only primary education or with only some secondary education are the most affected by unemployment. However, those with Grade 12 still show substantial unemployment rates. Young people between the ages of 18–24 years with only primary or some high school education are more likely to be unemployed than any other age group. This age group experiences high unemployment even when they have matric or tertiary education, with over 30 per cent of people with tertiary education being unemployed. This could be attributed to lack of experience (ibid.). Large numbers of young people leave the education system prematurely and possess no professional or technical skills, making them effectively unemployable. About 60 per cent of unemployed youth aged below 35 years have never worked (NYDA 2015).

Although young people are less likely to be employed than older people, they typically have more years of schooling and those with a tertiary degree have better chances of finding employment. In contrast to the low percentage of children attending secondary schools in sub-Saharan Africa, participation in South Africa is high and has increased from approximately 88 per cent in 2002, to 90 per cent in 2013 (GER) with a GPI of 1.03 (DBE 2014). In 2013, GER in tertiary education in South Africa was 19.7 per cent and the proportion of females 23.5 per cent in comparison to 16 per cent of male students (UIS 2014). Almost two-thirds (66.4 per cent) of these students were black, 22.3 per cent were white; 6.7 per cent were coloured and 4.7 per cent were Indian or Asian (NYDA 2015).

Even though most students were black, the student participation rate of this population group remained proportionally low in comparison with the Indian, Asian and White population groups. About 4.3 per cent of 18–29-year-olds were enrolled at a higher education institution in the country in 2013—up from 4 per cent in 2002. An estimated 18.7 per cent of white individuals in this age group and 9.2 per cent of Indian or Asian individuals were enrolled in higher education compared with 3.1 per cent and 3.2 per cent of the coloured and black population groups, respectively. The percentage of individuals aged 20 years and older who have attained Grade 12 has been growing since 2002, increasing from 21.9 per cent in 2002, to 27.7 per cent in 2013. Over the same period, the percentage of individuals with some post-school education increased from 9.3 per cent to 12.8 per cent. The percentage of individuals without any schooling decreased from 10.6 per cent in 2002 to 5.6 per cent in 2013.

The studies—materials and methods

The two studies on which this chapter draws were conducted at different points in time and both had specific research agendas and sets of research questions. This difference can also be seen in the way we represent our data and findings. A common interest was to understand why some young people succeed in education against the odds. The qualitative in-depth interview data for the Tanzania study (Tz) was acquired through three fieldwork periods, in 2005, 2006 and 2008. The study was about the experiences and insights of ten women who had reached higher education—placing them amongst a tiny proportion of Tanzanian women. Eight of the ten women were qualified teachers from professional backgrounds and they were studying education at the university. The women diverged in their backgrounds with regards to geographical location and ethnicity; their parental educational backgrounds varied from no schooling at all to doctorate level. They came from families with three to six children, and nearly all of their siblings were educated at least to secondary level education. The women defined their families as 'normal and middle-class' in the Tanzanian context; yet, they all emphasised financial constraints in pursuing education and described various modes of support from their extended families. At the time of carrying out the study, most of the women were in their early thirties, the youngest was 26 and the oldest 53 years old. With regard to living arrangements at the time of the interview, three women were living with their boyfriends; one was dating but living independently; four women were married and had children (1–4), and two were divorced.

The South African (SA) data is drawn from a three-year study (2014–2016) with final year teacher education students (pre-service and in-service). The study focused on understanding opportunities and constraints to reach university education; the value and relevance of higher education in general, and teacher education in particular, in relation to students' professional aspirations, the kind of life that they wish to achieve, *and* in building the future of South Africa within and beyond schools. A group of 14 students from diverse backgrounds (as was the case with the Tanzania study) were interviewed in 2014. The group included nine female and five male students. On the basis of the experiences from the Tanzania study, and to make gendered (not only female) claims, male participants were also included in the South African study. As per the official racial population groups in the country, black African ($N=6$; three females, three males), white ($N=5$; four females, one male) and coloured ($N=3$; two females, one male) students were represented. At the time of our encounters, most of the participants were in their early twenties (the four youngest were 22 years old; the oldest participant was 43); three of them were married, three were dating, and eight were single; four of them had children.

In this chapter, we base our empirical analysis mainly on the Tanzanian study with female participants only. We have selected, however, four South African students' stories to illustrate the importance of the social over the presumed autonomy and individualism in the formation of young people's lives regardless of the differences arising from the country context, gender and race. From South Africa, we introduce Ruth (black female), Isaac (coloured male), Nevaeh (white female) and PG (black male). It is not the purpose of our chapter to make comparisons. Instead, in considering our two sets of data, we have been struck by the similarities, and some differences, with respect to schooling, family and social environments that have enabled educational achievement amongst those who are typically marginalised within education.

School environment

It is common for educational stakeholders to look at the influence of the school environment on educational advancement, and the importance of enabling a learning environment is explicitly recognised, for instance, in the SDG 4 on quality education. On the grounds of the Tanzanian women's narratives, we may conclude that much of the quality of education and the enabling of a learning environment depends upon having 'sufficient school facilities'; yet, the most essential factors to construct educational pathways and well-being seemed to arise from the social aspects, referring particularly to the ambience of the school, peers and good teachers.

What seems to characterise the Tanzanian research participants' school experiences is the difference between their primary and secondary schools, regarding both the facilities, and the teaching and learning ethos. In brief, the women's primary schools were not that enabling, and failed to open up sets of capabilities for achieving such educational beings and doings that they had a reason to value. Instead, both the physical and the mental environments were rather poor: their schools were quite a distance away, water and toilet facilities existed, but the quality was poor, the food was non-existent or bad, the class-rooms were poorly equipped and fights over desks and chairs were habitual:

> I hated this moment of going to school.... At one time I even asked my parents if they could make me my own chair so that in the morning I could carry it to the school. Because it was so bad: you have this nice clean skirt, uniform, and then you go and sit on the floor; then when you go home you are totally dirty. That was worse ... the strong ones got the chance to sit on chair.
>
> (Wema, Tz)

All Tanzanian women reported how both female and male teachers frequently used corporal punishment as a method of learning as well as to maintain discipline, and the teachers held somewhat biased ideas towards girls' ability to study and learn. However, poor physical school environments, the many deficient experiences, and the low quality of education did not constrain the research participants to function; instead, such school environments were regarded 'as normal' and to embrace sufficient and supportive conditions enough to stay enrolled, to perform well enough, and to pursue education further (Okkolin 2017).

Most of the Tanzanian women got their perspective of what was 'normal' upon entering secondary education, since most of the prohibitive and constraining factors at the primary schools were no longer present. Therefore, the enabling factors to construct educational well-being at the secondary schools referred to: 'no more caning', 'all girls', 'good teachers' and a 'friendly environment'.

> For the first time, we went away from home and we used to like it because at home there was a lot of work to do, and we felt now we can become nice, the skin can be softer.... Everybody had a desk and chair of her own. We had had green lawns with roses, nice houses, there were not many of us in the dormitories, just four, and we had separate lockers, which you could lock if you wanted.... I still have very nice memories of my school.
>
> (Leyla, Tz)

The women valued their 'conducive and harassment-free school environments'. This implies, first, that their educational surroundings enabled them to calmly sit down and study hard and effectively; second, that their fellow students assisted them, helping them to study hard and catch up, so as to not be left behind. Apart from the fellow students' support for their academic agency achievements they mentioned like-minded friends with whom to have girly conversations, who seemed to play a great role in the process of the women's formation of identity.

> The best memory [in secondary education] was friends. I remember, I made lots of friends. We were a group of five ladies who were doing well; very close to each other, and we were teaching each other.… We were together during recess and after classes, playing, joking, and … yeah.
>
> (Tumaini, Tz)

Third, the harassment-free school was a single-sex school and had (almost) abolished corporal punishment and other physical disciplinary actions. The women's narratives included examples of some very good and encouraging teachers, who particularly supported their educational well-being and agency aspirations, especially after reaching the level of secondary education. The teachers significantly supported the women's academic attainments, in addition, they made an impact on their lives more generally, in terms of developing their female subjectivities (Okkolin 2017).

> Contrary to the former [primary, teachers [at secondary school in Dar es Salaam] were very committed. They [primary school teachers] were very lazy, they didn't attend the school and the performance … only one or two students passed to join secondary school.
>
> (Genefa, Tz)

> I don't know.… She [matron at the boarding school] just like … teaches you how to take care of yourself as a girl. As I said, my mother and I, we don't discuss like personal stuff, maybe something, but not so much how to manage my life as a woman or a girl.
>
> (Wema, Tz)

On observation, the South African narratives indicate that the demands of belonging to different socio-economic groups, school resources, teachers, peers, racial disparities and family resources, build up a spectrum of factors that the participants were challenged by within their school environments. With regard to the students' experiences, only PG had the challenge of studying in schools that quite severely lacked in resources. He had the sensitivity to note how it was the teachers' hard work that compensated for the lack of resources and he talked about why that was a reason he liked his teachers: it was their constant encouragement and belief that he would do well that led to his academic achievement and him remaining a committed learner all through school: 'So many teachers were committed and they had faith in me. I believe that's why I am who I am today'.

Nevaeh felt that she always got the attention from teachers that she needed. From her string of responses, it is evident that what appeals more is the warmth and personality of the person, and also—with specific teachers—their teaching abilities. She particularly liked her maths teacher since she built a community classroom with interactive learning, which introduced Nevaeh to team work and effective individual work. She also mentioned her biology teacher for being a humorous man and making the subject fun and full of surprises. Furthermore, she very much valued the good listening skills of one of her very 'sweetest' teachers:

> When she saw you struggling, she would come and say, 'all right, I think you must do that rather than this'. And she was always there when you needed her. She always listened to you when you wanted to speak or had something to say. She would always listen and then respond nicely to that. She wasn't one of the teachers that said 'I'm busy now; come back later!'
>
> (Nevaeh, SA)

Ruth, for her part, mentioned some very interesting characteristics of the teachers she liked:

> There's things that they teach you about how you should present yourself, how you should treat other people, how you should care for nature and how you should always see the world as one system that works together. So that just enlightened me.
>
> (Ruth, SA)

In his responses, Isaac shared that he loved going to school because the teachers loved him and because he was popular among his peers.

> The teachers loved me, I was sort of like the teacher's pet, you know, because I was always, what do you call it, class leader.... One Afrikaans teacher of ours made us feel like, I don't know how to explain; she made us feel like we were actually like one of her own kids, the whole class, like she really cared for us all.
>
> (Isaac, SA)

In Isaac's story, in particular, there are clear indications of the presence of various economic layers in the student community and also characteristics defined by the race factor. He stated that there were different levels of educational aspirations between the white and coloured kids, and he himself did not set high goals for himself: 'I affiliated myself with the coloured kids who didn't want much in life, I just settled for average; so, then you didn't have motivation to learn'. On the other hand, he had the pressure of being popular and to feel included among his peers, and he did have friends from all groups: 'with the lower class guys I got along perfectly, the middle class kids, some of them I got along with, and funnily enough, higher class kids affiliated themselves with me, which I always found weird' (Isaac, SA). The tension of fitting in with his peers was interspersed with Isaac's compulsion to perform and not fail in studies. He said that the fear of getting labelled by his peers still exists. All in all, however, to have friends from all groups and to enjoy an inclusive school environment played a subtle role in enabling his educational advancement. Ruth and PG did not have active social lives and the role of peers in their educational pathways seems limited. In their case, in contrast to Isaac, the *lack of* social life and friends, layered with the desire to be a committed learner, led to academic engagement that took priority during their studies.

To sum up, in the Tanzanian study, the participants shared stories of the school environments offering rather poor mental and physical environments, which included poor infrastructure, ill-equipped classrooms and teachers often using corporal punishment. Despite these challenges the participants regarded these environments as normal, continued to attend and to pursue their aspirations. However, in contrast, their secondary school experiences were very similar to the narratives from South Africa, with the presence of good teachers, no punishment, a friendly environment, and some even mentioned having supportive peers. Supportive peers appear to be only exceptional in the Tanzanian stories when compared to the South African narratives, where the positive impact of peers was minimal.

In contrast to the stories from Tanzania, the stories from South Africa indicate that the participants grew up in rather well-equipped schools with all basic facilities in place throughout their entire primary school life, except in the case of PG, who grew up in a school environment that severely lacked in resources. There was minimal punishment, almost an absence of it in any form. Yet, these schools did not have the most ideal physical and mental environment either, with challenges posed by peers, the socio-economic backgrounds of the participants, school resources, racial disparities and family influences. It must also be stressed that the learning environments were rather well supported by caring and affectionate teachers, who shared good work ethics and a sense of commitment to teaching. Nevertheless, despite all the advantages and disadvantages that these school environments might have posed it is critical to highlight that—very similarly to the Tanzanian narratives—the South African study also indicated that the participants managed these environments with all their limitations, while still being sensitive to what the positive elements were, that contributed to their educational well-being.

Enabling family

The research on education, gender and development is packed with literature discussing the importance of, and interlinks between, education, gender and *poverty*. In this section, we discuss the enabling conditions that were central in both country cases regarding students' families, and specifically address the topics of poverty/financial support *and* familial moral encouragement.

Although financial constraints did not restrict Tanzanian women's educational advancement, they did impact and intersect with their gendered identities and familial roles. On the other hand, the women felt that gender-based roles and hierarchies, which undoubtedly existed in their families, did not determine their familial position or diminish or deteriorate their educational options. The Tanzanian women defined their families as 'normal and middle-class' in the Tanzanian context; yet, they all emphasised familial financial constraints in pursuing education. Wema, for instance, recalled how she saw her mother (parents divorced; no support from the father) really trying to make the available money go far enough: 'She showed us that there is only this [amount of money] and you could really see that there really is only this' (Wema, Tz). In Naomi's family too, all four daughters were enrolled in a 'very good' Catholic missionary boarding school. Their parents 'were really, really struggling hard' to spend a lot on education; yet, they were taught that 'without education, life is harder; education is the key!'

Educating their children had been a big financial investment for their parents and this was often accomplished as a kin-initiative. Categorically, they were all 'educated by someone': parents, grandparents, other relatives and/or older siblings (to which we will return in the section on decision-making). All families had carried out gardening and farming, and generated additional income by selling agricultural products and baking bread, for instance, to raise the family income to maintain the household *and* to enable the children to be enrolled in school (a good school), and to learn and perform well (private tuition).

> My mum was the one who was doing business to add to the income.... The work which he [father] was doing was kind of enough for him. And maybe, because other men in the prison camp [where he worked as a guard] were not really doing any other business to add to their salary.... She was seen as not a normal woman by everybody in the camp ... sometimes they used to say, 'oh, she's Chagga' [ethnic group, famous for doing business].
>
> (Tumaini, Tz)

Yet, as an investment, the educational achievements of the women were supposed to pay back later, as a return of the financial benefits (instrumental value). At the time of the interviews, these women were able to sustain themselves through their professions and did not report facing critical financial constraints; they were relatively stable financially, either because of a scholarship, the support of their spouses and families, or their own income.

To strive for and gain enough financial resources was a pre-requisite for the educational achievements of the research participants. However, to convert the available resources into functionings critically depended on and was supported by social factors, identifiable in the women's cases as their parents, and *their ideas* concerning the value and relevance of education, *and* the schooling of their daughters. As highlighted within the capabilities approach, resources and opportunities are not synonymous with educational well-being and equality. For this reason, the critical issue is that 'to afford' and *the idea* of female education intertwine and intersect. Accordingly, the Tanzanian research participants' set of capabilities comprised of both 'financial' resources and 'moral' opportunities; the utilisation and conversion of which into educational achievements being enabled by their parents. In the research participants' families, the education and schooling of all of their children, boys and girls, was a prestige for them and a valuable 'mental' inheritance (intrinsic value): 'I don't have anything to give you.... There is no inheritance that I can give you. I'm giving you education: if you want something from me, then you have to go to school' (Amisa, Tz). In other words, for the Tanzanian women, the (relative) material poverty in their families did not imply aspirational poverty. Both fathers and mothers had a significant, albeit different role, in encouraging the women in their educational achievements and to pursue their educational goals. Apart from the support for constructing academic identities, for the women, their families represented a reservoir of the basic capabilities of joy, happiness and the feeling of togetherness.

In thinking of the circumstances of PG, Ruth, Nevaeh and Isaac in South Africa, it was PG who came from very challenging family background. His mother (who had passed away) had been the sole breadwinner in the family and PG grew up without knowing his father. PG had lived with an extended family (two uncles, two cousins and an aunt) and the eldest uncle had supported PG's education financially. According to him, they barely had minimum household resources:

> It wasn't easy! Even though there wasn't a day where maybe we would go to bed without a meal, but yes, like even though we did have a meal but it wasn't a proper one.... It wasn't really enjoyable taking account that when I came to university I didn't have a strong financial background and all that.
>
> (PG, SA)

PG received a bursary to finance his university studies and it seems that his challenging familial background was the prime factor in his motivation to study. Similarly, his family circumstances did not enable him to construct educational pathways; yet, his family background pushed him to work hard and made sure he progressed. He had no one to really talk to regarding his educational opportunities and choices, and it was his own self-driven aspiration for change and creating a better life that 'enabled' him to advance:

> I think it is I myself, basically. Also taking into account the family background, you know, I will tell myself, 'now this is the situation I'm in at the moment and I don't like it. And it's up to me to change my life and yes, no one else!'
>
> (PG, SA)

Like PG, Ruth studied with a bursary. In her case, however, the father had a predominant role and impact on her studies. Her father came from a family that had struggled with resources for education; nevertheless, he was passionate about schooling and education, and had worked as a plumber not only to educate himself, but also his siblings. Later in life he had the opportunity to pursue the studies he had wished for. Because of his passion and strong vision, Ruth's choice of what to study and have as a career was not without debate and constant strife with her father.

When it comes to careers, yes, we had to debate it a lot. Because my father, sort of had everything planned out. 'I want my first born to be this, my second born to be this'. So, he already had it all planned out.... Then when I came to university, like I want to study education. But then he said 'no, we already have a lot of teachers in our family. We are fine with that. How about going for occupational therapy or something like that?'

(Ruth, SA)

At the end of the day, supported and reassured by her siblings, Ruth was able to convince her father of her passion to study education and teaching. 'And now he's very proud. He can't wait to see me actually go into the workplace', Ruth stated. She also explained how her father owned a lot of cattle and that is how he paid for most of Ruth and her siblings' education. She described how their father was 'always the one stepping in and saying "if it's for school, I do not mind, I can spend!"'. To sum up, it was 'a better chance, a better shot at life' that their father wanted to provide for the children. Yet, another major factor that influenced and enabled Ruth to stay motivated and persevere further were her siblings (six sisters and one brother), who all graduated from university, found employment and were independent— in contrast to the mainstream perception of youth.

If her father was the enabler for Ruth, for Isaac it was his mother. He grew up in a community that was stigmatised by poverty, joblessness and high crime rates. Despite these challenges, his parents supported the children (two daughters, six sons) and made sure everything was comfortable enough to focus their energies on what they needed, according to their mother's interpretation and aspirations, for education. Isaac's mother was a trained nurse and he states how:

She felt like she knew best! We never discussed what you wanted to do; she only pushed you in the direction that she felt you should go.... But I really have to applaud here: she always made sure we had the best when it came to education.... Since we were in grade one, we always talked about education.... We had much more that most of our peers had in our community. Yes, my mother, my pillar of strength!

(Isaac, SA)

Neveah's parents had lost all that they had from a financial assets and income point of view, and were rebuilding their lives with scarce resources. In her narrative, it is both the mother and father who had an impressive influence on her pursuing higher education and aspiring to be a teacher.

I think my mother had a very big influence on that, as well as my father, because my father was studying law and he only needed to do two modules then he would have had his degree, but he didn't; and then he was always telling me 'don't make the same mistakes that I made'. And my mum always said she didn't have, her parents didn't have the funds to give her the opportunity to study further ... that if I have the opportunity to keep on studying and further myself and my knowledge, I must never stop!

(Neveah, SA)

Neveah had been thinking of studying drama, but her mother's subtle sugges-tions made her change the field of study that she intended to: 'Why don't you think about teaching? You've always been good at explaining things and doing things and achieving things—you would be a great teacher' she had said; and guided by her mother's observations and explicit guidelines, she decided to pursue education and a teaching profession.

The family environments of the participants from both countries came with their share of challenges and yet offered a supportive and loving environment. In the Tanzanian narratives, the women faced financial constraints and this had an impact on their gender identities and familial roles, yet it did not affect their options for educational advancement. In the South African narratives, the parti-cipants share stories of financial constraints in the family, either with experi-ences of being supported by a relative, a university bursary, or growing up in families where, despite a financial crisis, they had parents who were very com-mitted to ensuring their educational well-being was not compromised. It is inter-esting to see how, in the contexts of both countries, even though financial constraints were a common factor for almost all the participants, it never limited their opportunities for educational achievements or advancement, with either a parent or other relative being committed to the participants' education. When none of this existed, as in the case of PG (SA), the university bursary functioned as a support.

The influence of parents was significant in both narratives, with either the mother or the father or, in some rare cases, both the parents playing an influen-tial role in encouraging the participants to pursue their educational goals. In the Tanzanian narratives, there are indications of violence or difficult family situ-ations, with pressures of the father being a traditional figure whose decisions were overpowering. There were also the added challenges of gender bias of the women having to contribute to the household chores rather than being prepared for a school education. In contrast to the Tanzanian stories, these roles and factors are almost absent in the South African narratives, although they involve participants of both genders. Nevertheless, one of the female participants does share an experience of the father being the decision-maker at home, and how her initial compliance with his decisions later transforms into her pursuing her own educational aspirations with his support and involvement.

Conclusion

As shown by the studies in both countries, individual differences in response and experience emerge. Regardless of the differences arising from the context of country, the effects of gender and race and the strong impact of *the social* in enabling the construction of educational well-being, understood as the opportunity concept of freedom (capabilities) *and* outcome (functionings), have become evident in our studies on young people's lives in Tanzania and South Africa. The findings highlight the interrelations of economic and socio-cultural factors, the significance of parental and familial (with various meanings) support, and the importance of social relations within schools, when thinking of access to, participation in, and completion of education. Hence, our findings support the criticism of individually and autonomously focused definitions of the youth, and encourages further research on the diverse meanings of attaining adulthood, which helps us to better understand the complex and intersecting processes that most often take place simultaneously in young people's lives.

In both countries, access to schooling (including higher education) has increased. Nevertheless, not enough young people in the post-school phase are gaining training in the different skills needed to participate in the knowledge economy. Furthermore, even though there has been some improvement in the enrolment rate, there is still evidence of major inequality based on social class, gender and race. However, while racial disparities remain a serious concern in South Africa, the growth of a black middle class suggests that an over-simplified analysis of race and participation can downplay the intersectionality of race and class in participation patterns. All in all, a holistic and more analytical approach towards the complexities and socially constructed nature of each category, not to mention the intersectionalities of race *and* class *and* gender will provide a better understanding of the multidimensional nature of educational well-being in Tanzania and South Africa, and in other sub-Saharan African countries in addressing similar kinds of challenges, which manifest and actualise in the planning and implementation of youth policies.

Note

1 There are four official population groups in South Africa. Some agencies use the term black African while the other use only black or African; in addition to whites, coloured and Asian/Indians. In this chapter, we employ black and African synonymously as per the original reference.

References

Arnot, M., Chege, F. N. and Wawire, V. (2012). Gendered Constructions of Citizenship: Young Kenyans' Negotiations of Rights Discourse. *Comparative Education*, 48(1), 87–102.

Arnot, M., Jeffery, R., Casely-Hayford, L. and Noronha, C. (2012). Schooling and Domestic Transitions: Shifting Gender Relations and Female Agency in Rural Ghana and India. *Comparative Education*, 48, 181–194.

Helgesson, L. (2006). Getting Ready for Life: Life Strategies of Town Youth in Mozambique and Tanzania. PhD thesis. Sweden: Umeå University.

Latvala, J. (2006). Obligations, Loyalties, Conflicts. Highly Educated Women and Family Life in Nairobi, Kenya. Doctoral dissertation, University of Tampere.

MoEVT (Ministry of Education and Vocational Training). (2014). Education for All 2015 National Review Report: United Republic of Tanzania. Mainland.

National Bureau of Statistics (NBS) (2012). Tanzania—Population and Housing Census. Online, available at: http://catalog.ihsn.org/index.php/catalog/4618.

NYDA (National Youth Development Agency). (2011). Draft Integrated Youth Development Strategy for South Africa (May 2011).

NYDA (National Youth Development Agency). (2015). National Youth Policy 2015–2020 (April 2015).

Okkolin, M-A. (2017). *Education, Gender and Development: A Capabilities Perspective.* New York and London: Routledge.

Posti-Ahokas, H. (2014). Tanzanian Female Students' Perspectives on the Relevance of Secondary Education. Doctoral dissertation, University of Helsinki.

Posti-Ahokas, H. and Okkolin, M-A. (2015). Enabling and Constraining Family: Young Women Building their Educational Paths in Tanzania. *Community, Work and Family.* doi:10.1080/13668803.2015.1047737.

Tranberg Hansen, K. (2005). Getting Stuck in the Compound: Some Odds against Social Adulthood in Lusaka, Zambia. *Africa Today*, 51(4), 3–16.

UNESCO Institute for Statistics. (2014). Higher Education Statistics. Online, available at: www.uis.unesco.org/Home/Education/.

UNFPA. (2013). Young People. Fact Sheet. UNFPA South Africa Country Office.

Unterhalter, E. (2012). Poverty, Education, Gender and the Millennium Development Goals: Reflections on Boundaries and Intersectionality. *Theory and Research in Education*, 10(3), 253–274.

Unterhalter, E. (2016). Educating Adolescent Girls around the Globe: Challenges and Opportunities. *Comparative Education*, 52(2), 274–276.

URT (United Republic of Tanzania). (2011). Tanzania Demographic and Health Survey. Dar es Salaam: National Bureau of Statistics Ministry of Finance.

URT (United Republic of Tanzania) (2014). Basic Demographic and Socio-Economic Profile Statistical Tables Tanzania Mainland. Dar es Salaam: National Bureau of Statistics Ministry of Finance.

Waage, J., Banerji, R., Campbell, O., Chirwa, E., Collender, G., Dieltiens, V., Dorward, A., Godfrey-Faussett, P., Hanvoravongchai, P., Kingdon, G., Little, A., Mills, A., Mulholland, K., Mwinga, A., North, A., Patcharanarumol, W., Poulton, C., Tangcharoensathien, V. and Unterhalter, E. (2010). The Millennium Development Goals: A Cross-Sectoral Analysis and Principles for Goal Setting After 2015. *Lancet*, 376 (9745), 991–1023.

Wilson-Strydom, M. (2015). *University Access and Success. Capabilities, Diversity and Social Justice.* New York and London: Routledge.

Wilson-Strydom, M. and Okkolin, M-A. (2016). Enabling Environments for Equity, Access and Quality Learning Post-2015: Lessons from South Africa and Tanzania. *International Journal of Educational Development*, 49, 225–233.

3 A capability approach to participatory research platforms for young black women in South African higher education

Talita Calitz

Introduction

Interest in student participation in higher education is increasing in line with global patterns of widening university access (Tinto, 2012; Wilkins and Burke, 2015). In much of the Global South, access to university is accessible to a minority of the population, although in South Africa there has been a significant expansion in enrolments since 1994 (Ministry of Higher Education and Training, 2016). Despite this dramatic increase in access for students who have historically been excluded because of race, higher education institutions in the South African context have been unable to retain many university entrants (Ministry of Higher Education, 2016). At the same time, public higher education institutions face a myriad of structural fault lines, including entrenched racist and sexist violence (Ministerial Committee on Transformation and Social Cohesion and the Elimination of Discrimination in Public Higher Education Institutions, 2008); underfunding from the state, exacerbated by pressure from students to decrease or eliminate tuition fees; curricula and institutional cultures that fail to incorporate indigenous knowledge or to recognise diverse lives, identities or voices (Luckett, 2016; Mbembe, 2016); and a low-participation, high-attrition system in which up 46 per cent of first-time entrants will never graduate (Ministry of Higher Education and Training, 2016).

These structural constraints are particularly concerning when taking into account that a significant percentage of students who will never graduate are young black women, who are a social group vulnerable to violence, socio-economic exclusion, and marginalisation (UNDP, South Africa, 2015). For many black women from working-class and/or rural contexts, university enrolment has not translated to equal participation at university, or to academic success, graduation rates or employment (Council on Higher Education, 2013). The focus of this chapter is a research project that tracked the experiences of five young black undergraduate women students at a South African university, which investigated their freedom to participate within the context of these structural barriers. This chapter brings together the questions of poverty, gender, socio-economic class and race to the experiences of first-generation university students in the Global South, to contribute to a growing concern about poverty as a barrier to equal academic and social engagement in higher education (Case, 2013; Wilson-Strydom, 2015).

While from a social justice perspective it is necessary to acknowledge the structural vulnerabilities that decrease young black women's social and academic mobility, there is a risk of reproducing a deficit approach to student lives, where the individual is framed as a victim who lacks the resilience, agency or skills to navigate a negative environment or to pursue alternatives (Bozalek and Boughey, 2012; Pym and Kapp, 2013; Walton *et al.*, 2015). The chapter aims to challenge a deficit approach to black women within higher education, and this critique takes the form of women's own narratives, voices and experiences, which were collected during a longitudinal participatory research project. The first section of the chapter illustrates how black female students who face socio-economic vulnerability and academic marginality must navigate an intersecting range of conversion factors at university. The second section then shifts attention to the agency that individuals use to negotiate structural inequalities. Students' experiences and agency are explored using a capability approach (Nussbaum, 2010; Sen, 1999) which is framed alongside Nancy Fraser's redistributive theory of justice (Fraser, 2008, 2013). I now explore these two theoretical frameworks in greater detail.

The capability approach and redistributive justice

The capability approach offered a multidimensional analytical tool to evaluate the freedoms and opportunities available to students positioned precariously within institutional hierarchies. Student participation is theorised as the opportunities and the functionings that an individual has the freedom to access (Sen, 1999). According to the approach, capabilities are defined as individual abilities alongside the opportunities 'created by a combination of personal abilities and the political, social and economic environment' (Nussbaum, 2011: 20).

This exploration of student participation is grounded in the assumption that redistributive justice is required to address intersectional inequalities in higher education, and that social justice cannot be achieved without resource redistribution. As such, individual participation cannot be expanded unless individual students have equitable access to basic resources and services. While equitable access to resources is an important prerequisite for cultivating just institutions, the capability approach also takes into account whether an individual is able to convert available resources into capabilities (or opportunities) and functionings (or valued beings or doings) (Sen, 1999). The analysis frames structural barriers as conversion factors, which are defined as personal, social and environmental differences that inhibit an individual's freedom to convert available resources into capabilities or functionings (Robeyns, 2005). Structural conversion factors include for example, social norms about gender and discriminatory patterns of inclusion based on race, ethnicity or socio-economic class. I return to a detailed discussion of conversion factors in the analysis section of the chapter.

The research is also framed using Nancy Fraser's theory of redistributive justice and recognition, which strengthens the chapter's structural critique of unequal power embedded within higher education institutions. Given the participatory nature of the research process, the themes emerging from student narratives—the intersection of alienation and resource poverty within the context of structural inequalities—informed the decision to incorporate Fraser's model of justice into the theoretical framework. I draw on Fraser's model of justice to theorise 'the ways in which economic disadvantage and cultural disrespect are currently entwined with and support one another' (Fraser, 2008: 69), particularly for individuals acting within unequal social arrangements. Fraser also critiques the way that redistributive feminist agendas have been captured by the rise of neoliberal policies in politics, social life, activism, education and the labour market, which in turn are intimately connected to the increasingly corporate and instrumentalised forms of higher education to which young women aspire (Fraser, 2008). Drawing on her broad structural framing of injustice as both inextricably political and personal, Fraser's theory was applied as an evaluative tool for examining structural injustice and power-based hierarchies, since the capability approach in some instances takes for granted the existence of benevolent and functional state and social institutions (Nussbaum, 2011). Fraser however, builds a robust case for a redistributive model of justice that implicates the state as a perpetrator of injustice alongside other institutions such as universities. According to Fraser, social arrangements are unjust 'if they entrench obstacles that prevent the people from the possibility of parity of participation' (Fraser quoted in Bozalek, 2012: 147). The capabilities discussed later in this chapter were collaboratively selected with these principles in mind, and shaped the research discussions and questions that developed throughout the project.

Intersectional inequalities

Building on its redistributive theoretical framework, the chapter investigates intersectional injustices by examining how macro-economic inequalities play out in higher education institutions, and influence individual agency and freedom. The analysis foregrounds the intersection of race, gender, geography, language and socio-economic class, in order to expand a superficial focus on identity categories into an analysis of the structural rootedness of discrimination, marginalisation and violence (Fraser, 2008). This chapter examines how 'institutionalised value patterns cast some people as advantaged, as normal, as respected, and others as disadvantaged, as pathological, as unworthy of respect' (Bozalek interviewing Fraser, 2012: 146). The analysis of student narratives pays attention to the way that intersectional vulnerability correlates with decreased legitimacy and voice, devalued positionality within the institution, an unequal distribution of goods and resources, and dehumanising treatment from peers and people in authority. Finally, the intersectional analysis draws attention to how unjust structural conditions create conversion factors that appear to be individual, but on closer examination structurally exclude the individual from equal participation.

This has implications for transformative interventions, so that instead of blaming the individual for a deficit approach, we transform the structural barriers that exacerbate unequal participation.

Methodology and methods

Research design

The data presented is drawn from a qualitative, longitudinal research project conducted at a South African university between August 2013 and March 2015. The research project was organised into two distinct phases. During the first phase (August 2013–November 2013), I conducted individual interviews ($N=20$), facilitated digital narrative workshops ($N=4$), and assisted with the production of digital narratives ($N=8$). A digital narrative is a short multimedia film that can be used to explore life history. Some educators use digital narratives to explore complicated content in their classrooms. I chose digital narratives as a data collection tool that would expand participants' freedom to frame and narrate their experiences using creative multimedia forms. The narratives were conceptualised, designed and produced in a series of four collaborative workshops and individual production sessions. The aim of these digital narrative workshops was to create overlapping opportunities for participants to engage reflexively with their experiences, to expand their awareness of implicit structural arrangements, to develop technical and narrative capabilities, and to produce a multimedia artefact that they could share with others, if they chose to do so. Because of the creative freedom inherent in the design and production of narratives, this process destabilised the alienation between researcher and 'researched'. The narratives were also useful for enriching the interview data, especially for participants who were not as comfortable as their peers during individual interviews.

The second phase of the research emerged from participant requests to extend the research project beyond the original four-month data collection. Aligned with the participatory nature of the project, I had anticipated that the research design would be guided by participant agency and aspirations (Kemmis *et al.*, 2013). The project was extended into 2014 and was concluded in March 2015. During this second phase, the research dynamic shifted from primary researcher and participants to senior researcher and co-researchers. Although this new dynamic did not erase the power imbalance created by access to resources, educational opportunity and institutional positionality, it did offer fertile opportunities for research engagement and collaboration[1] (Mertens, 2008). First, students were involved in the inductive process of extracting themes and codes from their interview data, and then workshopping these themes in focus groups. The analysis was organised around a series of public events, workshops and research meetings throughout the academic year, which culminated in a community engagement event at a local school in October 2014. Second, the co-researchers converted these codes and themes into public presentations, where they shared findings and screened their digital narratives. The research process aimed to shift the conversation *about* vulnerable students to a conversation *with* students, informed by the tensions, complexities and agency embedded in their own experiences (Brown, 2009). These experiences played an important role in the selection of the capabilities that are discussed later in this chapter. In the section below, the participants are introduced in more detail.

Introducing the research participants

The chapter focuses on the experiences of the five female participants in the research. The students were recruited as volunteers in July 2013. All participants were registered on extended degree programmes,[2] which means that they entered university with lower admission scores than students on mainstream degree programmes. Table 3.1 provides an individual profile and the pseudonym used for each participant:

Analysis and discussion

The discussion of qualitative data is divided into two sections: the first investigates structural barriers as conversion factors that diminish individual freedom for equal participation, while the second section investigates the role of participatory research in expanding individual capability development and agency.[3] In the discussion below, student voices offer insight into both structural conversion factors and the agency used to navigate unjust structures.

Structural conversion factors that diminish participation

This section focuses on how structural conversion factors intersected with each individual's freedom to participate at university. As discussed earlier, students require a fair share of resources as well as structural arrangements that equally distribute the opportunities to convert resources into capabilities (Tickly and Barrett, 2011). The analysis found that the intersectionality of being female, black, rural and working-class at university is an accumulative disadvantage that increases structural barriers to equal participation (Wolff and de-Shalit, 2007). Although these conversion factors also affect black male working-class students, the analysis below is particularly interested in the intersection of female gender[4] with race, socio-economic status and rural geography.

Table 3.1 Research participant profile

Participant pseudonym	Race	Gender	Age	SES	Degree	Home
Aziza	Black	F	23	Working class	Social sciences	Rural
Clarice	Coloured	F	22	Lower middle class	Social sciences	Urban
Condorrera	Black	F	29	Working class	Humanities	Rural
Kea	Black	F	21	Lower middle class	Social sciences	Rural
Naledi	Black	F	21	Working class	Social sciences	Rural

Socio-economic status

The most significant structural barriers to equal participation identified across the five participant narratives were high levels of household poverty and low socio-economic status. This finding is not surprising, given South Africa's status as the fourth most unequal country in the world, with a current youth unemployment of 53.7 per cent (South Africa Youth Unemployment Rate 2013–2016). Poverty acts as a complex barrier to participation for a number of reasons. First, despite South Africa's strong focus on equity in its post-apartheid higher education legislation, most higher education institutions lack the structural arrangements and resource requirements needed to enable equal participation for vulnerable students, such as adequate funding for tuition and sufficient numbers of undergraduate teaching staff. Second because of increasing living costs and tuition fees, access to sufficient resources is an important condition for equal participation. Third, state funding for higher education is not aligned to increasing enrolments, and in real terms, government subsidy per student has decreased[5] (Bozzoli, 2015). Finally, poor students cannot rely on their families for financial support to cover tuition and other costs, leaving them in a precarious financial situation.

While all five participants are from households with relatively low socio-economic status, the intersectional analysis of qualitative data showed significant nuance, depending on the family structure, number of dependents, employment status of parents and/or caregivers and urban–rural geographic location. For instance, there are important socio-economic differences between Condorrera and Clarice. Condorrera was raised by a single parent in an informal settlement, while Clarice had two parents living in an urban area, who are both employed. While both families were under financial pressure to meet the costs of tuition, accommodation and other costs, Condorrera's situation was more precarious. Unlike Clarice, Condorrera attended a school in an informal settlement, while Clarice's parents enrolled her in a well-resourced high school. Clarice and Condorrera's interview extracts below illustrate the consequence of attending differently-resourced schools. Clarice's narrative included a detailed description of the various opportunities she had for enriching extramural activities, and the impact this had on her development: 'That's what changed my life, the school environment, the teachers … sports. That kept me busy' (Int. 1). Clarice explained that throughout her schooling, there were never more than 25 students in a class, which enhanced the quality of learning and created a supportive environment and affiliation with teachers. In contrast, Condorrera described the structural limitations that constrained her opportunities for development at school:

> If you … compare [well-resourced girls' school in an urban area] with [Condorrera's poorly resourced high school located in an informal settlement], it's just top class. They take drama, music. We didn't have that. Their labs are equipped. I remember our science teacher performed an experiment that

failed in front of class. [During a field trip] the same thing was done at [well-resourced school] and it worked.

(Int. 1)

In her digital narrative, Naledi focused on the challenge of growing up in an impoverished rural area. She foregrounded the struggle to adapt to academic expectations at university while her family had limited resources to support her studies. Similarly, because Kea was orphaned at a young age, her financial situation was precarious, as she narrated below: 'I had to start saving for my registration because that's the most important money that you need at varsity. And I told myself, I'm going to save, if I don't get a bursary. I don't have money at home' (Int. 1). In addition to concerns about resources for basic needs, poverty also meant that students spent much of their time and energy trying to find alternative sources of income and working part-time to cover tuition or accommodation fees, which negatively affected their academic participation (Wilson-Strydom, forthcoming).

Intergenerational vulnerability

Another aspect of pursuing higher education with limited resources was intergenerational vulnerability, which was reflected in gendered care relationships (Zembylas *et al.*, 2014). In Aziza's experience, being a mother and a university student created marginalisation and acted as a structural barrier. Aziza's narrative detailed how her participation at university was complicated by her duties as a mother to her young sons. Compared to participants without children, Aziza had to negotiate her studies and financial constraints alongside significant care responsibilities in her immediate and extended family. During the course of her degree, this exacerbated the stress of participating academically, without support structures or adequate resources to alleviate these responsibilities.

Physical and mental health

Physical and mental health was identified as structural barrier to participation which was exacerbated by the failing provincial health system (Ground Up, 2015). In their narratives, some students found it difficult to maintain physical and mental health, especially during the transitional first year or two of university study. As a result, a number of women were vulnerable to depression, anxiety and chronic stress, which had a negative effect on their freedom to participate. In Kea's experience, the pressure of accessing university with limited resources and support led to serious health problems, which compromised her academic success and left her with less time and energy to participate in her studies. Furthermore, it was concerning that Kea individualised this structural conversion factor by blaming herself for being 'weak' when she became ill, which she framed as an individual failure to adjust to university life.

Academic preparation

Undergraduate women from working class backgrounds were less likely to have access to well-resourced schools, which diminished their freedom for academic participation. Across the interviews and narratives, participants identified a lack of academic preparation for university-level study as a barrier that decreased their participation. In the extract below, Kea described the transition to university during her first year of study:

> I really did struggle with academics.… The amount of pressure and the amount of work.… It's really different from high school because … here in varsity you don't get people pushing you … especially from the school that I come from … when you come here [to university], no one cares.
>
> (Kea, Int. 1)

In the extract above, Kea's struggle to adjust to the autonomy expected from university students reflects other structural constraints at university, including a high staff–student ratio, and a corrosive hierarchy between students and staff, partly as a consequence of expanding enrolments alongside the challenge of insufficient funding to meet both individual and institutional needs (Bozzoli, 2015). In the analysis of the other narratives, academic struggle was framed by participants as a combination of structural and individual failures. It was significant that despite the deeply historical and structural grounding of inequalities in school provision, most participants blamed themselves for poor academic performance or academic failure, and as a consequence framed structural inequality as individual failure and weakness (Smit, 2012).

Epistemological access

Another structural conversion factor was participants' concern about whether knowledge was being transmitted and processed in a sustainable and meaningful way. Interestingly, both participants who were struggling academically and those who were struggling less were concerned about the quality and depth of knowledge transferred at university. There was a pervasive concern about the quality of teaching and learning methods that encouraged memorising and regurgitating knowledge for assessment, while there were fewer opportunities for developing critical academic capabilities. In the extract below, Clarice described how an instrumental approach to large classes of students decreased the quality of learning: 'When lecturers wonder why we've only studied to get our degrees and we've learned nothing else, it's because they don't share their knowledge with us either' (Int. 2). Because of these pedagogical barriers, Clarice had less freedom to convert information resources into epistemological access. Condorrera expressed a similar concern in reflecting on the depth of learning during the course of her four-year degree:

> I was saying to my lecturer, if before we graduate you were to give us an interview, or an exam that tests our knowledge from first year to fourth year,

I don't think most of us would graduate. Because we get information and then we forget about it. After writing the test, you forget about it.

(Condorrera, Int. 2)

As an alternative to rote learning, participants expressed the aspiration for discipline-specific academic support throughout the duration of their degree course, in order to develop the academic and social capabilities that they needed for equal participation.

Institutional culture

The final cluster of conversion factors relate to institutional cultures that exclude students from both academic participation and belonging. An important finding within the interview data was that socio-economic status was not necessarily aligned with the degree of engagement or alienation for individual students, because of alienating institutional cultures. In other words, Condorrera faced socio-economic challenges throughout her degree, but she was not less engaged or motivated in her studies, while Clarice, a more privileged student, described an ongoing struggle to engage academically. A closer look at Clarice's disengagement showed that she found aspects of the institutional culture alienating and demotivating, in particular the low academic expectations of students on extended degree programmes.

Another aspect of institutional culture was discriminatory attitudes towards black students from rural areas. Kea described the distinction made at her residence between students from urban and rural areas, in the extract below:

[At residence], there are labelled corridors, where this corridor is called … 'corridor of class' and the other corridor is called 'corridor of ghetto students' … it's saying that black people should go that way, white people should go that way.

(Int. 1)

Student experiences suggested that while resource scarcity contributes to alienation, a geographic identity that is located in an informal settlement or rural area made it more difficult for students to adapt to an institutional culture in an urban area. For this reason, students from rural areas also faced a more complex intersection of discrimination when they were marginalised, not only by white peers, but also by black middle-class peers. This marginality was exacerbated for students who were registered on the extended degree programme. Participants explained that while some aspects of the foundational support provided skills such as academic writing, the stigma attached to foundational support created a barrier between them and students on the mainstream degree programmes (Hlalele and Alexander, 2012; see also Leibowitz and Bozalek, 2015), which also diminished recognition.

Participants identified the struggle to prove their intelligence and worth by assimilating the discourse of English proficiency. In the context of a rural primary school, Kea explained how she was rewarded for speaking English and integrating into the dominant academic culture. Despite this skill, she experienced persistent discrimination within the university culture as a black woman from a rural area trying to prove her academic worth, and experienced pressure to assimilate by speaking English with an accent that was acceptable within a higher education environment. She described an incident that illustrates the value judgements connected to race and class: 'Because if [the lecturer] reads your essay, and she looks at you, and how you speak in class, she thinks, that person can't write this kind of essay'. Other participants also identified judgments about language proficiency as a barrier to engagement and participation, given an institutional culture, where students were mocked and devalued for English spoken with a rural or an 'ethnic' accent.

Having explored the structural conversion factors that constrain equal participation, I now turn to the second section of the chapter which shifts the focus to the agency that students used to negotiate these structural inequalities.

Equal participation and capability development

The next section outlines the capabilities required to enable equal participation. The capabilities outlined in this section were selected as part of the participatory research process described in the methodology section. Drawing on participant experiences, and their engagement in focus groups with the experiences of their peers, these capabilities emerged as significant. In relation to the focus on the intersection of gender, race and class, these capabilities also reflect, in particular, the vulnerability faced by black female working-class students, while also giving attention to their agency in resisting these obstacles.

In addition to the participatory process, the capabilities introduced in this section build upon the conceptualisation of equal participation as a critique of both access and outcomes as insufficient indicators of equity in higher education. Because of high attrition, enrolment rates offer an incomplete assessment of whether students are achieving meaningful participation. Yet at the same time, graduate output does not provide a nuanced understanding of the capabilities with which students leave an institution, and whether these benefits associated with graduate outcomes are spread evenly across the student body. Since neither enrolment rates nor graduate output adequately capture the question of participatory parity, the collaborative research process developed a framework based on qualitative data analysis that brings structural and individual conversion factors to bear in the capabilities required for equal participation.

The six capabilities originally associated with equal participation included the following:

1 Critical literacies
2 Practical reason
3 Research
4 Affiliation

5 Deliberative participation
6 Values for the public good

In later iterations of writing and analysis, the capabilities have been expanded to include:

7 Recognition and voice
8 Emotions
9 Narrative imagination
10 Confidence

A significant part of the research was to draw attention to agency that is often neglected by the deficit approach to students i.e. framing structural weaknesses as individual weakness. The aim was to shift attention to the agency with which students were navigating conversion factors at the institution. While all ten capabilities are relevant to the women involved in the research, this chapter focused on the six capabilities listed in the first set above, that resonated in particular with gender-based exclusions in higher education, which are discussed in detail below. The six capabilities that are discussed in this chapter respond in particular to gender-based injustices, alongside race- and class-based marginality, such as silencing of voice and participation, oppressive academic practices, undervalued indigenous and feminised knowledge, rejection and alienation in institutional spaces, and lack of freedom or real opportunities to conduct research. These capabilities also address the precarious circumstances in which vulnerable young women students find themselves, with less freedom to speak, to be heard, to participate, or to produce and own knowledge. In the section below, the importance of each capability is discussed in more detail.

Research

As detailed in the methodology section, the research process created sustained engagement with the participants, which positioned them as collaborators in the project. Instead of being on the margins due to their undervalued status as young black females, they participated in the process of producing knowledge, using platforms that are usually not available to first-generation, undergraduate students, especially when this intersects with black, female, working class identity, as the student narratives suggested.

The capability for research resisted the superficial learning identified earlier in the chapter, which Clarice described here: 'This research project has helped me change my approach to university life. It was an opportunity for me to participate freely and I was also then allowed to share my views with others' (Clarice, Pedagogy Colloquium, 31 July 2014). Clarice had explained in her narrative that as a young coloured female, she felt vulnerable to being excluded from university life, and that she experienced stigma and discrimination due to assumptions that lecturers made about her academic potential. The capability for research therefore challenged these hierarchies implicit in the deficit approach to young, black, female and working-class students by enabling them to contribute to the production of knowledge related to their experiences. By claiming this position, participants shifted the discourse around student deficit by including their own experiences about their lives, and critiqued the one-dimensional view of students as poor, weak and struggling.

In resistance to being silenced or marginalised, participants also showed agency in choosing to share their experiences in public platforms, where they could cultivate identities as co-producers of knowledge about their lives. The capability for research enabled students to incorporate valued capitals and existing capabilities into the conversation, as Kea described here: 'I became empowered in that I realised that the project was about the struggle to succeed … I gained the skill of becoming a researcher, and I am proud to say that I am now a researcher' (Pedagogies Colloquium, 31 July 2014).

Kea also described the importance of having a platform for impact as a young black female from a rural background. To her, the capability for research enabled her to expand her aspirations and to build up additional capabilities such as confidence. This capability was also valuable because it aimed to give excluded students access to the implicit discourses around knowledge, which participants explained had often been denied to them due to deficit assumptions of incompetence as working class black women.

Recognition and voice

From a gender perspective, the interconnected capabilities for recognition and voice are crucial for challenging the deep seated historical and political silencing of women, and especially for young women of colour who face socio-economic vulnerability. What emerged clearly during the in-depth interviews were concerns about the absence of platforms where students could be recognised as valued members of the institution. In response, the research process was intentional about expanding opportunities for recognition and voice, as Clarice explains below:

> When people ask you to participate … it's either a survey or a questionnaire. You fill it in but you never get the feedback. And this has really opened a platform where we are allowed to say what we feel and share our stories with other people.
>
> (Digital narrative seminar, 21 May 2014)

The project operationalised an understanding of student voice that stretches beyond the symbolic inclusion of student representatives in decision making. In this case, it was about whose voice was not being heard: women who had to resist both racial, gender-based and classed stereotypes in order to be given a platform to speak. The capability for voice extended to questions of knowledge, pedagogy and curriculum, to the everyday practices where student voice was missing at the institution. During the monthly research workshops, participants had the opportunity to analyse structural conditions that diminished their voice and recognition at the institution, by drawing on the findings in the interview data and digital narratives, and by looking at the intersection of gender, race and class in this silencing. Another component of the research process included evaluative meetings scheduled to encourage reflexive analysis and discussion of the research activities. During these sessions, students identified capabilities that were expanded by their involvement in the research process.

Students also designed and implemented strategies that could expand their visibility on campus. Three specific research initiatives were implemented to expand student voice and recognition: first, participants were invited to contribute to a public colloquium on higher education pedagogy; second, they presented their digital narratives at a seminar organised by the Centre for Research on Higher Education and Development, where a panel of higher education experts acted as respondents; and finally, they were interviewed for a student response video that was screened at a national teaching and learning conference in November 2014. The significance of these research platforms was that young black women claimed multiple opportunities to address institutional concerns related to teaching and learning.

Affiliation

In response to the institutional alienation described in the previous section in this chapter, all the women in the study identified affiliation as a capability that they valued, especially as a buffer against the intersectional discrimination and marginality facing first-generation, black, working class students. To the women in the research, affiliation was theorised not merely as companionship, but as a politicised set of opportunity freedoms that enable individuals to pursue meaningful alliances with peers and academic and support staff (see also Nussbaum, 2011; Walker, 2006). Across the women's narratives, there was also evidence of students who found support from their immediate and extended families, despite poverty, mobility and geographical location. In some cases, even when the student's family was unable to provide adequate financial support, they offered a cohesive structure based on culture, religion, language, and shared values, which students identified as a valuable capability.

In Condorrera's experience, her affiliation with lecturers facilitated access to knowledge, and increased her confidence to approach lecturers for assistance. For other women students, affiliation with peers and staff at university was important because of increasingly strained connections with family and community when they entered higher education. Across the narratives, students related experiences of being rejected or judged by community members as they developed unfamiliar ways of reasoning, speaking or relating. Kea describes this positionality in her narrative below:

When I was at school me and my friends … did everything together. But the moment I got to varsity, whenever I went home, we were now on a different level…. Your educational journey, doesn't really make you better, but it puts you in a different … place than the other people. People will call you names when you're in varsity.

In response to alienation, participants used their agency to create affiliation across a number of sites on campus, where they sought out non-racist and non-sexist allies with whom to connect. Students living at student residences on main campus had a distinct advantage in having access to multiple platforms for culti-vating affiliation. Kea's interview data gives evidence of an extensive network of support with other young women, including an interracial friendship with her residence head, a mentorship affiliation with a young female student leader, and interracial and intercultural friendships at residence.

In her experience, Thuli created affiliation by sharing her knowledge with other students: 'I think my ability to share what I have with other people. So I am one of those people, a people's person, and I am open and I get to help them' (Int. 1). In contrast, Naledi lived off campus, and described how she had made no friends on campus before joining the project. Once she joined the research team, she cultivated the confidence to build friendships and cultivate affiliation.

Narrative imagination

The fourth capability is narrative imagination, or the ability to imagine the experiences and challenges that other people face (Nussbaum, 2010). This capa-bility was valued by women who understood the importance of being treated with dignity, and who did not want to reproduce the alienation that they had experienced on campus. During the research, participants explained how their narrative imagination was enhanced through their exposure to the experiences of their peers, as Aziza described here: 'What the narrative part did was, it opened up that space where you could say, mmm, another person went through some-thing like that. It opened that level of understanding that … we don't all know how we got here' (Focus group, April 2016). Clarice described how the research process also enhanced her understanding of the challenges that other young black women with limited resources face in accessing higher education: 'Like the group we are—it's just made me respect everyone more … we just learned so much about people and their lives. People might seem happy but you don't really know what's going on' (Int. 2). For an isolated off-campus student like Naledi, the opportunity to engage with peers through research offered her insight into other people's struggles: 'I've learned a lot about other people … under-standing their history, backgrounds. Other people have been through a tough time, like myself' (Int. 2). During the course of the research, students used the capability for narrative imagination to reframe affiliation with the collaborative, which also played a role in challenging damaging stereotypes created by a deficit view of students.

Emotions

Emotions emerged as a crucial aspect of capability development during later iterations of qualitative analysis, and acted as signifiers of both inequality and agency. Since emotions have often been feminised and thus devalued in academia, it was significant that participants reclaimed space within the project to express emotions freely. Being intentional about allowing emotions into the research process challenged the cognition–emotion binary. In some narratives, repeated expressions of anger and frustration signalled unjust structural arrangements that silenced and denigrated the experience of being female, poor, young, and black. The capability for emotions also emerged during the second phase of the research process, as the research group presented their narratives in the public platforms. The freedom to share emotions with peers was identified as a capability that was often absent in academic environments. Because of the severe alienation, stress and socio-economic challenges faced by the women in this study, they identified the importance of having access to institutional spaces that allowed the expression of emotions in a non-judgmental and supportive way. In particular, there was a need for sustainable opportunities where emotions could be shared with peers and staff members. As part of the research process, students used their agency to create an informal network of support for each other, which was cultivated alongside the research project.

Confidence

The final capability identified was the freedom to act and speak with confidence. During their interviews and focus groups, all five women identified the lack of confidence as a consequence of discrimination and resource inequality. The research project was identified as a platform where students could expand their confidence by reframing their experiences and 'failures' as part of their resistance to structural violence across the institution. Instead of individualising their struggle for recognition and equality, they converted the research platform into opportunities to critique gender-blind, classist, and racist institutional arrangements and practices that reproduced unequal participation. The conversation shifted from individual self-blame and pathologising failure to a nuanced discourse where individual women identified patterns of exclusion and injustice. Individual confidence was also cultivated as students worked closely with their historical and educational trajectories, which deepened their awareness of their agency in navigating structural inequality.

Conclusion

In this chapter, I have proposed a capability approach to conceptualising equal participation, based on the qualitative findings emerging from participatory research. In response to the intersection of structural barriers that young black, working class women students face in trying to achieve equal participation in higher education, this approach suggests an alternative research practice with the potential to destabilise institutional hierarchies and inequalities. The alternative model is based on a capability set that draws on the experiences of students who have been marginalised at the intersection of race, gender, age and class. The capabilities discussed speak directly to the silencing, oppression and discrimination faced by the research participants in this study. At the core of the capability set is an intersectional lens that foregrounds how institutional injustices are exacerbated by multiple forms of discrimination against an individual whose voice is devalued due to her youth, gender, class and race. Instead of being a set of conditions imposed upon vulnerable students, the capability approach proposed in this chapter is inherently participatory, with a strong focus on narrative, individual knowledge, and the expansion of the individual's freedom to choose alternatives. Across the six capabilities, there is evidence of the agency that young women brought to the research process, in challenging hierarchies and in using institutional spaces to enact resistance to oppressive practices. As such, the collaborative project showed important potential for future research that could resist the silencing of young women at universities.

Crucially, however, there is an accompanying need for a commitment to the human and material resources required to enable participation at an institutional level. Without sufficient resources invested in institutional programmes and pedagogy, equal participation will remain unattainable for too many undergraduate students. As evidenced in the increasing intensity of student protests against fees in South Africa, there is an urgent need to ensure that more young South Africans who have been denied opportunities for education and development are given platforms to aspire towards and pursue valued freedoms.

Notes

1 I discuss these opportunities in detail in the analysis section of the chapter.
2 Extended degree programmes form part of the equity agenda in South African higher education. In some cases, extended programmes allow access for working-class students from poorly-resourced schools, whose admission scores may be an inadequate reflection of their academic ability (Council on Higher Education, 2013).
3 Sen (1992: 56–57) distinguishes agency achievement as goals that have been accomplished and agency freedom as the opportunity to pursue valued goals.
4 Women in this study are representative of the cohort of South Africa women between the ages of 16–35 years, who remain most vulnerable to associated risks of being poor: increased incidences of sexual violence, murder by intimate partners, unwanted pregnancy, HIV infection, food insecurity, and diseases linked to malnutrition and food insecurity, such as diabetes, heart disease and obesity (ONE.org, 2015).
5 The impact on poor students' participation has been captured most recently in national #FeesMustFall protests, in which students and contract workers challenged escalating tuition fees, and the outsourced labour practices adopted by higher education institutions.

References

Boni, A. and Walker, M. (2016). *Universities and Global Human Development: Theoretical and Empirical Insights for Social Change*. London: Routledge.

Bozalek, V. (2012). Interview with Nancy Fraser. *Social Work Practitioner/Researcher*, 24(1), 136–151.

Bozalek, V. and Boughey, C. (2012). (Mis)framing Higher Education in South Africa. *Social Policy and Administration*, 46(6), 688–703.

Bozzoli, B. (2015). On My Mind: Stuck in the Past. Opinion. *Financial Mail*. 10, April. Online, available at: www.pressreader.com/south-africa/financial-mail/20150410/282102045189193.

Brown, R. N. (2009). *Black Girlhood Celebration: Toward a Hip-hop Feminist Pedagogy*. New York: Peter Lang.

Calitz, T. M. L. (2017). Designing Capability-Informed Pedagogy Using Participatory Student Research. In: M. Walker and M. Wilson-Strydom (eds). *Socially Just Pedagogies, Capabilities and Quality in Higher Education: Global Perspectives*. London: Palgrave Macmillan.

Case, J. M. (2013). *Researching Student Learning in Higher Education: A Social Realist Approach*. London: Routledge.

Council on Higher Education. (2013). A Proposal for Undergraduate Curriculum Reform in South Africa: The Case for a Flexible Curriculum Structure. Pretoria: Council on Higher Education.

Fraser, N. (2008). *Scales of Justice. Reimagining Political Space in a Globalizing World*. Cambridge: Polity

Fraser, N. (2013). *The Fortunes of Feminism: From Women's Liberation to Identity Politics to Anti-Capitalism*. London: Verso.

Ground Up. (2015). How the Free State Health System is Being Destroyed. 27 February 2015. Online, available at: www.groundup.org.za/media/features/freestatehealth/freestatehealth.htm.

Hlalele, D. and Alexander, G. (2012). University Access, Inclusion and Social Justice. *South African Journal of Higher Education*, 26(3), 487–502.

Kemmis, S., McTaggart, R. and Nixon, R. (2013). *The Action Research Planner: Doing Critical Participatory Action Research*. Geelong: Springer Science and Business Media.

Leech, N. L. and Onwuegbuzie, A. J. (2007). An Array of Qualitative Data Analysis Tools: A Call for Data Analysis Triangulation. *School Psychology Quarterly*, 22(4), December, 557–584.

Leibowitz, B. and Bozalek, V. (2015). Foundation Provision—A Social Justice Perspective: Part 1: Leading Article. *South African Journal of Higher Education*, 29(1), 8–25.

Luckett, K. (2016). Curriculum Contestation in a Post-Colonial Context: A View from the South. *Teaching in Higher Education*, 21(4), 415–428.

Mbembe, A. J. (2016). Decolonizing the University: New Directions. *Arts and Humanities in Higher Education* 15(1), 29–45.

Mertens, D. M. (2008). *Transformative Research and Evaluation*. New York: Guildford Press.

Ministerial Committee on Transformation and Social Cohesion and the Elimination of Discrimination in Public Higher Education Institutions. (2008). Report of the Ministerial Committee on Transformation and Social Cohesion and the Elimination of Discrimination in Public Higher Education Institutions.

Ministry of Higher Education and Training. (31 March 2016). 2000 to 2008: First Time Entering Undergraduate Cohort Studies for Public Higher Education Institutions. Higher Education Management Information Systems.

Nussbaum. M (2010). *Not for Profit: Why Democracy Needs the Humanities*. Princeton: Princeton University Press.

Nussbaum, M. C. (2011). *Creating Capabilities*. Harvard: Harvard University Press.

ONE.org. (2015). Status of Women and Girls in South Africa 2015. Towards the United Nation General Assembly Meeting on the New Sustainable Development Goals (SDGs). Online, available at: https://s3.amazonaws.com/one.org/pdfs/Status-of-women-and-girls-in-South-Africa-2015.pdf.

Pym, J. and Kapp, R. (2013). Harnessing Agency: Towards a Learning Model for Undergraduate Students. *Studies in Higher Education*, 38(2), 272–284.

Robeyns, I. (2005). The Capability Approach: A Theoretical Survey. *Journal of Human Development and Capabilities*, 6(1), 93–114.

Scott, I., Hendry, N. and Yeld, J. (2007). Higher Education Monitor: A Case for Improving Teaching and Learning in South African Higher Education. Pretoria: Council on Higher Education.

Sen, A. (1992). *Inequality Re-Examined*. Oxford: Clarendon Press.

Sen, A. (1999). *Development as Freedom*. Oxford: Oxford University Press.

Smit, R. (2012). Towards a Clearer Understanding of Student Disadvantage in Higher Education: Problematising Deficit Thinking. *Higher Education Research and Development*, 31(3), 369–380.

South Africa Youth Unemployment Rate 2013–2016. (No date). Online, available at: www.tradingeconomics.com/southafricayouthunemploymentrate.

Tikly, L. and Barrett, A. M. (2011). Social Justice, Capabilities and the Quality of Education in Low Income Countries. *International Journal of Higher Education*, 31, 3–14.

Tinto, V. (2012). Enhancing Student Success: Taking the Classroom Success Seriously. *International Journal of the First Year in Higher Education*, 3(1), 1–8.

United Nations Development Programme (UNDP). South Africa. (2015). Human Development Report (HDR) Work for Human Development.

Walker, M. (2006). *Higher Education Pedagogies: A Capabilities Approach*. Berkshire: Open University Press.

Walker, M. and McLean, M. (2013). *Professional Education, Capabilities and the Public Good: The Role of Universities in Promoting Human Development*. London: Routledge.

Walton, E., Bowman, B. and Osman, R. (2015). Promoting Access to Higher Education in an Unequal Society: Part 2—Leading Article. *South African Journal of Higher Education*, 29(1), 262–269.

Wilkins, A. and Burke, P. J. (2015). Widening Participation in Higher Education: The Role of Professional and Social Class Identities and Commitments, *British Journal of Sociology of Education*, 36(3), 434–452.

Wilson-Strydom, M. G. (2015). *University Access and Success: Capabilities, Diversity and Social Justice*. London: Routledge.

Wilson-Strydom, M. G (ed.). (Forthcoming). *In Our Own Words: Perspectives on Being a Student at the UFS*.

Wolf, J. and de-Shalit, A. (2007). *Disadvantage*. Oxford: Oxford University Press.

Zembylas, M., Bozalek, V. and Shefer, T. (2014). Tronto's Notion of Privileged Irresponsibility and the Reconceptualisation of Care: Implications for Critical Pedagogies of Emotion in Higher Education. *Gender and Education*, 26(3), 200–214.

4 Young academics, gender and chairs at universities in Russia

Natalia Karmaeva

1 Introduction

Gender equality in education is a development goal of the highest importance worldwide. It is a situation where women and men are placed in similar conditions to be able to realise their human rights. According to the definition provided by UNESCO (2014), gender equality implies that the interests, needs and priorities of both women and men are taken into consideration and the diversity of different groups of women and men are recognised. Gender equality is 'a human rights principle, a precondition for sustainable, people-centred development, and it is a goal in and of itself' (UNESCO 2014: 11). Ensuring equal rights for women and men is not only an economic, but also a moral concern due to the wider transformative intent (Loots and Walker 2016). Ensuring gender equality in higher education and research may be a crucial factor for transforming society at large (Unterhalter 2007).

In Russia, the employment participation of females has been increasing throughout the twentieth century; however, the labour market remains differentiated into female and male occupations and sectors of employment (Ogloblin 1999). In the higher education system, the number of female academics has been increasing in recent decades (Berezina and Vitjuhovskaya 2014). The proportion of female academics hired in higher academic positions—such as rectors, vice-rectors, or chairs—is considerably lower (ibid.).

As has been argued, the primary concern within the capability perspective has been on quantifiable indicators of gender equality and measures of female participation in different spheres of society, including education (Loots and Walker 2016). This chapter follows the debate started by Loots and Walker by analysing gender beyond the 'equal representation' view, by focusing on 'qualitative, everyday, lived experiences of people' (ibid., 261). This strategy is especially relevant for the analysis of the academic system in Russia, where gender hierarchies persist in spite of a high involvement of women in academic work.

Existing hierarchies might be reinforced by growing competition in the sector, especially as a result of global rankings. The 'striving' context is characterised by higher education institutions' pursuit of prestige within the academic hierarchy, which changes the conditions and content of academic work (O'Meara

2007). This reproduces resource dependencies within the sector and triggers inequalities between the 'have' and 'have not' academics and institutions (Paradeise and Thoenig 2013).

Academics in positions below full professor are especially affected by academic job cuts, clientelist relationships in the departments and a growing accountability in their work (Karmaeva and Rodina 2016). Limited access to international library resources, English language learning and professional development programmes, together with a lack of funding for research and academic mobility, hinder academics' research capacities and shift their preferences away from research (Kozmina 2014).

In the 2000s, programmes based on excellence in Russian higher education were targeted at integrating Russian universities in the global field. Universities and public research foundations were identified by the government and provided with additional funding and many universities underwent mergers, restructuring, optimisation of the study process, faculty closures, staff redundancies and the introduction of performance-based pay for faculties (Kuzminov *et al.* 2013). In Russia, a considerable volume of literature has been produced that discusses the acceptance of recent policies by academics (Hagurov and Ostapenko 2014; Karmaeva and Rodina 2016). Surprisingly, few scholars have concerned themselves with the effects that these changes have had on young female academics, who are often considered as among the Russian higher education sector's most fragile actors (Djenina 2003). Many female academics already have a lower status within the academic hierarchy; they are at risk of further marginalisation vis-à-vis 'striving'.

This chapter has the goal of analysing the academic identities of young female academics as actors in a changing environment, when the academic system and academic institutions are 'striving' towards better positions in rankings. The analysis of how female academics struggle with their different roles in academia and outside is carried out from the perspective of the 'practical reason' capability defined as 'being able to form a conception of the good and to engage in critical reflection about the planning of one's life' (Nussbaum 2000). This capability is universal, meaning that human beings have the same capability in a wide variety of social and cultural settings.

The analysis of the qualitative interviews reveals that an academic career becomes too challenging for many female academics due to the increased demands on research productivity and a high workload. Low pay in the higher education sector increases the financial dependency of female academics on their families. This exacerbates the conflict between work and domestic responsibilities. Female academics feel that they lack control over their professional biographies. Practical reason capability is constrained by gendered structures in academia and in society. Many of the young academics interviewed are not considering the option of entering the next academic qualification phase—writing a second doctoral dissertation to obtain a professorship in the future. They may even leave academia if the academic job requirements and the demands at work increase any further.

The chapter proceeds with an introduction to the context of the academic system in Russia, provides a literature review and analytical framework, and continues with the presentation of methodology and results. The presentation of the professional identities and aspirations of young academics is followed by the conclusion and policy recommendations.

2 On being women and academic careers

A number of studies focus on the analysis of 'striving' in academic systems and its impact on faculty (Gonzales 2015). Feminist scholars criticise the term 'excellence' that is widely used in 'striving' environments as it delineates privilege and the power of elites (David 2009). A 'striving' university is defined as a setting 'where resources and energy have been committed to climbing up the rankings' (Gonzales 2015: 303).

'Striving' in different countries leads to the marginalisation of groups with already weak positions, such as scholars of colour (Baez 2000), women (Gardner 2013), and the young (Courtois and O'Keefe 2015). In many countries, female academics are marginalised. This is especially seen in the growing proportions of female academics hired in non-tenure track and adjunct positions, and in the distribution of work at the departments (Wolfinger *et al.* 2009). Women tend to perform less valued types of professional activities in different countries, such as teaching bachelor degree students in short-term positions. In Germany, for example, 'women tend to perform this kind of badly paid and hardly valued work for longer periods of their academic career than their male colleagues' (Quality in Academia and Life 2011: 16).

The position of female academics in universities is also defined by professional hierarchies. Scientific discovery is a social process that not only involves theoretical assumptions, but also the actual social context, traditions and customs. The social dimension of science is about the organisation of academic work, structures and hierarchies of the scientific community. The barriers women face are related to social structures that set specific time structures, forms of organisation and hierarchies, that are considered as 'natural' (Krais 2000).

Capability approach scholars advocate policies that see an individual as an end, as well as policies that promote individual agency and well-being (Otto *et al.* 2017). In such a situation, the capability approach can be a normative account that can strengthen policy making to promote justice in academia and beyond (Boni and Walker 2016). Researchers are involved in developing theoretical frameworks and interventions aimed at transforming unjust structures to expand freedoms and development opportunities for disadvantaged groups (Unterhalter 2007).

Gender injustices in different societies have long been a concern of the capability approach (Nussbaum 2000; Walker 2007; Unterhalter 2007). Within the capability perspective, the primary focus has been on developing approaches to evaluate existing gender injustice and to acquire information to develop policies aimed at the empowerment of women in different cultural contexts (Kabeer

1999). A list of capabilities for women in Western societies have been developed to delineate a threshold of capabilities that has to be provided for individual agency (Robeyns 2003; Walker 2007). The list includes 14 capabilities, such as life and physical health, mental well-being, and bodily integrity and safety.[1] Not only structural conditions, but also individual autonomy are important in overcoming unjust gendered structures, as soon as opportunities can be converted into valued functionings or achievements through decision-making (Loots and Walker 2015: 365).

The capability approach is normative as it advocates public policy guided by a conception of the human good (Alkire 2008). However, as the capability approach applies the principle of methodological individualism, there is a risk of underestimating the role of social context in the formation of actors' preferences. This limits the degree of contextualisation of agents (Qizilbash 2002). Still, Nussbaum's account includes individuals' commitments and cultural context in the analysis and provides tools for analysing female academics in a social context. Her account offers enough critical power derived from its general orientation of the universal goods of well-being and agency. The choice of using Nussbaum's perspective for this analysis was defined by the goal of considering academics as actors in the contexts of their biographies and social environment and, at the same time, as reflexive agents that can override oppressive structures.

Nussbaum considers practical reason capability and the related capability of affiliation to be central, as they organise other capabilities. Practical reason delineates the ability to be able to form a conception of the good and to be reflective about the planning of one's life. Practical reason is a good in itself and 'suffuses all other functions, making them human rather than animal' (Nussbaum 2000: 87). An individual is exercising practical reason capability in acting in accordance to his or her internal beliefs.

Affiliation includes two aspects: 'being able to live with and towards others, to show concern for other human beings, to engage in various forms of social interaction; to be able to imagine the situation of another'; and 'having the social bases of self-respect and non-humiliation; being able to be treated as a dignified being whose worth is equal to that of others' (Nussbaum 2011: 33). Her approach puts forward what people consider valuable and emphasises individual autonomy (Muñiz Castillo and Gasper 2012). Although one capability cannot be prioritised over another, practical reason and affiliation capabilities are of special importance, as they organise the capabilities (Alkire and Black 1997).[2]

Nussbaum's conceptualisation of practical reason has been debated by a number of capability approach theorists (Gasper 1997; Qizilbash 2002; Clark 2002; Srinivasan 2007). For example, Alkire and Black (1997) suggest going beyond the rather restrictedly Aristotelian approach proposed by Nussbaum's ethics. They formulate fundamental and incommensurable dimensions of human flourishing, and by this overcome the dichotomy of 'normativity versus consequentialism' in the conceptualisation of human development present in Nussbaum's theory. The advantage of Alkire and Black's account is that it makes the capability approach more operationalisable. They identify the dimensions of practical reason that 'open up the possibilities as for how human development must be pursued.... The task of deciding which possibilities are to be pursued and how to pursue them is the task of practical reason' (Alkire and Black 1997: 268). The actions are directed toward internal human fulfilment (ibid.). Alkire and Black propose a list of principles of practical reason that can be used for evaluations of community decision-making processes (see Table 4.1). These principles will also direct the analysis of the empirical data in this chapter.

These principles include, for example, to 'have a harmonious set of orientations, purposes and commitments', to 'seek to integrate the objectives and commitments and practices involved in and affected by any practical decision', and to 'employ efficient means to objectives' (see Table 4.1). The research literature on academic careers in Russian and in other countries suggests that the most relevant, among others, are those principles of practical reason that are related to the ability to integrate diverse experiences, to deal with changing conditions and postpone gratification, as well as to form an enduring and non-contradictive sense of identity (Kozmina 2014; Klecha and Reimer 2008).

In the present study, these intrinsically important dimensions of human life will be illustrated and specified based on the cultural context of academia and personal values of individuals. By doing this, the chapter will account for

Table 4.1 Principles of practical reason

N	Principles of practical reason
1	Have a harmonious set of orientations, purposes and commitments. Seek to integrate the objectives and commitments and practices involved in and affected by any practical decision.
2	Do not leave out of account, or arbitrarily discount or exaggerate any of the basic human goods.
3	Do not arbitrarily discriminate between people.
4	Do not attribute to any particular project the overriding and unconditional significance that only a basic human good and a general commitment can claim.
5	Pursue one's general commitments with creativity and do not abandon them lightly.
6	Employ efficient means to objectives.
7	Do not overlook the foreseeable undesirable consequences of your choices.
8	Seek to identify and take responsibility for predictable consequences of any decision on the full roster of well-being dimensions, even if these are unintended.
9	Do not deliberately harm any dimension of human well-being.
10	Foster the common good.
11	Do not act contrary to your conscience, i.e. against your best judgement about the implications for your actions on these requirements or practical reasonableness and the moral principles they generate.

Source: this table is adapted from Alkire and Black 1997.

commitments that are meaningful to young academics, and also their self-reflexivity exercised under structural constraints in academia. The commitments and self-reflexivity of academics are central to the formation of practical reason capability.

Being young in academia

Being a young academic at a university is defined by the position in professional and organisational hierarchies and also by a lower professional autonomy compared to senior academics. The unfavourable situation of young academics is reinforced by the differentiation of faculty into research-active and teaching-active and the prevarication of academic work (Musselin 2008). For young academics, this increases both uncertainty with regard to material resources and cultural uncertainty (Billot 2010). In a big university, the structures are precarious, which means that although young academics are highly educated, they are pushed to work for long hours, make little money, and are expected to carry out unpaid work. As a result, junior professionals in education tend to be neglected by those above them (Shills 1997). As a result, many young academics have to manage fragmented professional identities and struggle with discontinuity of careers.

Young academics are less autonomous as social actors: male and female academics are largely dependent on their families in pursuing academic careers, as long as their employment remains unstable and low paid (Abramov *et al.* 2015). In addition, many young academics are still at the stage of trying out different professional development paths, with some of them entering academia by chance or considering it as a transitional stage in their careers (ibid.). The characteristics of the structural position of young academics and their characteristics as actors define them as vulnerable actors in the academic labour market.

3 Russian academia: an overview

The modern higher education system is a successor to the Soviet system and has inherited its territorial centralisation, structure and bureaucratic hierarchy (Kuraev 2016). Other legacies include an orientation towards teaching for many institutions due to the separation of teaching and research during the Soviet era, insufficient funding of academic research since the beginning of the economic transition in the 1990s, and the reduced prestige of an academic career.

Russian higher education was subject to deregulation and commercialisation in the 1990s, faced a weakening of professional institutions and an expansion of survival-oriented entrepreneurial behaviours on individual and organisational levels (Kitaev 2004). The economic transformations during the 1990s and insufficient funding of higher education and academic research resulted in the exodus of many young academics from this sector. The general instability of the sector, characterised by low pay, changing formal requirements on academic work, and mergers of higher education institutions, have led to the migration of many male academics to other sectors of employment, such as business.

Since the 2000s, public funds have been invested in selected universities and in several programmes to improve the academic system. Universities and academics from the central locations in the federalist higher education system in Russia benefited from these policies the most. The traditional key universities maintained significant strength (Moscow State Lomonosov University and Saint Petersburg State University) and several new institutions have been established. Currently, the universities' capacities to pay a competitive salary are largely defined by the availability of extra-budget funding, usually formed by commercial education programmes and fee-paying students, as well as the participation of some universities in country-level research excellence programmes (Carnoy *et al.* 2014). Of the 21 universities in the 5–100 excellence programme, nine of them are from Moscow and Saint Petersburg. This programme accounted for funding worth 14.5 billion Russian roubles in 2016.[3] Two universities, the Moscow State Lomonosov University and Saint Petersburg State University, have a special status and receive special funding from the federal budget (two billion Russian roubles in 2016). Country-level funding opportunities for young academics increased with the Russian Scientific Fund (RNF) and the Russian Fund for Fundamental Research (RFFI).

During the social and economic crisis of the 1990s, the economic situation as well as the social status of many working women lowered, this was also due to the worsened situation of teachers and medical professionals, where the proportion of female workers was significant (Baskakova 2004: 7). Currently, the proportion of women employed in the education sector is very high, amounting to about 80 per cent (Baskakova 2004: 280). In higher education, the situation is slightly different, the proportion of women amounts to 33.7 per cent, although at universities with a specialisation in social sciences and humanities this proportion is above 50 per cent (Berezina and Vitjuhovskaya 2014).

The proportion of women in senior positions in academia, such as rectors, is only 6 per cent; those that are vice-rectors and directors of branch organisations, 20 per cent; for deans of the faculties and heads of department, 28 per cent; and senior lecturers and assistants 68 per cent (ibid.). The major reason for this, even though 78 per cent of total academic positions are held by women, is that 'men succeed in their careers better, because they have more time and opportunities, then women' (Matjushina 2007: 72). Public opinion sees education as a professional sphere for women, while research and scholarship is seen as predominantly a professional sphere for men (Berezina and Vitjuhovskaya 2014: 9).

According to Berezina and Vitjuhovskaya (2014), the economic crisis has also led to cuts in budget provision for nursery schools, kindergartens and education centres for children, and the number of such institutions has decreased. In this situation, families are increasingly involved in the functions of caring and educating. Women are challenged by the social expectation of success in a professional sphere, a personal expectation of social stability, and the provision of care and education for their children.

4 Methodology

Universities were selected purposefully based on the criteria of location and their involvement in research excellence programmes.[4] Two 'central' universities, one of which (A) was a younger university established in the early 1990s and developed from a specialised university to a comprehensive university; and the other (B) was an old comprehensive university, founded in the eighteenth century. One of these universities is located in Moscow, and the other in Saint Petersburg. Three other universities were selected from smaller towns in Central Russia and Siberia: a technical university (C) established in the 1930s; a smaller pedagogical university (D) founded in the 1950s; and a comprehensive university (E) founded in the 1910s (A, B and E are listed in the QS rankings, with E holding one of the lowest positions). The higher education institutions are universities with basic and applied research stated as one of their functions in the bylaws. Universities A and B receive extra research funding: university A is in the 5–100 programme, university B is one of two universities with special status.

A qualitative analysis was performed to capture the creativity of action and structural constraints. Problem-centred interviews focused on research in the context of other professional activities (Witzel 1985) were chosen to obtain a faculty's justifications of their actions. The face-to-face interviews were conducted in Russian, and the translations are the author's. Every participant was asked to describe their experiences related to their career path, their current involvement in different professional activities, their understanding of what makes good teaching and research, their future plans, plus subsequent clarification and open questions. The disciplinary specialisation of junior academics represented social sciences: sociology, social work, educational psychology and education.

Academic careers in Russia include several ranks: PhD candidate (*kandidat nauk*)/chair assistant, lecturer (*docent*), professor (*doctor nauk*). Professors can occupy a position of a chair holder. To qualify for a professorship, applicants are required to achieve 'habilitation' (a 'doctor of science' degree, by writing extra scholarly work). To be granted a PhD ('candidate of science' degree), applicants are required to write a PhD dissertation, to pass exams, and PhD candidates are usually involved in the activities of the chair (*kafedra*), including teaching.

The sample was purposefully selected based on the criteria of discipline and career stage, consisting of 16 young academics (eight female and eight male) from ranks lower than full professor. The interviews were conducted between autumn 2014 and spring 2015. Male academics were interviewed to identify how structural and symbolic barriers impact male and female academics differently. This helps to achieve insight into women's experiences in comparison to male experiences. The participants were in the middle of their PhDs (Anjelika, Anna, Petr, Roman, Tatjana, Vlad, Olesya, Milena), or had completed their doctorates (Michail, Marina, Oxana, Olya, Dmitriy, Svetlana, Milena, Alex), they were aged between 24–30 years. They were involved in teaching and other professional activities and were employed with short-term contracts (for one or two years) in the posts of assistants, docents or senior lecturers. Most of the academics interviewed combine university positions in teaching and administration or have jobs outside university.

Promotion is managed locally and, until recently, extension of the contract was rather a formal requirement due to the peer mechanisms and a relatively low competition for academic jobs. However, the situation has changed and now in order to extend contracts many universities request applicants to have made publications in journals listed in Scopus or the Thomson Reuters Web of Science database; as well as in local journals accredited by the academic All-Russian Attestation Commission (VAK).

In addition, 16 interviews with the professors/chair holders were carried out to inform the analysis of the interviews with young academics (Karmaeva and Rodina 2016). Participants were assured of confidentiality in the reporting of findings. Documents such as strategies and university policies were used as supplementary data.

The coding used the procedures of Grounded Theory (Strauss and Corbin 1998). Codes on teaching, research and other professional activities of academics were systematised depending on the context they refer to and how these activities were framed. Coding includes two dimensions of focus: self-reflection, meaning, understandings of work related to the context of action, such as academic and non-academic; and resources (symbolic and material structures).

5 Results

The results section compares conceptualisations of the academic work of a number of female and male academics, as well as describing the formative processes that affect the work and life choices of female academics. Illustrations from the interviews are provided where possible.

Female academics' views on departmental hierarchies

Senior academics, both female and male, describe young academics as lacking autonomy, stating that they must be 'raised', 'directed and guided' by the seniors because they do not know how things work. They also mention that the selection of candidates for academic posts is made informally: 'I am not interested in hiring a "pig in a poke". This is why I hire my former students or people I know' (Professor, University B). Senior academics allocate work in their departments based on informally defined criteria, which are usually not favourable to younger colleagues. There is a noticeable difference in the ways that female and male academics see their involvement in less beneficial or unpaid activities. While male academics are critical of work that is unpaid or does not bring professional recognition, female academics emphasise their general fulfilment at work and the commitments they make in their department.

The young male academics primarily see research as the production of publications. The academics from the research university perceive publications as a way to earn extra money. Roman, a senior academic teacher, notes that it makes sense to write papers in order to 'earn money from them'. He plans to pursue an academic career where writing papers is central: 'My career ideal is, first of all, to do research—nothing will work without it—and to write papers'. This indicates that individuals have instrumental aspirations aligned with performance demands. This results in a situation where an individual does not act in accordance with her intrinsic values and beliefs and therefore experiences alienation from her work. Therefore, the orientation of this male academic towards advancement within the academic hierarchy yields adjusted aspirations (Hart 2016).

Female academics, including those who publish in international journals, see their professional activities differently. To them, doing valuable work and caring for and helping others is important. Therefore, they focus on the non-material aspects of well-being in work, neglecting the material aspects. For example, Olya, an assistant professor involved in teaching, research and administration work, says:

> Nowadays, the courses are very small. In the past, they lasted for 45 hours, but now they have been reduced to 30 hours. It is very difficult to arrange role play, practical exercises and so on within this time limit. But sometimes my wonderful students ask me to meet a couple of times more. But this means that I teach some extra hours unpaid. I still do this because when there is such enthusiasm we should do it.

Olya establishes good relationships with students and is concerned about their needs. However, her commitment leads to a very high workload, as she later says in the interview: her working day ranges from 15–17 hours in duration, she does not meet deadlines and feels 'stressed and guilty'. She sees her situation as critical, referring to her inefficient time management as one of the reasons for this. Michail, a senior academic teacher with a comparable workload in teaching and research, but with a slightly lower administrative workload, is more critical about the university structures:

> On the one hand, they exploit you by including a lot of responsibilities in your contract. On the other hand, you are in between these subjects of decision-making on your performance or subjects of evaluation [of his teaching and research].

He adds that, in addition to being productive in research, 'you have to also be liked by the heads of education programmes, by the students'. This indicates that some female academics are less reflective about the oppressive structures in academia, instead they consider themselves responsible for their success or failure. Therefore, their actions are merely guided by commitments rather than reasoned evaluation of their circumstances (Alkire and Finnis 1997).

Both female and male academics are subject to clientelist relationships in their departments when the boundaries of the departments become difficult to penetrate by outsiders. However, half of the female academics interviewed justify these relationships by ascribing the professors a higher authority: they are often named 'venerable scholars', 'gurus' or 'coryphaeus'. This indicates a lack of autonomy (Alkire and Finnis 1997). Most of the female academics consider that policies are responsible for their unfavourable situations: for example, they criticise recent policies that led to position cuts at universities, from the per-spective of a lack of new positions. Some female academics are more critical of the hierarchies in their departments and discuss the issue of senior colleagues experiencing professional stagnation yet still occupying senior academic posi-tions, as well as controlling information flow.

The unstable and contradictory professional identity, as well as constrained decision-making, can be seen in Olesya's interview. She is a doctoral student and a department assistant, who teaches and performs supportive work in her department. Due to the high volume of paperwork related to the recent growth of accountability, she must often help the secretary by writing reports, filling out forms, revising colleagues' methodical work, among other activities. This kind of paperwork is not included in the contract of the faculty and is—formally—unpaid, as her salary is based on teaching hours. If the paperwork is urgent, she must sometimes work over the weekend. As a result, Olesya does not have enough time for her dissertation. She reflects on her situation:

> I always think: If I continue to do this [supportive work], what is the reason? Will there be any result? Is my behaviour effective? If I am just around [at the department], helping everybody for free, what will be the effect of this for me? Will I develop my career or achieve stability? Now the positions are cut and a degree [doctoral] does not guarantee any career [achievement]. What can guarantee it is to win a research grant, to publish papers, to have a high citation index, but this is not related to your [doctoral] dissertation.

In this narration, she questions a variety of her activities from different points of view and struggles to relate these activities to her developmental goals. The development of a career is a relevant goal. She sees her work in unity with her life and expects to achieve stability. She would also like to dedicate time to her own research (dissertation). However, it is not evident to her how she can relate her current activities to her goal, especially when the 'rules of the game' become unclear. For her, maintaining personal commitments in her department is important, as well as writing a dissertation, which she is currently doing. The unpaid supportive work does not bring her any closer to the achievement of her goals. She lacks harmony among her judgements, choices and performances (Alkire and Black 1997: 268). Therefore, her development is constrained to normative and procedural dimensions of action. In summary, female academics are oriented towards commitments in their work, while male academics are more aware of their structural positions and are oriented towards advancement within the academic hierarchy.

Gendered outcomes of postponed gratification and poor material conditions at work

Male academics see their poor remuneration as an investment in their future and develop an expectation of obtaining a 'gratification' later. They are also likely to critically reflect on the amount of money they earn at the university and take on additional paid work, either at the university or elsewhere.

Petr, a teaching assistant and doctoral student from a technical provincial university, combines small jobs in teaching and research with his work as an acrobat. He balances different jobs and is always looking for new ways to earn extra income. He describes his unstable situation:

> I was a contract teacher at the pedagogical university.... There were changes in the personnel structure and they got rid of contract teachers.... It is a paradox: for one hour of work as a university teacher I get 150–200 roubles [equal to 2 euros at the time of the interview], whereas for extra jobs [outside academia] it can be up to 1,000 roubles [equal to 20 euros at the time of the interview].

Half of the female academics interviewed emphasise the altruistic character of academic work and do not expect any improvement of pay. Some of them, for example, Svetlana, mentions the influence of their supervisors on their decisions to stay in academia despite the poor material conditions:

RESEARCHER: How do you manage it financially, does your family help you?
S: Sure, this is all the 'charity' of my family. In general, you know, I would like to feel comfortable and happy at work. Now I do [feel happy], and I think, to feel good is very important for self-realisation, for professional self-realisation. Besides, I was told by my doctoral thesis supervisor that the material side is not the decisive factor.

She associates herself with the altruistic-in-nature academic profession and justifies her material situation by referring to the authority of her supervisor. She sees the family support, which is the condition for her to stay in the profession, as 'charity'. The comparison of this quote to other parts of the interview, as well as to other cases, shows that female academics often rely on the support of their families regarding international mobility, e.g. to attend international conferences. However, they are also expected by their families to fulfil domestic responsibilities and not to change residence for career mobility. This dependence on family support again lowers their autonomy.

For all female academics, having good relationships at work is one of the main reasons for their choice to work in the departments where they studied as masters students. Here, 'harmony between and among individuals and groups of persons' is important, in Alkire and Black's words (1997: 268). Later Svetlana says: 'I agreed to this position because I had developed very good relationships with my colleagues here. I did not have any material motivation—the salary was very low'. A similar preference for good relationships at work was expressed by only one male academic, a senior lecturer from a provincial university, who has a very high teaching load and an extra job as an alumni manager.

The analysis shows that female academics are highly oriented towards the non-material aspects of well-being at work. As academic work is not professionalised in Russia, this orientation does not refer to academic research, but to other related outcomes that academic work can offer: affiliation and commitments. This leaves the female academics vulnerable to external requirements on research productivity.

Family commitments, social expectations and career decisions of female academics

The theme involving the interference of family commitments in the career decisions of academics was only identified in the interviews with female academics. Not only do female academics depend on their families for travelling abroad to conferences, as they often do not have academic mobility funding, but some of them also struggle with family commitments, demands at work and their professional developmental ambitions. Olya says:

> I had an opportunity to do my PhD in the UK. I was invited, but I refused— my mother was ill and I had my boyfriend here.... But maybe I regret that decision. I don't know. But I still reflect on this and I do regret: what if [I had done it]?

This situation, coupled with the stress and feeling of guilt she experiences at work (see earlier), negatively affects her well-being and may constrain her actions in the future. As a result, she struggles to harmoniously align her different roles in academia and her private life. To illustrate how the tensions became visible in the interview, two narrations will be presented.

In the extract below Olya describes leaving academia:

> My future plans, well, I will have to renew my contract in 2016, there are new requirements.... This is the plan. On the one hand, I would like to exit this 'rat race' now, maybe to have a baby. But for now this does not work. On the other hand, it would be good to write a dissertation [a second dissertation, for the doctor of sciences degree], and [professor] X is pushing me in this direction. He is, of course, right.

In the following abstract, she discusses the option of becoming a mother and refers to the social norm of having children (she is 30):

> Definitely, I should do it [have a baby], because of my age. But this is very abstract. I just know this is something rational, that I have to dedicate time

and effort to this, to have a baby and so on. But practically I can't imagine this, how my life will change, taking into account my workload. This is a very threatening hypothetical assumption; it makes me very nervous. It is very difficult to unite everything in my life this way. I am afraid. This is a big fear I have—that I will not manage in one of the spheres [of my life]—either I will be a bad mother, or a bad scholar, or everything will collapse, everything that I developed with such great effort.

Olya emphasises that she fears the future, as it is full of uncertainties, and she fails to rationally evaluate the different options in her current situation. In the changing context of the university she lacks resources that would support her as a mother and she must rely on herself. This increases her fears, as she defines the alternatives as either being a scholar or facing a collapse of everything in her life (based on the interview it can be concluded that she means not just her current academic position, but her life in general). She experiences difficulties in integrating her roles, and struggles to develop a harmonious sense of self that will also help her set priorities (Alkire and Black 1997).

Female academics who plan to have children also voice that, as employment contracts are now shorter (up to one year, with some exceptions), they cannot get paid maternity leave. Those academics who already have children feel overloaded, as in the past they expected to have more time for their families. Nowadays, the increased workload and high demand for publications make it difficult to combine work and family.

This leads Olesya to the conclusion that the academic career is a career for males:

'Career'—this is a male career, a successful, brilliant, powerful, top-level career. A woman should have no husband and no children so she can be free and have time for everything. Because a woman who has a family cannot come back home and write something, write all day long—she has children, a husband. She has relatives, a mother, she has to take care of the grandmother, do shopping, cook, tidy up—do all these things that she has to do.

Some female academics are dissatisfied and continuously reflect on their situations. They state that it is hard for them to leave academia because: first, employment is still flexible and this is convenient; second, they do not know where else they could find a job; third, they like this type of intellectual work; and finally, they feel involved and are committed to the profession. As Olesya says, she would need to have a good reason to leave academia. This in fact refers to external powers out of her control, such as a considerable salary cut or her contract not being extended. This shows how difficult the decision to leave academia can be, despite the worsening situation at work. The situation of young female academics is especially problematic, as although they are well-educated, they are pushed to work long hours, while making little money and are expected to carry out unpaid work. This demonstrates the relationship between academic hierarchies and gender, generating a precarious structure that hits female academics the hardest.

Conclusions

Being young and female in academia places higher demands on those who strive for professional recognition in a social context where traditional gender roles are persistent. The prevailing social norms and expectations delegate to men more control over various aspects of life, including careers. Structures of academia including hierarchies, beliefs, wages and the principles of pay, and informal rules at the departments, create an environment that does not support the development of practical reason capability among female academics. Many of the young female academics interviewed struggle to develop a coherent sense of professional identity under the pressures of increasing competition in academia and research productivity demands.

The capability approach as a framework helps us to disentangle the stories in order to reveal that, despite female integration at the university level, women are under greater pressure than their male counterparts, as long as professional and social expectations are intertwined. As the analysis shows, the pressures on young female academics come not only from formal requirements on research and teaching productivity, but also from their involvement in supportive work at their departments, which is usually unpaid and agreed on informally. As the material conditions at work are insecure, female academics rely on the support of their families. A variety of commitments, including family commitments, make them less active players in the increasingly individualist and competitive academic field.

Many female academics showed difficulties in harmoniously relating their professional activities at work, formulating professional development goals, and choosing adequate means to achieve them (Alkire and Black 1997). They also had difficulties in forming a harmonious set of orientations, purposes and commitments that would unite their work and their lives. This also refers to the conditions of human flourishing as action orientations for men and women (Alkire and Black 1997). Male academics are more reasoned and critical about their situation, whereas female academics are oriented towards establishing and maintaining commitments.

The formation of the identities of female academics and action orientations was affected by structures. The analysis of the practical reasoning capability of female academics shows that in the dimensions identified by Alkire and Black (1997), the following structural factors constrain this capability: rapidly changing structures at their universities; increasing demands in their profession, particularly, research productivity demands; and a lack of support for women at the universities. The latter not only includes such basic aspects as maternity leave, provision of a kindergarten and other support to female academics with children, but also career development support for women, including gender mainstreaming programmes.

Individual autonomy is crucial in combating unjust gendered structures, as soon as opportunities can be converted into valued functionings or achievements through decision-making (Loots and Walker 2015: 365). The interviews show that growing demands at work related to 'striving' policies in the academic system make it difficult for women to combine work and life, as well as being self-standing professionals. A greater number of male academics are more oriented towards research, but with research that they relate with publishing, rather than the process of scientific discovery. Female academics show greater acceptance of involvement in less beneficial professional activities at the departments. This creates disadvantages for females as young academic professionals by limiting their involvement in the process of the production of scientific knowledge (Boni and Walker 2016).

This corresponds to the results from previous studies that consider labour market outcomes for women. In Russia, females do not tend to attribute their achievements to internal forces, such as personal effort, instead, they tend to attribute personal success and failure to external forces, such as fate or chance (Semykina and Linz 2010). Female academics' families cover a part of their living costs, but also costs for professional mobility, publishing and other work-related issues. In addition, female academics combine formal employment with domestic responsibilities, as a result, they have less spare time than men (ibid.). This exacerbates the conflict between the various roles of female professionals and leads to their disempowerment.

On the basis of these young people's experiences as professionals, policy recommendations for universities would include the provision of support structures for female academics in the form of careers advice, flexible working hours and child-care facilities at the university. For both female and male academics, recommendations include: better pay and employment conditions, such as limitation of the application of one year or shorter employment contracts, and support of academic mobility should be provided. Other recommendations for universities include reducing the gender gap in higher university positions as well as strengthening role models for female academics as academic researchers at universities, and supporting and promoting the contributions of women to science, promoting women's participation in policy-making processes at different levels, and setting family-friendly legal frameworks, including guaranteed paid maternity leave.

Acknowledgement

The author acknowledges financial support from the Basic Research Program at the National Research University Higher School of Economics and from the Russian Academic Excellence Project '5–100'.

Notes

1 The full list includes these capabilities: Life and physical health, mental well-being, bodily integrity and safety, social relations, political empowerment, education and knowledge, domestic work and nonmarket care, paid work and other projects, shelter and environment, leisure activities, time-autonomy, respect, religion (Robeyns: 72).

2 This analytical construct that combines practical reason and affiliation was also applied by feminist scholars in the analysis of identities. For example, there is a shift towards the account of relational autonomy, a social sensitive concept of autonomy. Within this perspective, actions and decision-making are grounded in the practical identity of an individual: 'a normative self-conception, which embodies a person's sense of self-identity and her commitments, values, and beliefs' (Mackenzie 2014: 18).

3 This amounts to about US$223 million (Ministry of Finances of Russian Federation, viewed on 10 July 2016, online, available at: http:/minfin.ru/).

4 The names of participants and the titles of the universities were changed to ensure anonymity.

References

Abramov R. N., Gruzdev I. A. and Terentyev, E. A. (2015). Akademicheskii Professionalism v epohu peremen: rolevye subidentichnosti i transformaciya budjetov vremeni [Academic Professionalism in the Period of Changes: Role Subidentities and the Transformation of the Budgets of Time]. *Monitoring obshestvennogo mneniya: economicheskiye I socialnye peremeny*, 6(130), C, 136–152.

Alkire, S. (2008). Using the Capability Approach: Prospective and Evaluative Analyses. In: F. Comim, M. Qizilbash and S. Alkire (eds), *The Capability Approach: Concepts, Measures and Applications*, pp. 26–49. Cambridge: Cambridge University Press.

Alkire, S. and Black, R. (1997). A Practical Reasoning Theory of Development Ethics: Furthering the Capabilities Approach. *Journal of International Development*, 9, 263–279.

Baez, B. (2000). Race-Related Service and Faculty of Color: Conceptualizing Critical Agency in Academe. *Higher Education*, 39(3), 363–391.

Baskakova, M. E. (2004). Mujchiny i jenshiny v sisteme obrazovaniya [Men and Women in the Higher Education System]. In: *Gndernoe ravenstvo v sovremennoi Rossii skvoz' prizmu statistiki* [Gender Equality in Russia], pp. 276–303. Moscow: URSS.

Berezina A. V. and Vitjuhovskaya, Y. A. (2014). Obraz jenshiny-prepodavatelya v SMI i v rossiiskom obshestve [The Russian Female Teacher in Media and Society]. *Chelovek v mire kultury*, 1, 3–9.

Billot, J. (2010). The Imagined and the Real: Identifying the Tensions for Academic Identity. *Higher Education Research and Development*, 29(6), 709–721.

Boni, A. and Walker, M. (2016). *Universities, Development and Social Change: Theoretical and Empirical Insights*. London and New York: Routledge.

Carnoy, M., Froumin, I., Loyalka, P. K. and Tilak J. B. (2014). The Concept of Public Goods, the State, and Higher Education Finance: A View from the BRICs. *Higher Education*, 68(3), 25 February, pp. 359–378.

Castillo, M., Muñiz, R. and Gasper, D. (2012). Human Autonomy Effectiveness and Development Projects. *Oxford Development Studies*, 40(1), 49–67.

Clark, D. A. (2002). Development Ethics: A Research Agenda. *International Journal of Social Economics*, 29(11), 830–848.

Courtois, A. and O'Keefe, T. (2015). Precarity in the Ivory Cage: Neoliberalism and Casualization of Work in the Irish Higher Education Sector. *Journal for Critical Education Policy Studies*, 13(1), 43–56.

David, Miriam, E. (2009). Diversity, Gender and Widening Participation in Global Higher Education: A Feminist Perspective. *International Studies in Sociology of Education*, 19(1), 1–17.

Djenina, I. G. (2003). Molodej v Nauke [Youth in Science]. *Sociologicheskiyjurnal*, 1, 71–87.

Gardner, S. K. (2013). Women Faculty Departures from a Striving Institution: Between a Rock and a Hard Place. *Review of Higher Education*, 36(3), 349–370.

Gasper, D. (1997). Sen's Capability Approach and Nussbaum's Capabilities Ethic. *Journal of International Development*, 9(2), 281–302.

Gonzales, L. D. (2015). Faculty Agency in Striving University Contexts: Mundane yet Powerful Acts of Agency. *British Educational Research Journal*, 41(2), April, 303–323.

Hagurov, T. A. and Ostapenko, A. A. (2014). Реформа образования глазами учителей и преподавателей [Education Reform from the Perspective of School Teachers and Academic Teachers]. *Sociologicheskiye Issledovaniya*, 11, 103–107.

Hart, C. S. (2016). How Do Aspirations Matter? *Journal of Human Development and Capabilities*, 17(3), 324–341.

Kabeer, N. (1999). Resources, Agency, Achievements: Reflections on the Measurement of Women's Empowerment. *Development and Change*, 30, 435–464.

Karmaeva, N. and Rodina, N. (2016). Zaveduyushie kafedrami v usloviyah menyaushih-sya mehanismov upravleniya [Chair Holders in the Context of Changing Governance in Higher Education Institutions in Russia]. *Sociologicheskiye Issledovaniya*, 8, 24–32.

Kitaev, I. (2004). University Funding by the Central Russian Government: Where the Ends Meet? In: Shattock M. (ed.), *Entrepreneurialism and the Transformation of Russian Universities*, pp. 36–56. Paris: UNESCO, International Institute for Educational Planning. Online, available at: www.unesco.org/iiep.

Klecha, S. and Reimer, M. (2008). Wissenschaft als besonderer Arbeitsmarkt, Grund-typologien des Umgangs mit unsicherer Beschäftigung beim wissenschaftlichen Personal. In: S. Klecha and W. Krumbein (eds), *Die Beschäftigungssituation von wissenschaftlichem Nachwuchs*, pp. 13–87. Wiesbaden: VS Verlag.

Kozmina, Y. Y. (2014). Preferences of Academic Teachers for Research and Teaching. *Voprosy Obrazovaniya*, 3, 135–151.

Krais, B. (2000). Das Soziale Feld Wissenschaft und die Geschlechterverhältnisse: theoretische Sondierungen. In: *Wissenschaftskultur und Geschlechterordnung: über die verborgenen Mechanismen männlicher Dominanz in der akademischen Welt*, pp. 31–54. Frankfurt am Main: Campus-Verl.

Kuraev, A. (2016). Soviet Higher Education: An Alternative Construct to the Western University Paradigm. *Higher Education*, 71(2), 181–193.

Kuzminov, Y. I., Semyonov, D. S. and Frumin, I. D. (2013). The Structure of the Higher Education Institutions' Network: from the Soviet towards the Russian 'Master Plan'. *Voprosy Obrazovaniya*, 4, 8–69.

Loots, S. and Walker, M. (2015). Shaping a Gender Equality Policy in Higher Education: Which Human Capabilities Matter? *Gender and Education*, 27(4), 361–375.

Loots, S. and Walker, M. (2016). A Capabilities-based Gender Equality Policy for Higher Education: Conceptual and Methodological Considerations. *Journal of Human Development and Capabilities*, 17(2), 260–277.

Mackenzie, C. (2014). Three Dimensions of Autonomy. In: M. Piper and A. Veltman (eds), *Feminism and Autonomy*, pp. 15–41. New York: Oxford University Press.

Maltseva, I. O. (2005). *Gendernye razlichiya v professional'noi mobilnosti I segregaciya na rynke truda: opyt rossiiskoi ekonomiki* [Gender Differences in Professional Mobility in the Labour Market: The Experience from the Russian Economy]. Moscow: EERC.

Matjushina, Y. (2007). Gendernyu podhod k upravleniyu vyshei shkoly [Gender Approach to Higher Education Institution Management] *Kadrovik. Kadrovyi menedgment*, 1, 70–74.

Musselin, C. (2008). Towards the Sociology of Academic Work. In: A. Amaral, I. Bleikle and C. Musselin (eds), *From Governance to Identity*, pp. 47–56. Dordrecht: Springer.

Nussbaum, M. (2000). *Women and Human Development: The Capabilities Approach.* Cambridge: Cambridge University Press.

Nussbaum, M. (2011). *Creating Capabilities: The Human Development Approach.* Harvard: Harvard University Press.

Ogloblin, C. G. (1999). The Gender Earnings Differential in the Russian Transition Economy. *Industrial and Labor Relations Review*, 52, 602–627.

O'Meara, K. A. (2007). Striving for What: Exploiting the Pursuit of Prestige. In: J. C. Smart (ed.), *Higher Education: Handbook of Theory and Research*, Vol. 22, pp. 121–179. New York: Springer.

Otto, H-U., Walker, M. and Holger, Z. (eds) (2017). *Capability-Promoting Policies: Enhancing Individual and Social Development.* Bristol: Policy Press.

Paradeise, C. and Thoenig, J. C. (2013). Academic Institutions in Search for Quality. Local Orders and Global Standards. *Organization Studies*, 34(2), 196–224.

Robeyns, I. (2003). Sen's Capability Approach and Gender Inequality: Selecting Relevant Capabilities. *Feminist Economics*, 9(2–3), 61–92.

Semykina, A. and Linz, S. A. (2010). Analyzing the Gender Pay Gap in Transition Economies: How Much Does Personality Matter? *Human Relations*, 63(4), 447–469.

Qizilbash, M. (2002). Development, Common Foes and Shared Values. *Review of Political Economy*, 14(4), 463.

Quality in Academia and Life. (2011). A Joint Strategy to Improve Work-Life Balance by GEW, UCU and SULF. Higher Education and Research. Women's Policy. Frankfurt, Germany: Gewerkschaft Erziehung und Wissenschaft.

Srinivasan, S. (2007). No Democracy without Justice: Political Freedom in Amartya Sen's Capability Approach. *Journal of Human Development*, 8(3), 457–480.

Strauss, A. and Corbin J. (1998). *Basics of Qualitative Research Techniques and Procedures for Developing Grounded Theory* (2nd edition). London: Sage Publications.

United Nations. (2014). *Priority Gender Equality Action Plan 2014–2021.* Paris: United Nations Educational, Scientific and Cultural Organization (UNESCO). Online, available at: http://unesdoc.unesco.org/images/0022/002272/227222e.pdf.

Unterhalter, E. (2007). Gender Equality, Education and the Capability Approach. In: M. Walker and E. Unterhalter (eds), *Sen's Capability Approach and Social Justice in Education*, pp. 87–107. London: Palgrave.

Walker, M. (2007). Selecting Capabilities for Gender Equality in Education. In: M. Walker and E. Unterhalter (eds), *Amartya Sen's Capability Approach and Social Justice in Education*, pp. 178–195. London: Palgrave.

Witzel, A. (1985). Das Problemzentrierte Interview. In: Gerd Juettermann (ed.), *Qualitative Forschung in der Psychologie. Grundlagen.* Verfahrensweisen. Anwendungsfelder, pp. 227–256. Beltz: Weinheim und Basel.

Wolfinger, N. H., Mason, M. A. and Goulden, M. (2009). Stay in the Game: Gender, Family Formation, and Alternative Trajectories in the Academic Life Course. *Social Forces*, 87, 1591–1621.

5 Capitals and capabilities

Social reproduction of inequalities in Sripuram

Laksh Venkataraman

Introduction

The system of education in India often plays an instrumental role where the economic success of social groups is visualised by their employment outcome (Venkataraman 2016). In this human capital ideal, social groups generally treat education contrary to the essence of the capabilities approach. As a normative framework, the capabilities approach argues for freedom and welfare of human agency (Sen 1999). Against this backdrop, the current chapter highlights the complex interactions between human agency and social structure. For this, reflexive insights have been gathered from an ethnographic revisit to Sripuram, a south Indian village, analyses have been performed of the caste, class and education (CCE) of the poor to examine the role of capital in capabilities formation.[1]

Sripuram, one of the small villages in Tanjore district, is located on the banks of the River Kaveri in Tamil Nadu. Although Sripuram is a pseudonym, the exact location was introduced to the author by Andre Beteille. The classical works of Beteille in the 1960s, it must be noted, allowed him to produce one of the eminent sociological texts on India. His oft-cited book, *Caste, Class and Power*, is based on this multi-caste village (Beteille 1965). Like any other Tamil village, Sripuram is inhabited by diverse socio-economic groups where the presence of different castes is visible. The physical location of the village is divided into diverse streets, mainly along caste lines. For instance, the Agraharam, where the Brahmins or the erstwhile 'higher' caste live, are the first streets that anyone who enters the village from outside will encounter. This is parallel to other streets where fellow-villagers of other social groups live. For instance, the other backward classes (henceforth OBCs) who are also often addressed as *dominant castes* in the literature (Srinivas 1987) live in the nearby streets, which are adjacent to Agraharam. The OBCs in the village are a conglomeration of diverse caste groups of Kallar, Padayachi, Vellalars, among others. Socio-economically, they occupy the middle layer between the extreme positions of the Brahmins and the Pallars. The latter historically occupied the lower-rung of the physical, as well as the social hierarchies, and are often addressed in the village either as scheduled castes (SCs) or Dalits. Their erstwhile inferior socio-economic position seems to be the reason for their deprivation at present. For instance, they represent almost all indicators of ill-being, such as economic deprivation, illiteracy, unemployment and under-employment in the village.

The physical presence of these three broad social groups highlights distinct lifestyles that are remarkably different to each other. Even though OBCs and Pallars might look identical to outsiders, one can observe forms of social unrest. This unrest is often displayed to establish the primordial identities. In contrast, one can notice the involuntary social distancing of the Brahmins from the 'others' in the village. The Brahmins of Sripuram, like anywhere else in the country, are generally known for their cultural capital, as they have historically occupied the higher echelons of power. This is possible because of their socio-economic position, as they owned most of the land in the village until a few decades ago. Beteille has often addressed them as Mirasdars, or the landowners, in his work (Beteille 1965: 15). This gave them power to 'control' others who were economically dependent on these landholdings. Their social position as a 'higher' caste has allowed them to enhance their cultural capital over the years. The intersection of socio-economy and education has naturally ensured their growth and development. For instance, the Brahmin women are often more highly educated and knowledgeable than 'even' men of other castes in the village. This is in contrast to the general presumption where women occupy lower rungs of the patriarchy. On a similar note, the Brahmin men are comparatively superior in their education and other aspects of development where the intersection of caste and class play an essential role (Venkataraman 2015).

Against this backdrop, a revisit to the classical framework of caste, class and power with a new outline of CCE has convinced the author to provide a reflexive account on the intersection of human capital ideals and social capital influences on capabilities formation. The ethnographic research provides a necessary tool to understand the social construction of educational functionings. This is specially seen in light of the invisible contestation of the caste system in Sripuram.[2] This contestation is based on diminishing economic alternatives and social opportunities. This is further reinforced in the system, as the economic success of any caste is decided primarily by its employment outcome. Almost all caste groups currently treat education in terms of the instrumentalist notions of human capital. Any scholastic effort to conceive notions of capabilities seems to be initiated mainly from employment centrism. Along this structural reality, even human agency does not treat education in terms of the broader notions of capabilities, nor do their employment-centric approaches assure them any economic avenues. Thus, it underscores the social reproduction of inequalities in Sripuram at present.

Human capital

The human capital approach (HCA) considers human beings as the agents of wealth production. Accordingly, it approaches skills and knowledge as forms of capital by placing education as an economic good for growth. In the economic process of globalisation, one can observe a skill-centric market pressure on human agencies in India today. Structural withdrawal of the state from the knowledge domains leaves the agency alone.[3] In consequence, the Darwinian law 'naturally' gets applied, where only the 'fittest' survive. Any notions of capabilities, thus, must conceptualise the intersecting complexity of structure–agency dualism as the process of learning becomes a commodity in the market-centric 'knowledge' economy. The skill pressure and its role in competitiveness must be understood in the increasing withdrawal of the state in the globalised political economy. Consequently, the structural as well as systemic 'false consciousness' misunderstands the notions of capabilities merely as skills (Venkataraman 2011). This is seemingly 'facilitated' by neoliberal market fundamentals. As this falsity is convinced of the HCA ideals, the perpetuations of employment-centric notions are evidently available in everyday lives. This primarily conceives individuals in terms of their economic value, where education becomes an investment. In this context, individuals' survival in employment is mainly based on their skills. If anyone fails to 'market' her innate abilities and skills, she cannot be employable. Thus, educational functionings in India are increasingly being understood in terms of the notions of HCA. For instance, the Ministry of Human Resource Development argued that: 'The improvement in higher education is being brought through restructuring academic programmes to ensure their relevance to modern market demands' (GoI 2012–2013: 58).

Against this backdrop, the status of unemployability symbolises the systemic limitation of education. The inferior quality of pedagogy, as well as the curriculum, neither ensures broader notions of capabilities nor even functionings. The systematic withdrawal of the state from public policy commitments has gradually allowed the labour market to define 'quality' in education. These definitions are generally market-centric notions of employability instead of the constructivist ideals of the National Curriculum Framework (NCERT 2005) in India. Thus, the social reproduction of educational functionings is seemingly stabilising the status quo in favour of the non-poor and the erstwhile higher castes. In the neoliberal economic reality, children in private schools have current learning and future wage advantages over those in government schools. These schools often consider the ideals of human capital as an educational outcome.[4] Furthermore, it is to be noted that the inferior educational outcome of the social groups, including the erstwhile higher castes, limits their life opportunities to escape these economic unfreedoms. This causes a restructuring of the social roles and status among them.[5] For instance, the increasing un/under-employment among the Brahmins is compelling them to take up the revivalist role of the Brahmaniyam. Though, this profession is monetarily less-rewarding, one can see an intrinsic competition among the educated underemployed youths (EUYs) even for these positions. However, the recent political discourse has removed the traditional entry restriction according to caste for this traditional service in Tamil Nadu. The state government under the Hindu Religious and Charitable Endowment Department has decided that anyone can become Kurukkal by pursuing a degree in the institutions that are established by the Government of Tamil Nadu.[6] This decision would have been unthinkable in Beteille's period, when these jobs were traditionally only given to a particular sect of Brahmins. This sent a shock wave among the Brahmins, who are generally known for their orthodox living. Nevertheless, most of the unemployed Brahmin youths are increasingly taking up the roles of Kurukkal in any available temples in their locality, even without knowing the finer points of Ahamam rules. They often cite reservation policy as one of the 'entry barriers' in the current formal economy.

In contrast, the truants of the education system (who are mostly from the Pallar households) and the unemployed youths are developing a sub-culture. Though this has its own version of 'functional' capabilities, agentic effort to break their deprivation trap and economic mobility are drawn mainly from their educational functionings. For instance, Natesan, a Brahmin EUY with a bachelor's degree in Commerce had initially 'succeeded' by becoming an accountant in a small business in Meenakshipuram.[7] Individuals like him are gradually 'marketing' their un-employability for livelihood necessities in the informal economies. This structurally allows them to be 'active' in local affairs like that of Brahmothsavam and other festivals in Sripuram temples.[8] Most often, the temple activities provide them with the social approval of being a 'good person', as religious outlook is often correlated with character credentials. Thus, educational dysfunctionalities are indirectly accommodated by the informal economies. Though education-induced emigration provides economic benefits to the local Brahmins, the social structure has additional complexities. For instance, the older generation feel that they have been left out by their children at present. On the one hand, some of them are nostalgic for their earlier status in the caste system; on the other hand, they are emotionally constrained by their inability to permanently leave the village, unlike their children. However, emigration is seemingly the necessity where there are no economic avenues in Sripuram. Thus, the younger generation generally moves out of the village as the village does not have any lucrative opportunity for developing their socio-economic status. They often have their nuclear families in the nearby towns where they work. This, generally, leaves their parents in the village. As this is a predominant trend among the local Brahmins, Agraharam becomes an 'old age home' for the left-out elders at present.

However, the harsher sides of employment have not caught the 'other' castes so far. They rarely leave their elders as most often their *adaptive preferences* and agency rationality convince them to search for jobs in nearby towns in Tanjore and to continue to live in the village. It must be noted that the adaptive preferences are individuals' self-subordinating beliefs in life. In this background, it is seemingly also due to the fact that educational outcome for them is relatively low. Specifically, the Pallars stand again at the margins of development due to the vicious circle of educational deprivations and inferior cultural capital. For instance, given the same level of education, most of the Brahmin youths work in Chennai with stable jobs, but still 'ambitiously' look for further opportunities.[9] In contrast, EUYs of other castes, such as Jeeva, who has similar education credentials, look for opportunities only in Tanjore. He is yet to find one such due to the regular demands in assisting his father's small business in the village. As the fall-back strategies of the men are seemingly different, the essential point is that the erstwhile higher castes, given their historicity of knowledge-oriented liveli-hood, can afford to take the risk of investing their living only on education without getting 'diverted' by mundane issues. But for others, it is seemingly impossible, except in few rare cases of 'committed' individuals like Iyappan. This Pallar youth's educational 'commitments' are also seemingly due to the support structures available in his family. However, the situation of other Pallars is exceptionally depressing as their inferior socio-economic status limits their opportunities and choices in Sripuram.

Against this background, the reservation policy in the government sector is contrastingly perceived as a medium to slow down the avenues of promotion for the Brahmins. This is seemingly due to the preferential quota for the erstwhile lower castes. Consequently, the Brahmin youths concentrate mostly on their functionings by looking outside the public institutions. Their employment-centric education 'strategies' are contrary to the ideals of capabilities approach as the aspirations are predominantly career centric. They generally aspire for the 'meritocratic' private sector in lieu of the HCA perspective. Thus, the unsup-portive state structure, with its notorieties of quality and 'preferential' treatments to the erstwhile lower castes in the public institutions, seemingly pushes them towards the private sector. This is in light of the emerging market-driven neolib-eral economic values, where knowledge becomes a 'capital' for the surplus-drive for profit. In contrast, other castes generally 'depend' on welfare regimes at the street level bureaucracy.

Social capital of the educated youths

The notion of social capital is embedded in the resources of the networks the individual, as well as any group, has in life. The approaches to education as well as its functionings are mostly shaped by these resources.[10] In the present case, caste-based social capital plays both functional as well as dysfunctional roles. The nature of social capital is, thus, different across diverse social groups. The educated unemployed, for instance, do have the support structures to rely upon, according to the intersectional dynamics of CCE. However, these youths' lives are seemingly taken for granted in the local affairs in Sripuram, where differen-tial education outcomes negatively influence others in the village. For instance, if an EUY roams 'around' the village aimlessly, the poor receive an instant ref-erence to rationalise not sending their children to school at the cost of available economic avenues. The 'reluctant' justifications often get rationalised according to the intersectional family dynamics. Since, there are no official records of natality or mortality, it is not possible to know the demographic of the village. This reproduction of 'reasons' often substantiates the poor in opting out of learn-ing, even at a time of the mainstream compulsory narratives in education at present.

In addition, the unemployed individuals who are willing to work have to com-promise their 'market values' according to their socio-economic status. This is important given the reality, where emigration to the nearby towns is the only 'developmental' choice for the poor. However, those who are unwilling to emigrate out of Sripuram, as in the case of Raman and Natesan, will have to compromise their livelihood. The harsher realities of under-employment are invisible where most of them are depending on the informal economies of Sripuram or Meenakshipuram for meagre pecuniary benefits. An interaction with Natesan, a Brahmin EUY, for instance, has revealed that the poor, irrespective of their caste, often do not have the necessary social capital. His case highlights this complexity even in the time of need:

NATESAN: I was working in the cycle-mart in Meenakshipuram till 2006. Then, my brother had an accident.
AUTHOR: Yeah. He was telling me the other day.
NATESAN: Both my father and I were taking care of him as mother cannot do this work. So, I spent my entire time on him.
AUTHOR: So, you left the job?
NATESAN: No. I did not leave the job. They themselves told me not to come as I was not able to work regularly. He has to be in the hospital for three months. No one helped us even at that time. No financial help from the cycle-mart. I was just expecting them to help me at least with my future salary. No one enquired about care. Neither my colleagues nor *even* the boss bothered to visit my ailing brother.

(From the field)

In India, economic deprivation of the poor is generally conceptualised in terms of social exclusion. Though, the erstwhile lower castes are at the developmental margin, an essential point is that the poor, irrespective of caste background, often do not have the necessary social capital at present. Natesan's case highlighted the same. In addition, the economic realities of the poor also have a gender dimension, where women are unequally placed in the patriarchal social structure. In this, the role of caste is visible, where the Brahmin women are relatively better placed than 'others' in the village. The Pallar women, in contrast, are at the social margin where their livelihood is mostly dependent on the male members of their households. However, there are a few small economic opportunities, such as rearing cattle and casual labouring in the nearby agricultural fields, to avoid the deprivation trap. These modest options are visibly insufficient. In this context, Mala, a 24-year-old Pallar EUY woman opines that:

To a greater extent, people in village do not have any work to do. They idly sit at home. For me, it seems that the nature of economic suffering is severe at present. I mean, now people's opportunity to find food seems to be more difficult than the past. Today, people survive mostly due to people like me who are *only* educated to get something from outside to sustain the family.

(From the field)

However, Mala's underemployment from a complex social context like that of Sripuram has often been overlooked in India. This is due to the systemic challenge in employment, where even the men in patriarchy are failing to get decent jobs in relation to their education credentials at present. While this highlights the intricate social complexities, one can notice informal networks, which are often formed along caste lines.[11] This abstract arrangement is often exclusivist in nature due to the stratified social structure. The interplay of caste and class dynamics complicates the formation of these networks. Hence the structure–agency interactions are mostly influenced by these complications. For instance, some of the Brahmin youths, who have left the village and been successful in their economic mobility, share that they usually help the fellow villagers based on their 'level' of friendships. Given their 'superior' cultural and economic status, clearly, the social capital of the Brahmin youths is higher than that of others at present. For a non-Brahmin, the help will generally be from their sustained association in the Agraharam. Although no one deliberately does this at the time of economic need, there is an essential point that needs to be noted. The formation of peer groups since childhood is one of the foundations for developing a wider social network for later years. This is significantly absent for the Pallars, due to the structural 'restrictions', where their position is distant from the primordial power centres of the village. Their educational deprivation, and inferior occupational outcome, perpetuate this even for the privileged few. In contrast, individuals like Karthi, who is a 25-year-old male EUY from an OBC caste, has been actively assisting the temple services to the Agraharam. By his own admission, at times, it helpfully places him nearer to the 'networks' in Chennai.

Thus, the social capital of the Brahmins is ensured in the Agraharam. The membership in the neighbourhood is mostly ascriptive. This shall be further seen in terms of social change, where residential patterns are increasingly changing. The economically well-off OBCs from outside are replacing the emigrating Brahmin houses. Though there are structural tensions between the remaining Brahmins and the newcomers as 'full members' of the neighbourhood, it confirms the newer realities of caste today. The economic exodus of Brahmins towards the nearby towns facilitates this social process. The result is a newer social arrangement that is 'unacceptable' to the remaining orthodox Brahmins in the neighbourhood. This can be noticed in their nostalgic preference for the habitus similar to that of the earlier years, with exclusivist life styles.

In this social construction of capabilities, it is pertinent to conceptualise habitus as it is the disposition of the structural factors. In a complex social structure like that of Sripuram, the interaction order lays the foundation for the social capital. This, however, cannot ensure the basis for habitus formation given the structural location of different castes. Law prevents the visible forms of exclusion, whereas the 'invisible hands', at times, withdraw even from the interaction order. Often, this withdrawal itself provides the power to influence others for the erstwhile higher castes. In simpler terms, no one can legally challenge people of higher castes if they refuse interact with other castes.

The changing nature of economic opportunities and caste in its new avatar structurally convinces agential exodus for employment reasons. However, differential education functionings prevents the exodus in some cases due to diverse social capital. For instance, even the 'higher' levels of educational qualifications of the daughters of Karuppaiah, an OBC agriculturist, is failing them as 'the children are strongly affected by the human capital possessed by their parents' (Coleman 1988: S110). Their failure to find salaried employment negatively influences the neighbourhood. These functioning-failures and capabilities deprivation can be contrasted with the habitus of Brahmins. The life-cycle of Tamil Brahmins' celebrations starts from birth namely, Ayush-homam, Upanayanam marriage, Shashtiabdapoorthi, Sadhabishekam and death rites.[12] These are typical occasions where the kin-groups will congregate as a family. These *rites de passage* ensure their social capital as this is an exclusive life-cycle. No new entry can be allowed except through ascriptive membership and conjugal connections. However, this aspect of habitus-formation has increasingly been reduced with the economic exodus of the younger generation and the current urban lifestyles. In contrast, the social encounters of other castes happen to cross the social system mostly in Shiv temple in Sripuram. This is in contrast to the exclusivism of the Iyengars.[13] For this reason, the Shiv temple provides an avenue for the social capital formation both for Smartha Brahmins and the OBCs at present. Pallars are far removed from these institutional opportunities due to their marginal locations in the social structure. Thus, a caste groups' modernity and outlook most often decide the agencies' human capital at present. Though caste as an endogamous unit provides a social capital base, the agencies' successes or failures in human capital are often intersected by systemic and structural interactions.

In addition, the newer modes of communication, such as television and mobile phones, ensure the potential avenues of social capital for the villagers. As these were non-existent during Beteille's time, this in a way 'influences' newer forms. These avenues consolidate the existing cultural and social capital amidst the contestation of castes at present. Although the reach of telephones among the social groups reflects their social positions, they are to a large extent altering the nature of structural hierarchies. For instance, almost all Pallar households 'proudly' own a handset today. This can be seen even among the poorest of the poor, who often struggle financially to maintain it. However, this gives them a new space to improve their social capital in both market and non-market spheres of habitus-formation.

In contrast, the state's governance and developmental records are deficient even in ensuring the basic needs in Tamil Nadu.[14] This has not provided the necessary avenues of capabilities formation for the poor so far. Thus, the social reproduction of inequalities often reinforces the existing arrangements in new forms. For instance, given the stringent anti-untouchability laws, the nature and forms of social capital have increasingly been intangible over the years. However, one can see them in subtle forms where the display of economic success through education, for instance, can often be seen in the nameplates on houses. Their symbolic presence in the streets of Sripuram signals the educational functionings in particular, and social capital in general.

Conversion factors

Educated youths' social capital or the aggregate network of resources can broadly be categorised in terms of: caste, family, politics friends, institution and the village. The web of social organisation plays an essential role in individuals' functionings and capabilities formations. For instance, the un/underemployed youths' standard of living and quality of life are primarily influenced by their family-habitus. In this context, parental education is an important aspect. Social capital formations of the poor are generally determined by the intersection of these aspects, where politics-based local networks and influential 'connections' arise. This is primarily due to individuals' image-making and adaptive preferences in life. In addition, in the institution-based avenues—such as career-planning—skill-formations are shaped by the welfare regimes where reservation policy becomes important. This can be conceptualised as shown in Figure 5.1.

In the conceptualisation in Figure 5.1, the nature of interaction is diverse, as the intersections of social capital might be functional to the non-poor whereas the very same plays against the poor.[15] The result can be seen in the case of individuals' institutional dependency and adaptive preferences. The credential gaps of EUYs often push them to the margin, where their literacy becomes a dysfunctional factor. In addition, it is important to mention the underemployed youths. The case of Iyappan, an individual with multiple degrees, is an instance of qualification escalation. As a Pallar youth, his dispositions are seemingly limited by the intersections. This is important in the present-day welfare regimes, where the erstwhile lower castes approach the reservation policy as a state sponsored social capital in India. However, the very same patronage polarises the 'others', where the consequence can be seen in the creation of exclusivist social order. Nevertheless, the welfare regime successfully addresses the caste specific issues in terms of 'protective' discrimination, the erstwhile higher castes 'increasingly' withdraw themselves from everyday interaction orders. The result is the invisible forms of social exclusion, where the structure dictates the lives of the depending human agencies. These exclusive social processes can further be seen in terms of conversion factors.

According to the capabilities literature, the conversion factors represent how many functionings one can get out of a good or service. This, in the present context, is predominantly being understood by the educated un/under-employed youths in terms of corruption. As corruption is increasingly being 'rationalised', one can understand it in light of the institutional dependencies of the human agencies in Sripuram. In the fieldwork, the author's everyday observation and interactions with the youths confirms its centrality as a conversion factor. At times, it is shocking that most of them were justifying it as a crucial factor for functionings-formations. The author's regular attempts to understand it from

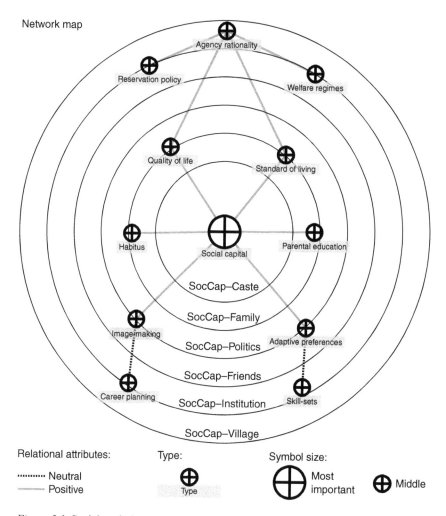

Network map

Relational attributes:

·········· Neutral
————— Positive

Type:

Type

Symbol size:

Most
important

Middle

Figure 5.1 Social capital.

moral perspectives was ridiculed and dismissed as 'idealistic talk'. Against this backdrop, one can depict the conversion factors as shown in Figure 5.2.

In terms of the factors shown in Figure 5.1, there are numerous aspects that further the complexities. These include institutional aspects like education quality and family based social capital. These factors have to be described as both are diverse in nature. For instance, the family-based social capital is gendered due to the patriarchal structure where women are socio-economically subservient. The nature of economic 'determinism' most often shapes the social structure, where gender is differentially institutionalised. Nevertheless, there are exceptions as the erstwhile higher caste women are generally assertive due to education and employment, the central point is their dependency to the

Network map

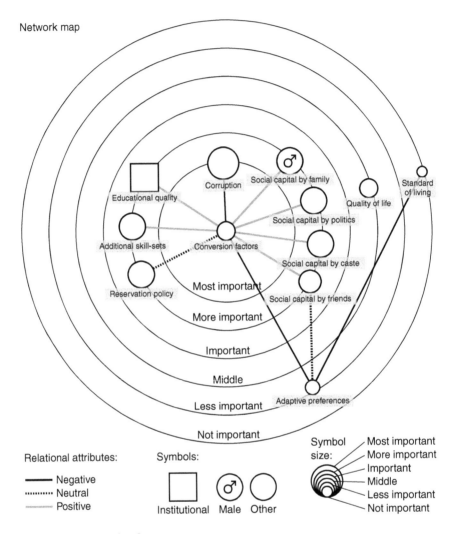

Figure 5.2 Conversion factors.

male-headship in the family. For this reason, social capital by family, caste, and even politics, plays a complex role, where the patriarchy often gets reproduced. In addition, the education quality and reservation policy play a significant role, where individuals are drawing the avenues of mobility. The social processes of these avenues altogether 'ensure' the standard of living and quality of life. Though this could be a social reproduction of inequalities, the poor's subjectivities seemingly rationalise them in the village today.

Social reproduction

As education is a process of human socialisation, diverse groups shape it according to their structural locations. This is mostly complicated by intersectional dynamics. Due to this, the educational outcomes of the Pallars are increasingly low in contrast to the 'others'. Cultural habitus and the social capital shape their functionings as intrinsically inferior to the hegemonic demands of the market. This can be contrasted, as the same system of education successfully produces 'employable' individuals among 'others'. The caste system invisibly plays its role, where the Brahmin youths with their social capital, at times, find it relatively easy to get a job in Chennai even if they have had a similar educative process to others. The gender dimension runs almost parallel to this complexity, where only very few women have been successful in shaping their educational functionings, with a 'natural' exception of Brahmanical supremacy.

The non-availability of economic resources and social opportunities convinces the Brahmin youth that emigration is the only avenue for economic mobility in Sripuram. However, the success of economic emigration to the nearby towns and cities is further influenced by the social capital. In this context, the emigration pattern of the Brahmins out of their education is seemingly similar, as their preferred destination is Chennai. Thus, the economic aspirations for mobility often drive the villagers out to where the role of social capital is significant. This is in sharp contrast to 'others' in Sripuram. The employability of the Pallars is mostly determined by the extent of their skills. As could be expected, they do not have adequate social capital due to historical reasons, nor do they have the opportunities to enhance their innate abilities at present. The process of learning from education enhances one's abilities with workable skills and capabilities. However, given their inferior socio-economic positions, Pallars have to depend on the mediocre services of government schools, which neither provide them enabling conditions for capabilities nor even functionings-formations. The result is the systemic label of being 'educated' in the village. In this education without freedom, when asked about the emigration among different castes, Santhanam, who is a teacher in the local school, suggested that 'The younger generation shall be educated well but at the same time they need to settle down in the village to uphold their caste traditions. Otherwise the livelihood balance will be lost. Consequently, people may suffer' (From the field). This correlates the educational functionings as a status stabiliser of the tradition. The structural interpretations of this nature structurally define the complexities of emigration in Sripuram. In addition, Bhairavi, an influential 'intellectual' in the village, argues that:

> Education-induced emigration creates nuclear families in society. This in turn produces households and individuals as islands in the urban anonymity. The result is even very close relatives cannot be entertained in these families. This is against our national tradition of having wider kinship networks. Therefore, the younger generation today do not have a higher level of social capital which we had from our family system.
>
> (From the field)

In light of these functionalist standpoints, one can conceptualise the educated youths where the limited social opportunities and economic mobility pushes them out of the village. The unemployed Brahmins (whether educated or not) normally take up odd-jobs like cook or Purohit. In this, the caste-based social capital readily assists them to be mobile. In contrast, others have to find out the possible economic avenues as caste-based division of labour has increasingly been eliminated. However, non-Brahmins do not have the cultural capital except the aforementioned state patronage of the Reservation policy. However, this is generally viewed by the Brahmins and other high castes as vote-bank politics. In their notion, the reservation policy generally promotes the backdoor entry of the 'unqualified' into the system.[16] Furthermore, the consequence of this can be seen in the newer social formation including the endogamous unification of castes to shake-off the sect-wise differences. This 'self-adjustment' of the status quo has additional aspects. For instance, the marital restrictions between different sects within the Brahmins are no longer perceived to be relevant. In fact, some of the present generation Brahmins do not even know these differences. This is a significant change in Sripuram today, in vast contrast to the earlier descriptions by Beteille.

The role of education in this newer social formation is important, where modernisation 'democratises' the institutions. As mentioned earlier, the Archahars[17] who have been traditionally occupied by a group of Brahmin, cannot claim their ascribed status in temples today. The role-allocation needs to have state approval, where politics has the final say as demography determines the political-economy of the state. The consequence is that the higher the caste, the lower the status in political system today. However, given the illiteracy figures, the erstwhile lower castes seemingly do not have the same level of cultural capital. Hence the reservation policy has to be understood from the perspective where the state provides the necessary capital for their empowerment to level the unequal society. However, the interplay of multiple factors like state-patronage for the Pallars and the increasing privatisation of both education and economic sectors provide a complex picture.

In addition, one must be aware that not all the Brahmins are highly educated as well as economically rich.[18] An aged Brahmin villager, Narashimhan, for instance, asserted that 'the only developmental option available for the Madapalli Brhamanan is to catch the next train to Madras *even* without a valid ticket' (From the field).[19] The Brahmins in general are rather seemingly skilful 'enough' to survive the economic deprivation in the village. Here, the role of social capital and educational functionings plays an important part. However, the Brahmin youths' failures in the labour market put them into another kind of deprivation in personhood. If they cannot migrate to the bigger cities like Chennai, they have the option of becoming a Purohit or doing odd *Vedic* jobs in the village. In consequence, most of them have not been able to find a match for marriage. As this is seemingly due to their 'higher' social status where the women are economically better placed, it consequently constructs inferior personhood in the Agraharam. This shall be understood in light of the positive gender dimensions in the neighbourhood, where Brahmin girls are often advised by the elders 'to study further to get a good husband' (From the field). In contrast, the other castes do not face such demands apparently, due to their lesser preferences on occupational outcome than the primordial identities. This is also seemingly due to the inferior educational past.

Conclusion

Mainstream literature treats education as an automatic solution for all development-ills. The capabilities approach shall not be misled by this human capital ideal. It is therefore essential to understand the intersectional complexities, as caste is not a homogeneous entity. In the present case, the threefold classification (of Brahmins; OBCs and SCs in the present case) highlights the complex heterogeneities, where the recognition of social structure could be a way out in capabilities approach-specific studies in India. This has been highlighted by how the knowledge-centric lifestyles of the Brahmins alongside the increasing modernity of the OBCs and the state-supportive political-economy to the erstwhile backward castes are seemingly convincing the diverse groups to come out of their orthodoxies. The changing social and economic reality alters the Brahmins. However, the adaptive preferences of their human agencies in relation to dynamic structural reality have often been overlooked by the mainstream academic narratives so far. The notions of capabilities are thus, seemingly initiated from the employment centrism, due to the intersectional dynamics of caste and class positions of the poor in India. Along this structural reality, even human agency does not treat education in the broader notion of capabilities, nor do Brahmins' employment-centric approaches assure them economic avenues out of it. The primary reason for this dichotomy is intersectional in nature. Thus, the chapter has analysed the complexities of capabilities formation and the limitations of capabilities approach in a collectivist social order. In this analysis, it has established that although caste-based division of labour has been increasingly eliminated due to its dysfunctionalities, the state has failed to create alternative social opportunities so far. Consequently, it complicates the social construction of capabilities by the reproduction of inequalities in newer forms of the structure; systemic and human agencies. Against this backdrop, the chapter argues that the perspective of a capabilities approach can conceptualise how these three-dimensional spheres could decide the capabilities alternatives. This is important as capabilities without normative listing could be an 'absolute' entitlement. This is evidently crucial, as theoretical engagements between capitals and capabilities can enrich the sociological contributions in development studies.

Notes

1 According to the literature, capabilities are 'the real opportunities to achieve valuable states of being and doing' (Robeyns 2006: 78).
2 Functionings, according to the capabilities approach, are 'the outcomes or achievements' (Robeyns 2006: 78).

3 See for instance Jha 2005.
4 In contrast, Sen argues that, despite the usefulness of the concept of human capital as a productive resource, 'it is important to see human beings in a broader perspective than that of human capital' (1997 [1960]).
5 For instance, the Brahmaniyam of the revivalist youths in Sripuram often takes the forms of Kurukkal today. This is in sharp contrast to the tradition where Kurukkals were from a particular sect of Brahmin where they used to study the rules of Ahamam in the separate system of Vedic schools. Thus, the role dilution between Purohit and Kurukkal by the Brahmin EUYs underscores newer forms of caste in the village. It is to be mentioned that Brahmaniyam is a colloquial Brahmin term for the priestly roles in their caste. This is mostly for rites and rituals performed. In contrast, Kurukkals' ways of life are both caste as well as religiously mandated in nature. They professionally thrive by their role in officiating Smartha temples in the village according to the rules of Ahamam, i.e. the Vedic knowledge about the priestly roles for the Smartha Brahmins in Tamil Nadu. Normally, it is studied at Vedic schools or the Vedha Pathsalas (a kind of school system where one graduates to become a Kurukkal). In addition, Purohit is a priestly role, officiating rituals in Smartha Brahmin households.
6 For further details see website, online, available at: www.hrce.tn.nic.in/.
7 Meenakshipuram is a pseudonymously named small town located near to Sripuram. It is one of the block headquarters in Tanjore district in Tamil Nadu.
8 Brahmothsavam is a typical Brahmin festival in both Vaishnava as well as Smartha temples.
9 Chennai is formerly known as Madras. It is the Capital of Tamil Nadu (which is one of the four southern states), with a population of nearly 70 million people in India.
10 See for instance, Cleaver (2005), Coleman (1988) and Migheli (2011) among others.
11 For instance, Jackson explains that 'Allowing for the social context of capabilities requires explicit recognition of social structures, both personal and impersonal, as some capabilities may be due to employment or other roles and membership of social networks' (Jackson 2005: 107).
12 First, Ayush-homam means the ritual naming of the child. Though the naming ceremony is widely done in all the caste groups, the Brahmins specifically call it *Ayush-homam*. It roughly means the 'prayer for a long life' for the one-year-old child. In contrast, the 'others' (including the OBCs and Pallars) generally call it *Punniyajanam* in Tamil. The expression of *punniyajanam* symbolises the 'purification' after the birth out of 'human-dirt'. Second, Upanayanam is the ceremony of sacred thread for the adolescent Brahmins. According to the Hindu scriptures, this ceremony will baptise the boys into the Brahmacharya (or the Bachelorhood). Third, *Shashtiabdapoorthi* is where the married Brahmin couples celebrate their marriage after the 'groom' attains 60 years of age. This is in contrast to *Sadhabhishekam*, where the grooms who are 80 years of age will be celebrated as having a successful married life. It must be noted that the non-Brahmins (including all the OBCs and Pallars) do not have these ceremonies, with the exception of *Punniyajanam*.
13 There are four varieties of Brahmins in Sripuram. Smarthas predominantly worship Shiva; Sri Vaishnava/Iyengars are the followers of the deity Vishnu; Madhwas are the followers of Sri Raghavendra; and lastly the Kurukkals are the priestly sub-caste for the Smartha. Though these are endogamous sub-units within the Brahmin caste, one can observe changes over the years.
14 In the fieldwork period in 2012, the author found that the entire state of Tamil Nadu lacked a regular supply of electricity and water. For instance, electricity was available only for 15 or so hours a day. This shall be seen in light of various official reports claiming it as one of the 'developed' states in India.
15 It must be mentioned that the local Brahmins generally represent the former, and the Pallars the latter in Sripuram.

16 This shall be seen in light of the role of the state in development discourse in India. The distributive justice ideals of the state have been addressing the unjust issues, where caste-based division of labour has increasingly been restructured in light of the modern democratic ideals.

17 Archahars are often called Kurukkals in Tamil, which means priests in the Hindu temples. Though, it primarily denotes a priest for the Smartha temples, the colloquial usage also denotes the non-Brahmins in the state.

18 For example, Driver has established that the caste hierarchy and occupational hierarchy are no longer parallel to one another (Driver 1982: 228).

19 Madapalli Brahmins in colloquial terms denotes the economically poor Brahmin

References

Beteille, Andre (1965). *Caste, Class and Power: Changing Patterns of Stratification in a Tanjore Village*. New Delhi: Oxford University Press (Sixth Impression).

Cleaver, Frances (2005). The Inequality of Social Capital and the Reproduction of Chronic Poverty. *World Development*, 33(6), 893–906.

Coleman, James S. (1988). Social Capital in the Creation of Human Capital. *American Journal of Sociology*, 94 (Supplement S95–S120).

Government of India (GoI) (2012–2013). *Ministry of Human Resource Development Annual Report*, New Delhi.

Jackson, William A. (2005). Capabilities, Culture and Social Structure. *Review of Social Economy*, LXIII(1), 101–124.

Jha, Praveen (2005). Withering Commitments and Weakening Progress: State and Education in the Era of Neoliberal Reforms. *Economic and Political Weekly*, 40(33), 3677–3684.

Migheli, Matteo (2011). Capabilities and Functionings: The Role of Social Capital for Accessing New Capabilities. *Review of Political Economy*, 23(1), 133–142.

NCERT (2005). *National Curriculum Framework 2005*. New Delhi: National Council of Educational Research and Training (NCERT).

Robeyns, Ingrid (2006). Three Models of Education: Rights, Capabilities and Human Capital. *Theory and Research in Education*, 4(1), 69–84.

Sen, Amartya (1997). Human Capital and Human Capability. *World Development*, 25(12), 1959–1961.

Sen, Amartya (1999). *Development as Freedom*. New Delhi: Oxford University Press.

Srinivas, M. N. (1987). *The Dominant Caste and Other Essays*. New Delhi: Oxford University Press.

Venkataraman, L. N. (2011). False Consciousness. *Economic and Political Weekly*, XLVI(22), 4.

Venkataraman, L. N. (2015). Social Construction of Capabilities and Intersectional Complexities in a Tamil Village. *Development in Practice*, 25(8), 1170–1181.

Venkataraman, L. N. (2016). New Education Policy and the Continuing Contentions in India. *Economic and Political Weekly*, 51(35), 47–50.

Part II

Political and public space

Development and enactment of agency
and capabilities for change and justice

6 Ciudad Comuna

Re-signifying territory based on communitarian communication

Ángela Garcés Montoya and
Leonardo Jiménez García

Introduction

Ciudad Comuna works in peripheral neighbourhoods located in the city of Medellín, Colombia. There, two antagonistic notions of territory come together. On one hand, there is an "official" conception of borders, involving the city's planning and administration. This is supported by technical and rational knowledge, and regards recent conditions of the population in Medellín—in which these settlements appeared—as areas of urban conflict, since they promote "informal", "irregular" and "illegal" neighbourhoods that, besides deteriorating Medellín's urban borders, are focuses of urban violence. On the other hand, settlement dwellers uphold human rights, human security and life with dignity, which forcefully imply the reconfiguration of the notion of urban borders. It is understood that the communication practices developed by Ciudad Comuna in the urban border territories promote processes of social, political and cultural mobilisation and empowerment, so that the settlement dwellers can be included as citizens and their "popular"[1] territories can be dignified.

For the local administration, an urban border refers to a conflict zone for urban planning (technical and rational) and considers the dwellers as people carrying out illegal activities.

Amidst such antagonism, it is important to consider Ciudad Comuna's labour. Ciudad Comuna is a social organisation focused on communication and which resulted from an initiative by young people—most of them living in neighbourhoods located in the urban borders—who have been particularly exposed to armed violence and conditions of social inequity. Ciudad Comuna is a communications collective whose radius of action is in Medellín's Comuna 8. It intends to generate spaces for participation and inclusiveness based on the creation of communitarian communication media, so that young men and women from such territories can reclaim inclusiveness and be regarded as legal populations who should both be consulted and considered when it comes to planning their spaces. In this respect, the community values collective freedoms and agency that can lead to collective action to bring about better conditions for people.

Ciudad Comuna has consolidated youth communication groups in Comuna 8, and is organised into work collectives according to the projects developed in the field of communitarian communication. It is worth mentioning the communitarian newspaper *Visión 8*, consisting of five young women and three young men; the *Común-audiovisual Collective*, consisting of three young women and two young men; the community radio project *Voces de la 8* (Voices of *Comuna* 8), composed of five young women; and the *Escuela de Comunicación Comunitaria* (School of Communitarian Communication), Ciudad Comuna's educational project, which has between 40 and 60 young people from many different areas of the city, with equitable participation of both men and women. The communication projects implement a gender positive imbalance, by encouraging more women to participate in their activities than men. This is to compensate their daily realities, where women have less formal spaces to articulate their desires or opinions. The purpose of the communication processes promoted by the youth communication collectives may be synthesised by their motto: *communication for social mobilisation and change*. They are aimed at the community's integration and participation in the construction of its own development, and at the qualification of cohabitation processes within *Comuna 8*'s territory (see Ciudad Comuna website, online, available at: www.ciudadcomuna. org/medios.html).

   The case of the Ciudad Comuna youth collective will be approached as a communication process resisting hierarchical, male, individualistic and adult-centred forms of organisation. Collectivity is key to understanding Ciudad Comuna. They favour assembly-centred forms of participation, as well as collective decision-making, dialogue of knowledge, the construction of relations acknowledging gender-based subjectivities, and the social, political and economic self-management of processes. All of which are evidence of their commitment to the expansion of freedoms and the recognition of their collective agency freedom by using their collective decision-making for the well-being of the community. It is a collective struggling for the culturalisation of politics through plural direct actions. A state-of-the-art will be approached in the present chapter, referring to the emergence of youth collectives, an alternative modality of grouping built by young people from "popular" sectors. The second section refers to the theoretical and film references that inspire Ciudad Comuna. The third section goes into detail and explains the communicative practices, and provides examples of some of them. Finally, the conclusion shows how youth collectives such as Ciudad Comuna are spaces for aesthetics and communication that are realms for collective action, thus fostering different media-centred forms of social empowerment and building a critical political discourse in regard to territory, memory, and rights, which is important to explore thoroughly.

1   Ciudad Comuna's context of action: gender, collectivity and territory

Ciudad Comuna focuses its action on Comuna 8. In such urban borders, various conflicts develop, characteristic of a city that has been populated irregularly under the effects of the armed conflict experienced in Colombia, which generates the violation of human and social rights. According to Sisbén's report, dated August 2015, the total population of Comuna 8 is 152,430 people, out of which 62 per cent are adult women. Of the total population, 0.68 per cent people live in stratum 0 (tenement houses), 44.89 per cent live in stratum 1 (lower), 40.24 per cent live in stratum 2 (low), 14.16 per cent live in stratum 3 (lower-medium), and 0.03 per cent live in stratum 4 (medium).[2] Further regarding the population, 4.5 per cent are Afro-descendant, 0.3 per cent identify themselves as indigenous, and 12,000 people identify themselves as being displaced by the armed conflict. Over 6,000 people from five peripheral neighbourhoods still lack a sewage and fresh water system. There are 32 expressions of communitarian and social organisations in defence of human rights; most of the people participating in their bodies of representation and acting as their spokespeople are women affected by displacement, who, in turn, are the leaders of organisational processes in their neighbourhoods. This sign of women's empowerment can be seen in the video *Relatos desde la frontera* (Ciudad Comuna, 2013). This is based on the neighbourhood Pinares de Oriente and primarily features the social leader Isela Quintero. Her testimony enables an understanding of the fact that the most significant experiences of social organisation and participation for the dignity of Comuna 8's communities have arisen from women's empowerment and commitment to human rights. Her testimony reveals how this is a response to her reality, where women, alongside children, are those most affected by their unclear status that does not allow them to find a job, nor to have a sense of security in their own homes.

Ciudad Comuna is a collective following the path of audiovisual realisation, it consists of young men and women, communicators with a social and communitarian sense. Some of them have professional training in the field of communication. Their aim is to position the participatory social documentary (PSD) methodology, which seeks to move from individualistic ways of working to collective ones. This translates into the implication of the community at all stages of video production (thinking of the idea, filming and screening). By following this procedure, the young communicators act upon their territory and, at the same time, generate political commitment through experiences of communication. These young people, bound to the particular realities they experience every day, have managed to reassert their sense of belonging to their territory and their commitment to generate social transformations based on communitarian media. Furthermore, the members of Ciudad Comuna's communitarian communication collectives build their own critical reading of conventional media[3] (Jiminez, 2013). The videos and documentaries produced involve the community and foster a sense of fulfilment and empowerment to each of them as individuals, but also as a group. Thanks to the commitment of Ciudad Comuna for giving voice to women, the results are videos that deal with topics considered taboo in the Colombian culture. Issues such as teenage pregnancy, symbolic and direct violence against women, or domination and power relations faced by women in realms such as their school or family have been documented, worked in the community and finally projected. This process and methodology brings debate and awareness. For instance, in 2014, Ciudad Comuna's radio collective *Voces de la 8*, consisting of young women, carried out a pedagogical campaign to deal with sexuality related issues at state schools in Comuna 8. For this, they resorted to the production of radio programmes in which the main actors were young women who engaged in gender-centred dialogues related to issues associated to young people's sexuality,[4] *La Radio Suena a Sexo* (The Radio Sounds Like Sex) is one such programme, in which Garavito (2014) analysed the impact of gender on young people's sexuality.

Alongside the issue of gender, the collective methodology has a second area of work. The struggle for borders and conception of territory. These concepts, intersected with gender, have resulted in the documentary *Semillas del Pan de Azúcar*[5] (Seeds from Pan de Azúcar Hill, 2010), which pays homage to the women from Pinares de Oriente—one of the territories regarded as "an invasion" in Comuna 8—and their commitment to the struggle for dignity, life and the construction of social and material conditions to make this a more liveable territory. Such productions highlight and preserve for posterity the character and courage of those women who, amidst the social and armed conflict, have been able to forge equitable and dignified conditions for the dwellers of peripheral territories. This brings light to the mobilising role of women and allows an inclusive collective memory building. Hence, women's interests and voices are also incorporated in collective actions, dialogues and discussions.

2 Networks and borders: understanding social movements associated with marginal territories

It is interesting to recover reflections about the differences between the concepts of marginality, territorial appropriation and rural–urban borders. An undervaluation of *urban borders* underlies such reflections, as they are regarded as liminal spaces that have not managed to integrate into the city.

A resignification of the status of urban marginality can be found in Svampa's (2004) studies, as he preserves the strength of social networks of reciprocal interchange. He regards these as the most meaningful structuring element of neighbourhoods, allowing outcasts to migrate from the countryside, to settle in the city, to get a roof over their heads, and survive. His studies highlight the emergence of renovated community relations, in which the *compadrazgo* (joint fatherhood) and family relations and bonds, based on solidarity and reciprocity, outline a world where trust is the key to social relations, to such a point that in a stateless world, without any political parties or associations, the network of reciprocal interchange constitutes the urban outcast's actual community.

In turn, in his work *Cómo sobre viven los marginados* (1989) Lomnitz highlights the importance of family and neighbour networks in the configuration of shantytown subjectivities. However, he also underscores that kinship is not a determining factor in reciprocity in contexts of marginality, and that, on the contrary, geographic proximity is capable of establishing true flows of continuity in the relations between social actors. To Lomnitz, networks offer the marginalised individual emotional and moral support, and centralise their cultural life, given the virtual lack of any other kind of organised participation in the life of the city and the nation. Therefore, it could be claimed that the reciprocal interchange network constitutes the effective community of the urban outcast in Latin American shanty towns.

(1989: 223)

Together with reciprocal interchange, solidarity practices amidst social adversity have emerged from the social struggles of marginalised communities. In Comuna 8, one can see the importance of these informal structures and networks. The territorial actors are called convites. Convites are sites of assembly-like meetings where neighbour networks are activated in order to cooperate on tasks such as the building of streets, houses, community aqueduct networks, paths and parks, among others. Ciudad Comuna has carried out research to explore this through the project Memorias en Diálogo (Dialoguing Memories, 2013) and the magazine Para Qué La Memoria (Niño and Jimenez, 2013). The results confirmed that the solidarity-based convites carried out in Comuna 8 have been the initiative of female leaders from the territories. This highlights the special leading role played by women in the processes of weaving solidarity-based networks to achieve more dignified conditions in their territories.

Regarding territory, Ciudad Comuna is inspired by Zibechi (2008), who highlights the importance of territory in the constitution of social relations and as something that re-signifies the concept of *social movement*. A clear evidence of the discrepancies in the ways to understand and produce territory is the existence, in Medellín, of two Comuna 8 maps. On the one hand, there is a political administrative map made by experts in urban planning, which is regarded as the legitimate map; on the other hand, another one, regarded as a communitarian map,[6] has been made by the communities as a result of their processes of territorial appropriation. The latter transcends the land management plans proposed by the city's administrative planning department, and is made from the communities' perspective, from which renewed approaches on urban borders and settlements are collected.[7]

Comparing these two maps reveals two ways to *produce territory*, as the official approach reveals the notion of *marginal population* within the urban imaginary, which is supported by the particular logic of "technical and rational knowledge": according to Oslender (2002), such technical knowledge positions "the representations of space", referring to:

The spaces conceived and derived from a particular logic and from technical and rational knowledge, become a conceptualised space "the space of scientists, urbanists, technocrats and social engineers" (Lefebvre 1991:38). Such knowledge is associated to the institutions of dominating power and to the normalised representations generated by a hegemonic "logic of visualisation". They are represented as "readable spaces", such as maps, statistics, etc. They produce the normalised visions and representations which can be

Figure 6.1 Planning versus social imaginaries in Comuna 8.
Source: Ciudad Comuna, 2015.

found in State structures, the economy and civil society. This readability, in fact, produces a simplification of space, as if it were a translucent surface. A particular normalised vision is thus produced, which ignores struggles, ambiguities, and other ways to see, perceive and imagine the world. This abstract space is, precisely, "the space of contemporary capitalism".

(Oslender, 2002: 5)

Technical knowledge within city hall plans the city under concepts associated to urban landscaping, an innovative city and sustainable mobility. Furthermore, city hall generates high-impact mega-projects, in order to transform the city according to international standards of urban modernisation. In spite of being at the forefront of urbanism and megalopolis-style city planning, they leave the living conditions of the "marginal population" aside. This population has been pushed into living on the borders, given the status of the displaced population, and it finds itself forced to establish settlements as its only means to inhabit the city. This is where Ciudad Comuna has its greatest scope. It claims the reconceptualisation of networks and borders through the existence of different expressions of organisation and resistance.

3 Ciudad Comuna's communication practices based on a youth-centred approach

Within Medellín's context of urban violence in the 1990s, the figure of the "violent young person" was instilled and widely disseminated through the mass media (TV news, radio and newspapers). Simultaneously, universities' and NGOs' research lines focused on the "vulnerable young person" or the "young person at risk" (Acosta and Garcés, 2015). Such figures of "popular" young people are realised in the image of the "*sicario*" (hitman), that is:

> A young man who is not a drug dealer but participates in the war of cartels against the State; who is not a political activist, but mediates in the struggle between political actors; who does not belong to any organisation from which to vindicate a fair cause, but is regarded as an actor whose actions disturb collective life; and to top it all does not study, does not care much about school matters, and is barely over 15 years of age. This figure of the young person determined the course of research on youth in Colombia, as concern about violent expressions became the ordering and mandatory question.
>
> (Perea, 2008: 266)

This prevailing image of the "popular" young man as a *sicario* determined the path followed by youth-related studies throughout the 1980s and 1990s. Moreover, it was a really strong element in Medellín's audiovisual production, which was concerned with the violent expressions of gangs, and *milicias populares* (urban guerrilla groups). As noted by Sierra (2004), some landmark films from Medellín are *Rosario Tijeras* (2005), *La Virgen de los sicarios* (Our Lady of the Assassins) (2000), *Rodrigo D: No futuro* (Rodrigo D: No Future) (1989), *La vendedora de rosas* (1998), which tend to generalise a national imaginary of youth violence in Medellín's comunas. This imaginary is still valid in everyday life, as can be seen from the news outlook in Colombia in the late 1980s and early 1990s:

> In 1984, two young men riding on a motorbike killed Minister of Justice, Rodrigo Lara Bonilla, in Bogotá. Some years later, on 18 August 1989, Galán was killed [he was running for president at the time]; on 22 March 1990, Jaramillo Ossa was killed [also running for president for the left wing party *Unión Patriótica*]; on 26 April 1990, Pizarro was killed [running for president for M19]. And the news was always the same: a young *sicario* did it under Pablo Escobar's orders. Simultaneously, not many great political

meetings were held in that context, as Pablo Escobar's bombings forced them to hold all the meetings indoors. Such were the daily reports supporting the representations of the *sicarios* school based in Medellín.

(Martín-Barbero, 2015: 142)

On the other hand, the "popular" imagery also installed the image of the "*mujer-prepago*" (call girl) represented by a young woman (almost a teenager), associated with sexual traffic in the world generated by tough male drug dealers. The best representation can be found in the novel *Sin tetas no hay paraíso* (Without Breasts There Is No Paradise, 2006), which tells the story of a 14-year-old girl, Catalina, who lives in a poor neighbourhood in Pereira (a city located in the central western part of Colombia), in a region with great influence of drug traffickers. She witnesses how her girlfriends "live off the *narcos*", and make lots of money thanks to those relations. Catalina associates her neighbourhood girlfriends' prosperity with the size of their breasts. Therefore, those with small breasts, such as her, had to be content with living in poverty. This is why she decided, as her sole goal, to follow in her girlfriends' footsteps, and get silicone implants in her breasts so that she could get some *traqueto*[8] boyfriends.

The novel *Sin tetas no hay paraíso* was adapted into a TV series in Colombia (Caracol, 2006) and managed to stir up fierce controversy, due to the treatment it gave to the issue of aesthetic breast surgery and teenage prostitution, as means of social climbing within the context of drug trafficking. The novel not only reveals the artificial standard of beauty that prevails in the present, but it stresses the subjective experience of the young girls who submit to such standards and to diverse forms of domination, with the purpose of participating in the lavish world of drug traffickers.

These figures of "young *sicarios*" and "*mujeres prepagos*" become the starring roles in film shootings and in TV series called *narconovelas*[9] (*narco*-themed soap operas). The latter become audiovisual productions that have eclipsed other expressions of the masculine and the feminine—diverse and alternative—of "popular" young people from Medellín's peripheries, who had to wait until well into the 2000s to find a stage for their representation and dissemination. On the one hand, different research projects recreate other forms of youth grouping in impoverished neighbourhoods, with bonds stressing aesthetic-musical bonds (rock, punk, reggae, hip hop). On the other hand, alternative audiovisual productions, centred on communitarian and educational video, become stronger; they contribute to the emergence of "other forms of being together in the urban peripheries" (Román, 2009).[10]

Ciudad Comuna try, above all, to distance themselves from the traditional forms of organisation; they explore other forms of the young subject, such as the social actor and the cultural agent. They are firmly committed to social and cultural dynamics in their environs, which make communication a key element in their group; given that they appropriate communication media, based on their own processes of self-teaching, group collaboration, self-management and pluralism.

In addition to media, in recent years the organisational dynamics of the youth have centred on art, pop and rap, and other aesthetic resistance has been explored. Previous research undertaken regarding Ciudad Comuna reveals the power of these pursuits.

> Youth cultures will then acknowledge the central role of music, understood as a youth's identity force, which also strengthens the likelihood of cultural creation and production from and for the young. It is a choice that goes beyond taste and affinity for one genre or musical style, to become the force branding their existence and collective identity, thus making it possible for young people to face each other; this meeting, in turn, complies with conditions of reciprocity [as they share their taste for the same music] and co-presence [they come together in the same territories]. Such are the main conditions to build a collective identity.
>
> (Garcés *et al.*, 2007: 201)

This is why it is not gratuitous that local documentary films distribute landmark films on "*sicarios* from Medellín", as they conceal other—diverse and alternative—images of "popular" young people dwelling in Medellín's urban peripheries. As it is true that young people living in "popular" areas have

> an enormous capability to suffer, as the feeling of death is latent in their everyday lives, they survive bound to urban guerrilla groups, to *parches*[11] in the comuna, to paramilitary groups, but also associated to communitarian organisations in their neighbourhood, cultural or countercultural movements [music, graffiti, theatre].
>
> (Martín-Barbero, 2015: 143)

Great richness in DSP production occurred between 2010 and 2015. The voices and approaches on the territory related to the realities faced by youth in Medellín is thus made visible by Ciudad Comuna, as well as their own views on the social conflicts suffered by their territories. In this regard, the documentary *Gritos de Arte* (Art Screams), produced by Ciudad Comuna (2014), proposes a reflection on counterculture, understood as an artistic and social vindication of young people from Medellín's Comuna 1, and on how young participants of artistic collectives may build respectful and equitable relations, based on artistic expression, and, simultaneously, propose critical perspectives on the social realities of Medellín's peripheries, based on the expression of street theatre and the theatre of the oppressed.

The documentary *Memorias en Diálogo* (Dialogue of Memories, 2016)[12] acknowledges the implication of many young people from different comunas from Medellín in processes aimed at building new references for peace, based on the construction of stories of community life allowing the acknowledgment of other approaches on memory—different from the memory of war—in which art, youth groups and community meeting places, become the way to build a new narrative of hope, life and solidarity, so that the present of the communities in Medellín's peripheries can be built.

The documentary *Encuentro de Juventudes y Despliegues de lo Posible* (Youth Meeting, Deployments of What Is Possible), filmed by the Universidad Autonoma Latinoamericana (2016)[13] allows the recognition of processes of articulation, meeting and dialogue of knowledge between diverse youth processes, as well as between youth and academic processes, as a means to go beyond the academic-centred view on youth's realities and issues in Medellín. This Latin American meeting of researchers on youth, and young people from different youth collectives from Medellín—among which was Ciudad Comuna— enabled the consolidation of a debate on how young people have managed to break away either from the stigma of being violent young men, or from the submission to patriarchal domination (in the case of women), through what they do within their communities and their organisations. It also allowed the acknowledgment of emerging proactive subjectivities of the young, which circulate through culture, their own readings of city realities, and the construction of stages to develop their own knowledge, in dialogue with appraisals from the academia and the adult-centred culture.

The documentary *Resistencias Diversas* (Diverse Resistances, 2013)[14] allows the acknowledgment of an important and timely reflection on the building of young subjectivities based on sexual diversity, in the voice of young homosexuals who have built their own processes of youth organisation and participation within Comuna 8's territory. Spaces emerge from it for young people to expose and reflect upon the stigmatisation of a sexually diverse young population; upon the weight of religious, patriarchal, heterosexual education that increases the rejection of diverse young people; and upon the importance of generating spaces for meeting, interchange and dialogue with the general citizenship, for the young members of organisations vindicating the right to sexual diversity; they thus seek to overcome the conditions of stigmatisation and violence that still persist, due to the homophobia that lingers in the territories.

The documentary *Hip Hop Elemento de Vida* (Hip Hop an Element for Life, 2014)[15] could be the film made by Ciudad Comuna that best reflects the possibilities of transformation and social improvement represented by hip hop for the young in Comuna 8, who have been historically stigmatised by violence in their neighbourhoods. Comuna 8's hip hop movement has re-signified the idea of *school* from the perspective of its young participants. Relations of respect and mutual aid are developed between young men and women in such hip hop schools. Children have a chance, from very early age, to get closer to and learn about the four elements comprising the hip hop culture; and, at the same time, they adopt hip hop as an art and a means of expression, an attitude towards life, a path to explore, acknowledge, re-construct and tell their social reality, a way to express the critical interpretations they make of social inequities, and a chance to weave a proactive, humane and sensitive narrative. It offers hope about what the new generations, who make hip hop their political school, can achieve.

This documentary also makes it possible to acknowledge how young people, based on hip hop, reconstruct their family and neighbourhood ties, thus projecting themselves before their families and friends as male and female bearers of change, of conscience and life transformation, as men and women who take hip hop as an element to feed life and change.

The communicational initiatives developed by Ciudad Comuna provide new images of young people associated with urban cultures, which claim to be outside the armed conflict, and regard themselves as active political actors. They use art, music and aesthetics as an option of a non-violent life. The young person is, hence, considered as an individual with potentiality for collective action who is carrying a specific culture (subculture, microculture, youth culture), is highlighted, and the young subject is regarded as a creator of local and global senses and practices (Garcés, 2010; Acosta and Garcés, 2013; Garcés and García, 2016). The artistic expressions also help them question the inequalities in their lives, leading the capability of awareness and transformative change, forming a public deliberation and creating a productive place to start working for change, and to bring about change during and beyond the production of documentaries. As Barnett (1997) describes, the capability of awareness also being critical, developing critical self-reflection, and critical action, all of which contribute to reading the world through participation and dialogue

Conclusions

In Medellín's impoverished neighbourhoods, in spite of the grave situation of violence and destructuration of everyday life, the collective strength of youth groups can only surprise us, as they discover and renew the importance of creating space and time shared in collective processes. Such is the strength of youth collective capabilities, which enhance diverse expressions of territorial entrenchment and integration, allowed and empowered by their collective actions and by local communicational processes. These actions and processes emerge from the needs of information and of the construction of social weave in their territories, but also from their desire to narrate the realities of their own territories in a transparent manner. The work done by Ciudad Comuna reveals two things. First, that there is a political capability and articulate voice of youth, and especially women, that seeks collective action for breaking social taboos or stereotypes and institutional conceptions of territory, and second, that media, art and aesthetics are good tools for channelling it.

Thanks to young people's association with collectives, they discover they can act, not as isolated individuals, but as members of a collective environment where their action creates political communities. Their acts of communication and participation, within young social organisations, generate a collective body that breaches, transforms and questions prior frames of reflection, and proposes new ones to understand the realities and dynamics of the young amidst the diverse and complex realities faced by the comunas in Medellín, particularly in the peripheral neighbourhoods of Comuna 8.

Using the concept of collective capabilities (Ibrahim, 2006) and the work carried out by the authors in Egypt, Ciudad Comuna also demonstrates how the vulnerable can act together to expand and exercise their agency in a most effective way. The chapter argues that the capability approach, with its emphasis on freedoms and agency, is a suitable framework; however, the work developed by Ciudad Comuna cannot be attributed to one person. Hence, the idea of agency as concerned with the individual freedom to choose and bring about the things he/she values (Sen, 1992) is insufficient because it is not necessarily concerned with the state of affairs. This chapter has shown how the issues of gender, networks and territories are variables that affect all the inhabitants of Comuna 8, or people in a similar situation. This "collective" dimension of collective capabilities is seen by the intrinsic and instrumental value of social structures in the case of informal networks, the discrepancies about administrative and perceived borders, or the imaginary of youth and gender projected by mass media.

The work Comuna 8 have made through PSD since the early 1990s not only strengthens the formation of collective capabilities, it goes beyond that and leads, first of all, to a nurturing of the capability of participation that enables an expansion of the capabilities of others, working for public good, advancing democratic relations, having political representation in a project. Second, it also prepares a fertile ground for gender awareness through deliberation on the gender dimensions of inequalities or incorporating women's voices, which in return boosts the empowerment and confidence of women. Last, the capabilities for dignity and respect and affiliation are nourished and people have started to value treating each other with dignity and respect and developing empathy and recognising their interdependence. All these can be read as a process of well-being and agency as well as human development for a better community for youth in Colombia.

In conclusion, the aforementioned Ciudad Comuna's communication processes underscore the interest in people's participation in Comuna 8, and thus become experiences of citizen's journalism. These allow the members of the collective to assess the power generated when they share knowledge and approaches on the communities' reality, thus contributing to the building of communitarian identity. This identity is expressed in the content spread by these media, and in the deep roots of these young people in their territories, their communities, and their commitment to change the present.

Notes

1 In the context of Medellín's communitarian movement the word "popular" implies a broader sense than in English. It refers to a set of critical social counterhegemonic discourses and practices, emerging in contexts of advocacy of rights which are assumed by subjects who share conditions of exclusion.
2 Medellín's society is divided into socio-economic strata ranging from 1 (the lowest) to 6 (the highest). This classification is based on the public utilities tax, which has assigned a different stratum to each neighbourhood in the city.

3 Video in which young people express their politics regarding the hegemonic audio-visual sector in Medellín, 2013. Online, available at: www.youtube.com/watch? v=gmNbrZvSy-c.
4 Video memoire of Ciudad Comuna's campaign *la Radio Suena a Sexo*, 2014. Online, available at: www.youtube.com/watch?v=avWgwpD6XJY.
5 The documentary *Semillas del Pan de Azúcar* (Seeds from Pan de Azúcar Hill, 2010). Online, available at: www.youtube.com/watch?v=K5mdrkDIeAY.
6 See special edition of the Visión 8 newspaper *Memoria del Mapa político de las comunidades de la Comuna 8* (Memoire of the Comuna 8 communities' political map). Online, available at: http://issuu.com/ciudadcomuna/docs/namef08ae4.
7 The municipality's political administrative map—which was last updated in the 1980s—is intended to structure the current land management plan and includes the delimitation of 18 neighbourhoods in Comuna 8's map. In turn, the communities dwelling in the urban–rural border, together with social and organisational processes of all Comuna 8's neighbourhoods, built a communitarian map through negotiation processes revolving around the local development plan, a political map of their territory. The result of this exercise, which was open to the participation of the communities constituting the settlements in the borders, is the construction of a map with communitarian roots and identity. In this map, the communities present 34 neighbourhoods with their respective territorial delimitations, their history, their social constructions and processes of social and cultural participation, as well as population censuses carried out in participatory ways.
8 "*Traqueto*" is a common term in Colombia to refer to drug dealers and the issues associated with their lifestyle. The terms "*cultura traqueta*" (*traqueto* culture) and "*moda traqueta*" (*traqueto* fashion) appear repeatedly in the novel *Sin tetas no hay paraíso*.
9 Due to its particular way to introduce the *mujeres prepago*, the Colombian TV series *Sin tetas no hay paraíso*, realised by Caracol TV (2006), is an outstanding example based on the novel of the same name, written by Gustavo Bolívar. This series was broadcast in 2006 and, by the end of that year it had been released on DVD. The last chapter managed to beat rating records in Colombia, thus becoming the most widely watched TV show to date at that time; it achieved a 63-point rating. Later, Caracol announced that the rights of format and broadcasting had been sold to the Spanish channel Telecinco, which released its own version, called the same as the original *Sin tetas no hay paraíso*, in January 2008. Never before did another Colombian production centre so rigidly on the country's reality linking teenage women and prostitution, which had been generated by drug trafficking. It is understood that "*narconovelas* reflect Colombia's recent history and represent *narcos* as heroes and women as merchandise, thus becoming weapons of show business and the consumer society, aimed at selling Colombia's misery in a satirical, vulgar and exaggerated way" (Amado, 2016).
10 Communitarian video is made by youth collectives in "popular" contexts, which undertake pedagogical tasks and audiovisual production in marginal or minority communities, in some cases, the very communities to which the collective belongs. An intense work of re-seeing and re-signifying their own neighbourhood contexts is achieved through communitarian video. It is a demanding labour of re-programming one's look: re-signifying, rethinking, reinterpreting, representing, relating, reconstructing, reaffirming, reuniting, replying, reporting, revealing, rewinding, remembering, recollecting, recovering, re-trying, recreating, roaming, grumbling, recriminating (not re-electing), rekindling, re-incorporating, solving, reiterating, resisting, reflecting, renovating, reacting.
11 The word "*parche*" (patch) refers in Medellín either to a group of friends (a gang; the word "*combo*" is also used with this meaning), the place where they hang out, or a party or event they hold.

124 *Á. Garcés Montoya and L. Jiménez García*

12 Documentary *Memorias en Diálogo* (2016). Promotional video of *Memorias en Diálogo*, a territory-based process of memory building and peace construction, promoted by *Corporación Con-Vivamos*, *Corporación Picacho con Futuro* from Comuna 6, *Corporación Ciudad Comuna* from Comuna 8, and the local branch of YMCA from Comuna 13.

13 Audiovisual memoire of the *II Encuentro Latinoamericano Juventudes Despliegues de lo Posible* held in Medellín, in November, 2015. It is a production of the Universidad Autónoma Latinoamericana, and it was realised by Ciudad Comuna. Online, available at: www.youtube.com/watch?v=B8_LZNnD2Bs.

14 Documentary series *Repensando la Seguridad* (Re-Thinking About Security). Chapter: *Resistencias Diversas Experiencia del Colectivo Conexión Diversa de la Comuna 8 de Medellín* (Diverse Resistances Experience of the *Conexión Diversa* Collective from Comuna 8 in Medellín). This production was realised by the Centre of Audiovisual Production. Online, available at: www.youtube.com/watch?v=juYvX_3sLas.

15 The short film *Hip Hop Elemento de Vida* was realised by young people articulated to Ciudad Comuna's seedbed of audiovisual training, within the frame of the *Cineastas del Futuro* (Future Filmmakers) project, an educational proposal for young film producers supported by *Medellín Inteligente*. This short film pays homage to the hip hop culture and to the mobilisation and participation processes to overcome the stigmatisation that it has generated for the life of young people from Comuna 8 in Medellín. Online, available at: www.youtube.com/watch?v=fXZUXHJnbIE.

References

Acosta, G. and Garcés, A. (2013). *Colectivos de comunicación y apropiación de medios*. Medellín: Sello Editorial Universidad de Medellín.

Amado, J. (2016). La sociedad de consumo, el narcotráfico y la mujer, un acercamiento a la obra "Sin tetas no hay paraíso". Tesis de maestría Comunicación, Literatura y Educación. Universidad Distrital Francisco José de Caldas.

Barnett, R. (1997). *Higher Education: A Critical Business*. Buckingham: Society for Research into Higher Education and Open University Press.

Cinep and Justicia y Paz (2003). Panorama de los derechos humanos. *Noche, niebla y violencia política en Colombia*. Bogotá: Banco de datos de Violencia Política.

Ciudad Comuna (2013). *Serie Audiovisual Relatos desde la Frontera*. Medellín. Online, available at: www.youtube.com/ciudadcomuna.

Ciudad Comuna (2014). *Serie Videográfica sobre conflictos y realidades juveniles*. Medellín.

Colombia (1993). Consejería Presidencial para Medellín y su Área Metropolitana, Programa integral de Mejoramiento de barrios subnormales en Medellín (PRIMED). Estudios de factibilidad. Colombia: Municipio de Medellín.

Garavito, Y. (2014). *Sistematización de la Experiencia de Formación Radial La Radio Suena a Sexo*. Medellín: Editorial Ciudad Comuna.

Garcés, Á. (2010). *Nos-otros los jóvenes: polisemias de las culturas y los territorios musicales en Medellín*. Sello Editorial Universidad de Medellín.

Garcés, A. (2016). Colectivos juveniles en Medellín. Configuración de subjetividades juveniles vinculadas a la Comunicación Audiovisual (participativa y comunitaria). Tesis Doctoral, Universidad Nacional de La Plata, Argentina. Online, available at: http://sedici.unlp.edu.ar/handle/10915/49916.

Garcés, Á. and García, L. (2016). *Comunicación para la movilización y el cambio social*. Medellín: Sello Editorial Universidad de Medellín y CIESPAL.

Garcés, Á. and Medina, D. (2011). Músicas de Resistencia. El hip hop en Medellín. In: Mutuverria, Marcos, Palozzolo, Fernando and Otrocki, Laura (eds). *Cuestiones sobre jóvenes y juventudes, diez años después*. Argentina: Universidad Nacional de La Plata.

Garcés, A., Tamayo. A. and Medina, D. (2007). Territorialidad e identidad hip hop: raperos en Medellín. *Anagramas*, 5(10), 125–137.

Ibrahim, S. (2006). From Individual to Collective Capabilities: The Capability Approach as a Conceptual Framework for Self-help. *Journal of Human Development*, 7(3), 397–416.

Ibrahim, S. and Alkire, S. (2007). Agency and Empowerment: A Proposal for International Comparable Indicators. OPHI Working Paper Series (4), May 2007.

Jimenez, L (2013). La Comunicación Haciendo Escuela. Medellín: Editorial Ciudad Comuna. Video Memoria. Online, available at: www.youtube.com/ciudadcomuna.

Lomnitz, L. (1989). *Cómo sobre viven los marginados*. México: Editores Siglo XXI.

Martín-Barbero, J. (1996). "Comunicación y ciudad: Sensibilidades, paradigmas, escenarios". In: Giraldo, Fabio and Viviescas, Fernando. *Pensar la ciudad*. Bogotá: Tercer Mundo Editores.

Martín-Barbero, J. (2002). Jóvenes: Comunicación e Identidad. In: *Pensar Iberoamérica. Revista de Cultura*. 1. Online, available at: www.oei.es/pensariberoamerica/ric00a03.htm (accessed 15 January 2013).

Martín-Barbero, J. (ed.) (2009). Entre saberes desechables, y saberes indispensables. Agenda de país desde la comunicación. Friedrich Ebert Stiftung– Centro de Competencia en Comunicación para América Latina. Online, available at: www.C3fes.net (accessed 15 November 2012).

Martín-Barbero, J. (2015). Jóvenes: una ciudadanía de raíces móviles. In: *Jóvenes un fuego vital: Reflexiones y conocimiento en juventud*. Alcaldía de Medellín, pp. 138–157.

Mongin, O. (2006). *La condición urbana. La ciudad a la hora de la mundialización*. Buenos Aires: Paidós.

Niño, E. and Jimenez, L. (2013). *Memorias en Diálogo: Diálogos y circulación de memorias locales*. Medellín: Editorial Ciudad Comuna.

Oslender, U. (2002-junio). "Espacio, lugar y movimientos sociales: hacia una espacialidad de resistencia". *Scripta Nova*, VI, 115. Revista electrónica de geografía y ciencias sociales, Universidad de Barcelona.

Perea, Carlos. (2008). *¿Qué nos une? Jóvenes, cultura y ciudadanía*. Bogotá: La Carreta Social.

Riaño Alcalá, P. (2000). Recuerdos metodológicos, el taller y la investigación etnográfica. In: *Revista Estudios sobre las Culturas Contemporáneas*, 10, pp. 143–168. Mexico: Universidad de Colima.

Román, M. J. (2009). Mirar la mirada: para disfrutar el audiovisual alternativo y comunitario. 21, pp. 141–164. Facultad de Comunicaciones, Universidad de Antioquia.

Sen, A. (1992) *Inequality Re-examined*. Oxford: Clarendon Press.

Serrano, J. (2003). Saber joven: miradas a la juventud bogotana 1990–2000. In: José Serrano (ed.). *Juventud. Estado del arte. Saber joven: miradas a la juventud bogotana, 1900–2000*. Bogotá: DAAC/DASB, Universidad Central, DIUC.

Svampa, M. (2004). "Cinco tesis sobre la nueva matriz popular". *Cambio Social*, 15. Primavera.

Universidad Autónoma Latinoamericana (2016). *Memorias Encuentro Latinoamericano Despliegues de lo Posible*. Medellín: Fondo Editorial Universidad Autónoma.

Wortman, A. (2010). En Kriger, M. (Dir., 2010): *Globalización, sentidos e identidades en América Latina*. Buenos Aires: CAICYT CONICET.

Zibechi, R. (2008). *América Latina: periferias urbanas, territorios en resistencia*. Bogotá: Ediciones Desde Abajo.

Web references

Ciudad Comuna. Online, available at: www.ciudadcomuna.org.

Comuna 8. Online, available at: www.comuna8.org.

Mesa Interbarrial Medellín: Online, available at: http://mesainterbarrialdedesconectados. blogspot.com/.

Repensando la Seguridad. Online, available at: www.repensandolaseguridad.org.

7 If you can see me, then I am here

Using participatory video in researching young people's aspirations*

Aurora Lopez-Fogues, Alejandra Boni Aristizábal,
Gynna Millán Franco and Sergio Belda-Miquel

Introduction

Using the theoretical framework of the capability approach (Sen 1999, 2009) and participatory video (PV) as a method to articulate the voice of young people (Milne *et al.* 2012), this chapter offers an insight into the use of PV as a methodology for the research and analysis of youth participation and its impact on public policy that directly affects their aspirations and realities. This chapter is the product of our reflections and analysis throughout the process and is an opportunity to establish a dialogue between PV and the capability approach perspective.

The fieldwork was conducted in the municipality of Quart de Poblet, located near the city of Valencia (Spain). The PV process lasted from February–April 2014. The participants were 11 young people aged 16–24 years old. For three months, the group engaged in a PV process to reflect on their aspirations and visions concerning issues they had identified as relevant during the earliest stage of engagement. In a context of severe crisis and continuous economic reforms, the young people selected three relevant topics after reflecting on the following question: "If you had five minutes to talk with policy-makers or influential politicians, what would you like them to hear?" The three themes that emerged, and that are central to the narratives of the videos later developed through the PV process, were migration, education and youth participation. The PV methodology was proposed as a way to engage with the interests and motivations of the group of young people. All the co-authors of this chapter participated in the process: Aurora Lopez-Fogues was the main facilitator, maintaining constant contact with the group; she was also in charge of interviewing the participants once the PV had concluded. Gynna Millán Franco was the main PV trainer. Sergio Belda-Miquel was in charge of the institutional network and conducted prior work within the SocIEtY project. Alejandra Boni Aristizábal was a participant observer during the PV process and the principal researcher of the SocIEtY project.

Building this chapter upon this research, we first describe the case study and the context and then present the main characteristics of the PV methodology. The fourth section explores the stages of the PV process during the case study.

In the fifth section, an analysis of the process and content of the videos using a capability approach perspective is performed. Finally, we conclude by examining what the PV methodology can offer as a tool for the analysis of young people's perspectives at the conceptual, empirical and methodological level.

Research context

The Spanish case study: Quart de Poblet (Valencia)

Quart de Poblet is a town of 25,174 inhabitants in the metropolitan area of Valencia, Spain. It can be considered an average Spanish municipality in terms of socio-economic indicators. Of this population, 93.1 per cent is of Spanish nationality. Since 2009, immigration has almost halved as a consequence of the economic crisis and the end of jobs in the construction industry, the municipal budget has decreased by around 30 per cent, around 16 per cent of the population is under 29, and nearly 43 per cent of the youth are unemployed (IVE 2014).

Despite the brief data provided above, which serves to illustrate the context of crisis and austerity, Quart de Poblet presents a lively civil society, a long-standing culture of citizen engagement promoted by the municipality and an active involvement in national and international projects. As examples of this: Quart de Poblet has one of the 33 youth councils in the Valencian community (from 600 municipalities); provides young people with municipal spaces for community use (e.g. *Espai de Creació Jove*); there are clubs and associations (the *Esplais*) that offer activities for youngsters, from toddlers to adolescents; there is a municipal building devoted to youth issues (*Quart de Poblet Jove*); and it has a feature known as youth houses (*Casas de Juventud*), a physical space where young people can propose and carry out their own projects and activities. Apart from the representability, uniqueness and the reasons presented above to choose Quart de Poblet as the case study for conducting the PV process, another important reason was access. The municipality had previous experience participating in European projects and (through the *Espai de Creació Jove* and the *Casas de Juventud*) had an interest in using audiovisual techniques to engage with the youth.

Who was the sample?—Participants

The selection of the participants had the goal of garnering a wide spectrum of voices, but focused on those who were already actively involved in youth activities. Thanks to close collaboration with the professional youth workers from the municipal youth area (*Quart de Poblet Jove*), 11 young people, aged 16–24 years old, were finally selected:

1   Interns of *Quart de Poblet Jove* (Youth Department of Quart de Poblet). Five participants represented young people who were at that moment doing an internship in the Youth Department of the municipality. The participants

were three women and two men. Age range: 20–22. Level of studies: Vocational Education and Training (3), University (1), Secondary education (1).

2   *Cremant*. Cremant is an audiovisual association promoted by young people linked to the *Espai de Creació Jove*, one of the spaces promoted by the municipality of Quart de Poblet. Three participants were from this group, comprising two women and one man. Age range: 22–24. Level of studies: University (3).

3   *Esplai*. Esplai youth club promoting play and recreational activities. Three young people took part in the PV process, one woman and two men. Age range: 16–18. Level of studies: Secondary level (3).

PV as a process and as a product

Participatory research was envisioned as the central methodology for approaching the overall goal of the FP7 SocIEtY project, which was to improve the quality of life of disadvantaged young people through social innovation. PV emerged as a key innovative and social tool for putting together participants as co-researchers and opening up new spaces and capabilities for young people via new digital technologies. The choice for the method was made mainly because PV has the potential to give a voice to young people and to transform the usual social dynamics through the production of collaboratively authored videos (White 2003) that show and tell young people's own stories (Humphreys and Jones 2006).

Video in research has been used in numerous ways and under different labels. Terms such as collaborative video, community video or social video (Mitchell and de Lange 2012) are used to refer to such practices. Although the arguments on which is the best term to employ have been disputed in several articles (Pink 2001; Nair and White 2003). It is important to highlight that the distinctive feature of PV is that it is a research and communication method for social change (Wheeler 2012) and that this necessarily involves "a group of participants who will primary construct their own videos and texts with minimal assistance from the research team" (Mitchell and de Lange 2012: 171). The key notion of the PV is that participants become researchers. It allows collaborative knowledge production, embodied in online platforms, which depend upon discussions, consensus building and the co-existence of contradictory knowledge (Wheeler 2011: 47). This is slowly trickling into academic research and practice, and implies a change of paradigm in the relationship with research participants, not as subjects, but as peers. Another reason for selecting PV as a method for this research was the flexibility of the tool to act as the lens through which the ideas, voices, aspirations and barriers experienced by young people, could be visually shaped and made legible to others. The aim was not only to foster reflection and change within the group of young people, but also to have a final product (the videos) that would have the potential to shape and amplify a reality and to enhance processes of social transformation.

In the following subsections, we examine the potential of PV in its two forms and the relation of PV with the work dynamics, using gender and youth as the focus variables.

PV as a process

PV, as one of the family of participatory methodologies (Kindon 2003; Ramella and Olmos 2005), is an interactive practice that intends to shift power and increase group agency towards social improvement. It is used worldwide by practitioners in the realm of empowering communities and giving voice to those who are invisible to mainstream academic research (Gomez 2003; Shaw 2007, 2013).

As a process, it is a method that impulses communication, strengthening the process of individual and collective empowerment, the sharing of realities and awareness and giving voice to collectives that traditionally have been silenced. Through the steps involved in the making of a PV process, the main emphasis is placed on the aspect of group dynamics, respect and the figure of participants as co-researchers. These aspects are familiar to other participatory approaches. In essence, the PV aims to focus on the flourishing of people, their communities and the broader ecology (Reason and Bradbury 2001), in the framework of the participatory action research (PAR) methodology. As with other participatory approaches, the PV seeks to invert the relationship between the researcher and the researched (Chambers 1997), while recognising power imbalances and barriers to achieving equality, e.g. the different levels of education among the participants and structural gender barriers. It implies that individuals—principally the collective—take action to identify their own reality, define a set of problems and come up with potential solutions. As noted by Bery (2003: 105), "the participatory video process puts communication tools into the hands of ordinary people who have something to share".

PV as a product

As noted above, one of the reasons that motivated the municipality and the youngsters to engage in the process was the audiovisual component. In addition to its engagement value, video is an attractive tool that provides immediate results that can be disseminated to a wider audience. The final product is a "particular audiovisual product that may bring consequences in terms of visibility, public impact or generation changes" (Montero and Moreno 2014: 73). Visibility is crucial in many cases because PV stories identify and validate people's realities, which are often invisible to the larger community or political context (Bery 2003: 108). Additionally, even when the focus could solely be on the final product, the PV process entails applying technical skills (script writing, filming, audio, formatting, etc.) and soft skills (teamwork, listening, self-esteem, analytical skills). The products—the videos—also have the potential to reach out to people that conventional reports or policy briefs lack. In Table 7.1 we summarise aspects of the final videos produced.

Table 7.1 Videos produced

Group	Title	Keywords	Video intention	Link
Quart de Poblet Jove	*Adiós España* (Goodbye Spain)	Youth opportunities Entrepreneurship Migration	To show that young people have ideas but not enough opportunities and that something needs to be done about it.	https://vimeo.com/145614948
Cremant	Educational laws	Legal instability Politics Education Conservatism Religion Segregation Social justice	To show that the government changes the law all the time, as they want, asking for more money or for more time, and we cannot do anything about it.	https://vimeo.com/128790965
Esplai	*Esplai*	Participation Voluntarism Young people Monitors Free time	To show the good and the bad things of being a community volunteer and the values attached to it.	https://vimeo.com/126901812

Source: this table has been developed by the authors.

The stages of PV—methodology

Ideas on exactly which steps or stages are needed for a PV process vary according to the literature and the practice (White 2003). Nevertheless, most of them seem to have common patterns, for example, to put together a dynamic group process facilitated by external people, which turns into an evolving process of exploration and dialogue about shared issues among the group of co-researchers. Through processes of action and reflexion, the group message finally takes the shape of a video (short or long, depending on the needs of the process) aiming to communicate to a wider audience.

The steps in which the PV process has evolved, were based on previous PV projects developed by some of the authors of this chapter. There are five main stages, as described in Figure 7.1.

First stage: diagnosis

This phase was divided into an initial group-building presentation of one day and a diagnosis of half a day. On the first day, a shared purpose of community sense was created and an introduction to the PV was given through examples and experiences in other projects. In this phase, the three groups were established

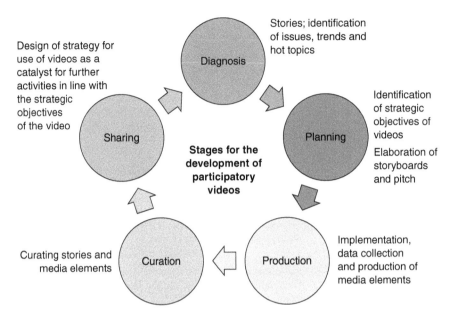

Figure 7.1 Stages of participatory video.

based on previous affiliations, the facilitators were introduced and the research question presented. Under the question: "If you had five minutes to talk with policy-makers or influential politicians, what would you like them to hear?", the three groups of young people started to discuss, share and evaluate their daily barriers and obstacles to leading a life that is meaningful for them and for others (Sen 1999). Two milestones of this phase were: (1) the debate about the themes presented in the introduction; and (2) the "elevator pitch" technique, a technique that implies explaining your idea in one minute. This minute symbolises the time that an elevator takes to travel from the first to the eighth floor. Each group held a debate on the issues that they felt were involved in order for them to lead a meaningful life. Using the starting point of their immediate realities, the discussion helped to identify areas that were relevant for each of them. Afterwards, within their groups, they had to select one and explore its sub-layers. Then, each group had 60 seconds to convince the rest of the attendees that their ideas (which were written with bullet points or drawn in 4–8 vignettes) were worth making a video about. At the end of the phase, each group had decided on one topic to work on, and on the message they wanted to come across through their PV.

Second stage: planning

For two weeks, each group worked autonomously to agree on which vignettes would be transformed into shots to form their video narrative. The storyboard was continuously modified through the process due to issues of access, but also to redefine the meaning and value of the images used to transmit their idea. Even though, in this planning phase, each of the young people was assigned a role within the group (editor, director, interviewer, etc.), this later became much more flexible and based each young person's ability or experience.

Third stage: production

This phase lasted two weeks. It centred on learning filming techniques (focus, background, setting, audio, etc.) thanks to the assistance of a facilitator who was an expert in the field. The development of this phase was very distinct in each of the groups. The Esplai group required the assistance of a tutor to accompany them and provide them with access to the people that were going to be interviewed in their video. For Quart de Poblet Jove, due to issues of schedules and technical unfamiliarity, only one person was responsible for filming all the agreed scenes. Finally, the Cremant group did not need any assistance because they were the most advanced in audiovisual techniques and they decided to make the video using icons, fonts, and visual effects rather than interviews (Esplai) or real images (Quart de Poblet Jove).

Fourth stage: curation

The phase also lasted two weeks. It focused on editing the video while the group dynamics described in the third phase continued. The youngest group (Esplai) required more facilitation to edit the video than the other two groups. Quart de Poblet Jove relied on the same person that produced the video, although they shared ideas and opinions about the progress made on it. The Cremant group worked more autonomously. All of them benefited from the insights of an audiovisual expert in the facilitator group, as well as from the comments of other co-researchers. Two days of collaborative work, in the same physical space, were arranged to make this possible.

Fifth stage: sharing

This last stage was conducted in three different spaces: the first was on 29 April 2015, as part of a series of conferences organised by the municipality. In this space, the target audience were civil servants working for the municipality, associations, and professionals interested in the topic of youth in Quart de Poblet. We organised a round table where four specialists (education, labour, culture and youth) were invited as guest speakers. A total of 30 people attended the event, including key persons from the youth department of the municipality. The participation of the young people was limited (one per group), but the debate was lively despite this. The second space took place on 7 June, in an open and informal event at the Valencian festival *Fira Alternativa* (Alternative Fair). This festival is an annual open space where associations and groups with a social background use stands to promote and showcase their work and projects. The number of people stopping at the stand and asking questions was high, and during the day we provided information to many visitors. Attendance by the young people was sizeable and almost half of the group came to this event. The third event was on 9 December 2015, at the final conference of the SocIEtY project, which took place at the European Parliament in Brussels. The three videos were explained and one of them was projected in the auditorium. The target public were parliamentarians and relevant policy-makers. However, despite the number of invitations sent out, their attendance was still low. Although the team had invited one of the young people to come to this event, she was unable to attend. One positive aspect was the number of academics in the audience, as all the SocIEtY team (more than 30 researchers from all across Europe) attended the conference, and we received positive comments on the work and narratives presented through the videos. These were shared with the young people through social media channels.

Analysis from a capability approach perspective: agency, voice and participation

Our analysis centred on information obtained through the PV process, the analysis of the three final videos and a final interview with each of the young people who were part of the project. The three videos show that voice, agency and aspirations have been limited for young people and that, given the space and platform to communicate, they are interested in raising their voices and communicating the issues of concern to them to others.

During the workshops, the young people talked about their personal stories and also those of their families, in which disengagement, deprivation and lack of opportunities were recurrent topics. Even though these stories largely centred on the consequences of the economic crisis (unemployment, precarity, etc.), they were not limited to the economic sphere. Group conversations touched issues such as school dynamics, sexual preferences, leisure and intergenerational relations. The process aimed at providing a "safe space" where topics could be discussed openly in order to encourage them not only to start creating their own storyboard but also to foster socialisation between themselves. We did not detect any gender imbalance in these sessions, because the number of attendees varied, without one gender dominating over the other. Although the theme of gender and its relation to economic revenues or educational achievements were issues discussed in the workshops, the voices were mostly centred on three or four participants, evidencing the difficulties of some of the young people to debate or provide a solid opinion about it. This, in our perception, had to do mostly with the variable of age.

Regarding the aspect of age, the youngest participants (those that formed Esplai) had greater difficulties in engaging with and attending the encounters. This may have been due to restrictions in their schedules linked to their age. The members argued that they had many "afterschool" activities, homework, exams and a time for being back at home. Despite this, thanks to the creation of a telephone group for instant communication, all the participants could follow the debate. Additionally, in the final meetings, the Cremant group, who were the most familiar with audiovisual techniques, helped the other two groups with technical questions and other design aspects.

Through the project, the participants shared their concerns and finally each group decided on one issue as the most significant, which would form the main theme of their video. Their concerns were mostly about their future because they felt unable to change structural practices (i.e. corruption, political instability, discrimination) that directly affect their opportunities. This was evident in the videos by Cremant and the interns of Quart de Poblet Jove, in which unfair practices (in education and in economics, respectively) were the trigger for producing the videos. One young participant expressed her opinion about social exclusion in one of the online debates made during the PV process:

> When I think about vulnerable youth, I think about all of us that are in total disagreement with the things that are being done politically and are affecting us in the short and long term, and mainly I think that our critiques are not being heard. Individually we cannot do anything to improve this situation "there is strength in numbers". I think that we all need to do our part, but support each other.
>
> (Female, Intern of Quart de Poblet Jove)

The quote reflects a strong agency in terms of the willingness to be an actor of change (Sen 1999) but, as Crocker (2008) notes, this capability needs to be more than a possibility and should be understood as the power of the individual to exercise it. It is within this conceptualisation of power that PV is seen as a methodology that reveals hierarchical power relations—going from *researching about* to *researching alongside*—and gains relevance and suitability as a means of transformation, in terms of the enhancement of capabilities. The other aspect included in this quote is the aspect of voice and the possibility of change.

The capability approach, as a framework, provides us with the informational basis to understand participation beyond formal spaces such as education, and puts emphasis on the ability of individuals to have a voice in public participation to "the extent to which people have the opportunity to achieve outcomes that they value and have reason to value" (Sen 1999: 291). Focusing on the videos, a recurrent theme in all three of them are references to the ability to engage, or in the words of Bonvin and Farvaque (2006), the capability for voice understood as the real opportunity people have to express their opinion, perspectives and aspirations. The following two quotes express how the process has influenced this capability, but also the limitations that a process like this can have.

> During the process of participatory video ... I think I gave my ideas and suggestions for achieving a common final product at the same time that I was hearing the arguments and ideas of the others.
>
> (Female, Intern of Quart de Poblet Jove)

I like to be part of things like this one, because I feel identified and I like it. I want to improve things. However, some days I do not want to be part of anything, because I think it will not make any difference.

(Male, Cremant)

These two young people express their engagement into the project, but also, as the second one says, there is a concern about the impact of it in the long term.

The video produced by Cremant is a critique motivated by the shared experience of the three members of the group, all undergraduate students. It constitutes a critique of the new educational law and a response to their feelings that the political forces are playing with their educational opportunities. By comparing the number of legislative educational changes in Spain with those in other EU countries, the video denounces that the reason for so many changes is not due to educational motives, but rather to political and ideological battles. The video is also based on the experience of friends and on the concerns, also expressed, in the video made by the group of interns at Quart de Poblet. There was a shared anxiety about their professional future once their studies have finished. The video of the interns of Quart de Poblet represents the forced migration that many youngsters face due to the barriers to lead a life that is meaningful for them in Spain. The main message concerns the lack of employment, but it is also accompanied by a critical view on the message of entrepreneurship, presenting, based on testimonies of people who started a business in Quart de Poblet recently, the difficulties of becoming an entrepreneur in Spain if one lacks personal savings. Consequently, the video goes beyond attributing the lack of opportunities that young people face to the economic crisis alone, illustrating the discourse of entrepreneurship as well as presenting the executive and legislative powers that play a role in the impossibility many young people feel of being able to plan for a future. Based on the argument of the video, these powers are responsible due to their preference to rescue banks (executive) and due to the impunity towards cases of monetary frauds and corruption (legislative). This anxiety is highlighted in the words of one of the producers of the video:

I want to keep studying and to find a job, here or outside, I guess that outside, because here in Spain there are no jobs, there are no young people. Everyone has to leave, the ones remaining are people who cannot run away or people who are too old.

(Male, Intern of Quart de Poblet Jove)

The third video, by Esplai, depicts the everyday experiences of the members as volunteers in the youth club. It narrates the value that the club adds in empowering individuals through collective play and activities. Contrary to the other two videos, Esplai as an institution is portrayed as a place where young people have the real freedom to voice their opinions and to make them count. The experience of one participant acknowledges this: "Quart is giving me tons of new experiences thanks to the Esplai. When the moment arrives I also want to be a mentor, to share the values that they have given to me" (Male, Esplai). On a more general level, the PV showed that young people, as a group, felt that their capability for voice within public policy processes was very limited. Linked to the capability for voice, the videos and testimonies make clear references to the issue of aspirations, which in this project emerged as uniform regardless of intersectional aspects such as level of education, gender or age. The capability to aspire, understood as the capability to envision a desired future (Conradie and Robeyns 2013), increased through the PV process as they revised and redefined their video message. Based upon strong critiques (Cremant and Quart de Poblet) and upon a good practice (Esplai), the three videos combine a critical side with a view of how things ought to be in order to have a fair educational system (Cremant) or a fair country (Quart de Poblet). Consequently, the videos draw attention to the facts that the capability to aspire is unevenly distributed in society (Appadurai 2004) and its distribution corresponds to issues of power. Hence, some people are favoured because, using the informational basis provided by the capability approach, policies and practices were not designed with well-being at the core.

The topics of the three videos and the final interviews, where all the young people shared their enthusiasm about the process and the final results, evidenced that the PV fostered young people's ability to carry out self-critical investigation and an analysis of their own reality (Gaventa and Cornwall 2008) and also contributed towards rethinking and reframing the particular practices of society and young people's roles within them (Kemmis and McTaggart 2005). These two young people express it as follows, the first referring to the process of video and the second with a critical view about structural limitations:

> I have learned to make a short film, to edit it … but mostly I learned to see all the problems that we as youth face … and it is an opportunity to express our needs and discontents with the current situation.
>
> (Female, Intern of Quart de Poblet Jove)

> Here in Spain, we don't have much of a future. My aspirations, I cannot know them, because when I finish my studies … it is in one year, and many things may or may not change in one year, I prefer to focus on now, on today.
>
> (Female, Cremant)

Examining the PV brings to the fore the question of why gender was not a topic when choosing the themes for their videos, nor a discussion fostered through the use of PV. Although gender and sexual orientation were raised at the initial workshop, when the young people presented the themes that felt relevant for them as young people, none of the groups worked in that direction. It was recognised that gender had a relation with economic progress and that multiple socio-economic gender constraints as well as stereotypes were still present. However, perhaps due to group dynamics and the need for finding a consensus, or perhaps due to the proximity of the topic, the three groups decided to opt for topics that all of them could easily feel part of: migration, education and associational activities.

The results from a capability lens shows that, through the five stages, the process provided the necessary spaces (internal and external) for young people to formulate and express how they understand the challenges they are facing, especially in a context of crises; how economic and social factors are constraining their opportunities, and the possibilities they imagine they have of being able to achieve their aspirations. Although the PV process did not reveal gender and youth-education differences, it offers the view of youth as a group that is cohesive based on their capabilities as well as providing a method to give voice to those who are traditionally left aside. The absence of references in the PV as a product may have been triggered by the cooperative character of the PV as a process, the homogenous character of the group (all of them were students), as well as by the most notorious aspect of other issues (such as education, employment and leisure) that seemed more evident to them.

With regard to agency, we can say that even though young people's level of consultation, participation and power in Quart de Poblet is higher than in many other municipalities, they still experience a general exclusion from participating in the design and implementation of public policies. This influences their ideas of self-organisation and the perceived power that they, as young people, have of changing or transforming their daily realities and, hence, on their aspirations and agency. Agency understood as being active *doers* (Sen 1999) and the ability for them as individuals to foster change, was a topic discussed throughout the PV process. The PV has been a successful method in terms of fostering the engagement of different voices in the community, talking about what topics they envisage are of concern to them, and in reaching different levels of audiences. The method enhanced collaborative work between young women and men. We perceived that there was solidarity between them as a group as through the process they understood that the reason they were taking part in it was, perhaps, because they needed to find their voice. In interviews with them at the end of the process, some of them had become more aware of their situation.

To conclude, the capability approach provides the lenses to explore the process of PV in terms of agency, aspiration, voice and participation. Through the process, these areas have been fostered and knowledge has been produced at three levels: personal, analytical and technical. At the personal level, the PV has enabled self-exploration and the outlining and reflecting of one's life plans. At the analytical level, thanks mostly to the stages of diagnosis, production and sharing, the PV has provided spaces in which topics and issues were debated among colleagues (workshops and meetings), professionals (dissemination at the municipality) or the general public (event at the Alternative Fair). Finally, on the technical level, each individual at the planning, production and curation stage has learned the process of video making and some of the basic techniques involved. Despite the shortcomings mentioned throughout the text, the level of analysis in the videos and the final interviews show that the capability for voice, aspiration and agency has been enhanced. This has been a learning process for the participants as researchers and in terms of awareness of the impact of their own assumptions and practices (Gaventa and Cornwall 2008), which makes this PV a small contribution towards opening up possibilities for "interaction, sharing and cooperation … for personal, social and cultural change" (White 2003: 64). The PV brings together young women and men to discuss issues that matter to both equally and to blend their voices to make visible very concerning issues that affect them on a daily basis.

Final reflections and some conclusions

This chapter has investigated how PV—an incipient methodology in formal academic research—may enable a practice of researching that does not perpetuate unequal power relations between the researcher and the researched and does not perpetuate the idea that knowledge is only produced from the top down. The PV fostered a cooperative bottom-up exercise of knowledge. The chapter showed how there is a shared experience of what it means to be young in the municipality of Quart de Poblet. The use of video through the five-stage process has brought about a series of conclusions.

At the theoretical level, the use of the capability approach as a framework has helped to highlight, disentangle and focus the research design by asking the young people about their daily barriers and obstacles to leading a life that is meaningful for them and for others (Sen 1999). It helped to focus on the aspect of voice, genuine opportunities and equity through the dynamics of video production as well as on the product itself.

At the empirical level, the conclusions are that the weekly work, in the form of workshops, discussions, social media interactions, video interviews and the final video production; has contributed voices and perspectives not often heard by policy-makers. Even though the young people shared the idea that their opinions were invisible to policy-makers, they also shared the resilience and enthusiasm to produce a short film that could be circulated and disseminated in different areas. The process of PV has juxtaposed different perspectives of what the concerns of youth in a locality in Spain are, and articulated them in an audiovisual product that has allowed them to share it in different spaces and with a variety of audiences. Although the dissemination has not engaged as many young people as would have been desirable, the aesthetics of PV have proven to be an important tool to explore, understand and record the stories and voices of young people. The PV shifted the power relations between researchers and researched, and what emerged is that some of the young people shifted and enhanced their agency through this process. It is also relevant to notice how young people identify themselves as a group regardless of other variables.

The group was spontaneously formed of six females and five males, hence purposive selection was not necessary. Looking at other variables, such as gender and level of education (mainly based on issues of age), the dynamics of PV illustrate that there were two levels of participation, determined mainly by the second variable. This was most noticeable, because on one hand, the Esplai and Cremant groups were already involved in municipal activities (through the youth club and through the *Casa de Juventud*), and on the other hand, the interns of Quart de Poblet Jove (interns at the municipal youth department), for the first time, were connected with social activities. The difference between these two levels of participation (committed and permanent vs accidental and temporal), may have had a possible influence on the dynamics of group work within each team, and on the ability to give weight to all the voices in the group. For instance, Cremant, which was formed of University students and had the advantage of being a group focused on audiovisual techniques, was the most cohesive group with the strongest voice during the PV, while the Esplai group were accompanied by a tutor and there was a reduced participation of the youngest members during the meetings and social media exchanges and discussions. Finally, regarding the group of interns of Quart de Poblet Jove, many of whom had never been actively involved in any municipal clubs and did not know each other in advance, they had difficulties engaging all the members throughout all the stages, and work became focused mainly on one person. As noted throughout the chapter, gender did not seem to play a role in the interactions. It may have been due to the cohesion within the group (all of whom were students), the participatory process itself, which emphasised the aspect of equal participation, or due to the fact that the group tacitly decided to focus on common aspects previously familiar to all of them, discussed through different channels and, hence, where they could more easily articulate an opinion about such topics (quality in education, migration and leisure activities).

Agency in the sense of being an active doer is not an easy measurable result; however, the effort put into learning the skills, cooperating and articulating an opinion within a group, defining the stories and researching and analysing the issues that were going to be shared, proves that PV is "a vehicle for people to see themselves as citizens in new ways and for them to learn a new mode of citizenship" (Wheeler 2011: 50). The concluding message of this PV—from a capability perspective—is that, contrary to the top-down perspective of employment as the single and biggest concern for young people; the participants expressed a shared diverse list of areas and topics that were relevant to them. Employment in itself did not represent a goal, instead insecurity, fairness or the future were more prominent topics, especially when referring to their future and their aspirations. Additionally, the PV as a method in this process proved not to be marked by gender differences, hence being a very useful tool to provide youth with a platform to design and engage on policies that directly affect them. The process showed that the fact they are deprived of this increases the climate of scepticism and mistrust towards the top authorities, as well as a general feeling of depression. Although in this municipality young people feel more active and included than at the national level, there is a gap between the needs of young people and the existing public policies that mostly focus on employment. For this reason, the young people that participated in the project did not feel safe referring to their future and downsized their expectations or centred them on migration as the only alternative.

Finally, on the methodological side, the conclusion to be learnt is that the use of digital or innovative tools such as the PV are highly recommended to engage young people as a cohesive group and to help them to articulate a powerful discourse (in terms of visibility and content). The PV not only had the potential to engage young people, but also to enhance their agency in terms of critical thinking and aiming for social change. Through the process, perhaps greater attention could have been paid to the equity aspect for choosing the topic or for fostering the inclusion of transversal issues such as gender and the relation of migration, education, or activities associated with this variable. However, the PV has provided the space where young people reflected on their relations with others, on hierarchical power, on the meaning of participation in a full sense, on their role in society, and provided them with the chance to share and discuss their visions (through the dissemination stage) with a wide range of audiences. Therefore, despite the challenges encountered in terms of engaging all the young people or having a greater audience in the public disseminations, the PV process, by providing a practice of co-researching, shared analysis and participatory discussions, created a space for agency to be enhanced and, hence, for transformation.

Note

* The results of this chapter are bsed on the work of a European Commission funded FP7 project SocIEtY "Social Innovation, Empowering the Young for the Common Good".

References

Appadurai, A. (2004). The Capacity to Aspire: Culture and the Terms of Recognition. In: Rao, V. and Walton, M. (eds), *Culture and Public Action*, pp. 59–79. California: Stanford University Press.

Bonvin, J. and Farvaque, N. (2006). Promoting Capability for Work: The Role of Local Actors. In: Deneulin, S., Nebel, M. and Sagovsky, N. (eds), *Transforming Unjust Structures. The Capability Approach*, pp. 121–142. London: Springer.

Bery, R. (2003). Participatory Video that Empowers. In White, S. A. (ed.), *Participatory Video Images that Transform and Empower*, pp. 102–121. New Delhi: Sage.

Chambers, R. (1997). *Whose Reality Counts? Putting the First Last*. London: Intermediate Technology Publications.

Chambers, R. (2015). PARA, PLA and Pluralism: Practice and Theory. In: Bradbury, H. (ed.), *Handbook of Action Research: Participative Inquiry and Practice*, 3rd edition, pp. 31–46. London: Sage.

Conradie, I. and Robeyns, I. (2013). Aspirations and Human Development Interventions. *Journal of Human Development and Capabilities*, 14, 559–580.

Crocker, D. (2008). *Ethics of Global Development: Agency, Capability, and Deliberative Democracy*. New York: Cambridge University Press.

Gaventa, J. and Cornwall, A. (2008). Power and Knowledge. In: Reason, P. and Bradbury, H. (eds), *Handbook of Action Research: Participative Inquiry and Practice*, 2nd edition, pp. 71–81. London: Sage.

Gomez, G. (2003). Magic Roots: Children Explore Participatory Video. In: White, S. A. *Participatory Video: Images That Transform and Empower*, pp. 215–231. New Delhi: Sage Publications.

Humphreys, P. and Jones, G. (2006). The Evolution of Group Decision Support Systems to Enable Collaborative Authoring of Outcomes. *World Futures*, 62, 171–192.

Institut Valencià d'Estadística (IVE). (2014). Datos y cifras por municipio. Ficha municipal. Online, available at: www.ive.es/portal/page/portal/IVE_PEGV/CONTENTS/fichas_mun/cas/Fichas/46102.pdf.

Kemmis, S. and McTaggart, R. (2005). Participatory Action Research. *Communicative Action and the Public Sphere*. In: Denzin, Norman K. and Lincoln, Yvonna S. (eds), *The Sage Handbook of Qualitative Research*, pp. 559–603. California: Sage Publications.

Kindon, S. (2003). Participatory Video in Geographic Research: A Feminist Practice of Looking. *Area*, 35(2), 142–153.

Millan, G. F. and Frediani, A. A. (2014). *Terms of Reference of the Summer School.* Castellón: UJI.

Mitchell, C. and de Lange, N. (2012). Community Based Participatory Video and Social Action in Rural South Africa. In: Margolis, E. and Pauwels, L. (eds), *The SAGE Handbook of Visual Research Methods*, pp. 171–200. London: Sage.

Montero, D. and Moreno, J. M. (2014). *El cambio social a través de las imágenes. Guía para entender y utilizar el video participativo.* Madrid: Catarata.

Nair, K. S. and White, S. (2003). Trapped: Women Take Control of Video Storytelling. In: S. A. White, *Participatory Video: Images that Transform and Empower*, pp. 195–214. New Delhi: Sage Publications.

Nussbaum, M. (2000). *Women and Human Development.* Cambridge: Cambridge University Press.

Pink, S. (2001). *Doing Visual Ethnography.* Thousand Oaks, CA: Sage.

Ramella, M. and Olmos, G. (2005). Participant Authored Audiovisual Stories (PAAS): Giving the Camera Away or Giving the Camera a Way? Discussion Papers in Qualitative Research. London: Methodology Institute, LSE.

Reason, P. and Bradbury, H. (2001). *Sage Handbook of Action Research: Participative Inquiry and Practice.* London: Sage.

Sen, A. (1999). *Development as Freedom.* New York: Knopf.

Shaw, J. (2007). Including the Excluded: Collaborative Knowledge Production Through Participatory Video. In: Dowmunt, T., Dunford, M. and von Hemert, N., *Inclusion Through Media*. London: Goldsmiths, University of London.

Shaw, J. (2013). Using Participatory Video for Action Research. *Real Time*. Online, available at: real-time.org.uk (accessed 5 February 2016).

Wheeler, J. (2011). Seeing Like a Citizen: Participatory Video and Action Research for Citizen Action. In: Nishant, S. and Fieke, J. (eds), *Digital (Alter)Natives with a Cause? Book 2—To Think.* Online, available at: https://issuu.com/hivos/docs/book_2_final_print_rev/:147-60.

Wheeler, J. (2012). Using Participatory Video to Engage in Policy Processes: Representation, Power, and Knowledge in Public Screenings. In: Milne, E. J., Mitchell, C. and De Lange, N. (eds), *Handbook of Participatory Video*, pp. 365–382. Lanham, MD: Alta Mira Press.

White, S. A. (2003). *Participatory Video: Images that Transform and Empower.* Thousand Oaks: Sage Publications.

8 Gender, subjective well-being and capabilities

An application to the Moroccan youth

El-Mahdi Khouaja, Noémie Olympio and Gwendoline Promsopha

Introduction

The capabilities framework (Sen, 2001) has been introduced as a criticism of welfarist approaches that use utility, i.e. satisfaction, as the main benchmark for social outcomes. However, research on subjective well-being (SWB), i.e. a subjective assessment of the concept of "utility" or "satisfaction", has seen a swift development in recent years. This literature is sometimes referred to as "happiness economics". Despite this recent popularity, SWB fails to account for situations of adaptive preferences, an issue widely discussed by Sen (1992).

In this chapter, we propose to compare the capabilities approach and the SWB framework in an analysis of gender inequalities among young Moroccan people. The literature does not provide consistent evidence of the effects of gender on happiness, while gender inequalities are frequently observed with the capabilities approach.

Our research has three objectives: the first is to provide a general framework to understand how SWB and the capabilities approach relate in their approach of gender issues. In order to do this, we analyse processual capabilities as resulting from two dimensions: the freedom to choose, and the achievements of valuable functionings—also called capability to achieve. This allows us to identify four case scenarios in the capability space applied to the Moroccan case, each of them leading to different SWB levels. Gender differences in SWB are only fully understood if men and women have first been positioned within these four scenarios. The second objective is to evaluate the relevance of SWB indicators for the analysis of key gender inequalities in developing countries. The third is to provide new insights on the issue of gender inequalities among young Moroccans, and to shed light on the most relevant indicators of progress or decline in gender equality.

We use mixed methods based on the 2013 OCEMO quantitative survey, which collects information on economic status and aspirations of young Moroccans; and qualitative work with 15 young Moroccans interviewed in August 2015.

The chapter proceeds as follows: Section 1 is a literature review on gender, SWB and the capabilities approach; Section 2 presents our theoretical frameworks and its four case scenarios. Section 3 reviews the Moroccan context for the youth. Section 4 presents the empirical methodology and main variables. Section 5 gives the main results, which are discussed in Section 6. Section 7 concludes.

1 A review of the literature on capabilities, SWB and gender

Three different streams of literature apply to our analysis. The first is a growing field of research on SWB. SWB has been highlighted as an alternative to income or consumption as measures of well-being. It broadly covers two generic terms—happiness and life satisfaction—and can be defined as individuals' self-assessment of their lives and choices. Gender inequalities have not been directly targeted by research on SWB, with minor empirical results coming from gender as a control variable in regressions. Yet, the results are surprisingly ambiguous, with some studies reporting lower happiness among women (Clark and Oswald, 1994), highest satisfaction among women (Fujita *et al.*, 1991; Asadullah *et al.*, 2015; Di Tella and MacCulloch, 2005), or no significant results at all (Louis and Zhao, 2002). An emerging part of this literature works on SWB in developing countries and consistently shows that women are happier than men, which is a very counterintuitive result in countries where women score poorer in other indicators.

Inconsistent or counterintuitive results in the SWB literature can partly be explained by the diversity of methodologies used to measure SWB (Tesch-Römer *et al.*, 2008), the capture of the gender effect by other regression correlates such as education and health (Dolan *et al.*, 2008), or the fact that gender has an indirect effect on SWB, passing through other factors such as social participation (Humpert, 2013) or parenthood (Kroll, 2011). Gender appears significant only in specific subgroups, such as age subgroup or the unemployed, or acts as an intensifier of other existing inequalities. Yet, if this can explain the lack of significance of gender variables sometimes observed, it does not help clarify why poorer and discriminated women frequently report higher happiness.

The second stream of literature analyses how gender shapes capabilities. According to Sen (1985, 1992, 2008), an individual's capabilities are defined as a set of freedoms to achieve that which enhances an individual's quality of life. Accordingly, a life is made up of a set of "*functionings*" each linked to the other and composed of "*beings*" and "*doings*". In the functionings space, capabilities reflect the individual freedom to choose between different lifestyles. Equality of capabilities represents equality in the freedom "to lead the lives they [individuals] have reasons to value" (Sen, 1992).

The capabilities approach is particularly relevant for gender issues in that it does not assume atomistic individuals but rather an ethically—or normatively—individualistic theory where individuals' freedom depends on their environment (Robeyns, 2003). Robeyns (2000) also accounts for a number of societal features, such as social norms or discriminatory practices—called conversion factors—that contribute to the conversion of resources into capabilities and that particularly matter for women. In the capabilities approach, gender inequalities have mostly been analysed with the prism of a definite list of valuable capabilities developed by Nussbaum (2000), a methodology aimed at avoiding adaptive preferences, i.e. women who do not desire what they believe inaccessible. The empirical research using capabilities lists finds women worse off than men except for very specific domains, such as social activity, and with context-specific variations (Picchio, 2005).

Lastly, an emerging literature looks at the complementarities between SWB and the capabilities approach in measuring social and economic inequalities, with the underlying assumption that more capabilities correlates with higher levels of well-being (Anand *et al.*, 2005a). As Sen reminds us, SWB is one of the functionings resulting from more capabilities: "Happiness is not all that matters, but first of all, it does matter (and that is important), and second, it can often provide useful evidence on whether or not we are achieving our objectives in general" (Sen, 2008). Meara *et al.* (2015) interpret the capabilities approach as a relevant framework or "space" for the evaluation of well-being.

Most of the empirical results in this field confirm a strong causal relation between capabilities and SWB (Anand *et al.*, 2005a, 2011; Suppa, 2015). Yet, while most of this literature tackles individual heterogeneity, endogeneity and personality biases, it relies on objective indicators of capabilities, i.e. a list of dimensions, therefore not fully reflecting the subjective evaluation of valuable functionings and the idea of freedom theorised by Sen (2001).

To summarise, empirical research in these three strands of literature gives the following sets of relations:

- Women may report a higher SWB than men.
- Being a woman systematically leads to lower capabilities.
- People with more capabilities are found to be happier.

Yet, if capabilities positively influence SWB, but are themselves negatively affected by gender, then we should also expect a negative effect of gender on SWB.

We conclude that the general results on gender, SWB and capabilities are both incomplete and conflicting.

2 Theoretical framework

2.1 SWB and the capabilities approach: differences and complementarities

We now propose a general framework to apprehend concomitant gender inequalities in terms of the capabilities approach and SWB and to solve the puzzle highlighted in Section 1. Such a framework requires rethinking the differences and complementarities between the capabilities approach and SWB approaches.

The evaluation of capabilities requires a broader informational basis[1] than the social evaluation of SWB alone. First, focusing on SWB leads to a consequentialist approach in which actions matter only in their outcomes, i.e.

satisfaction, therefore conflicting with processual approaches analysing the processes and the means of the justice.

Second and more fundamentally, subjective measures of individual well-being can produce pernicious effects among which adaptive preferences are probably the most emblematic (Sen, 1992). Adaptive preferences are formed without the awareness of opportunities and alternative options, by a casual mechanism that is not of one's own choosing (Nussbaum, 2000: 137). They are defined as a situation in which constrained individuals limit their preferences to a small set of "realistic" choices and as a result stop perceiving their situation as enforced. The "opportunities space" is thus limited by a low "capability to aspire" (Appadurai, 2004: 29). Objective indicators of capabilities such as capabilities lists are therefore proposed to avoid the issue of adaptive preferences.

However, objective indicators of capabilities such as capabilities lists have their own limits: they involve a top-down value judgment sometimes called paternalistic and ethnocentric (Kingdon and Knight, 2006).

Rather than objective indicators such as capabilities lists, Bonvin and Thelen (2003) put forward the importance of a "capability for voice" that represents "the ability to express one's opinions and thoughts and to make them count in the course of public discussion" (Bonvin and Thelen, 2003: 3) produced by the individuals themselves. Such a processual approach accounts for what individuals have good reasons to value: in other words, only individuals are subjectively entitled to define which functionings matter in their informational basis judgment of justice. On the empirical ground, individuals must participate in the selection of their relevant functionings, hence avoiding exogenous—if objective—evaluations of what constitutes a good quality of life (Kingdon and Knight, 2006).

To summarise, a good measure of capabilities should stand somewhere between objective indicators—to avoid issues of adaptive preferences and to avoid subjective assessment—to account for individuals' own perceptions of valuable lifestyles, and to avoid external value judgments. An attempt to capture autonomy and not only "means" is proposed in Graham and Nikolova (2015).

2.2 Freedom to choose, achieved valuable functionings and SWB

The capabilities approach places emphasis on people's empowerment (in terms of an increase of the degree of autonomy in order to enable individuals to represent their interests in a self-determined way). It offers a central role for two things: their agency together with their capability-set expansion (Keleher, 2014). Thus, we conceptualise capabilities as a *two-step process* that starts with the capability to make choices or decide which valuable life to pursue, called "*freedom to choose*"; followed by the capability to achieve the subsequent valuable functionings (called "*achievement of valuable functionings*"), and ending with an outcome, i.e. the final functionings and a certain level of well-being.[2] The definition of valuable functionings is by essence subjective and individual.

Observable functionings can be evaluated in terms of capabilities depending on whether they result: (1) from a full freedom to make choices among all the potentially valuable functionings; and (2) from a full capability to achieve the subsequent valuable functionings. Two different individuals may score equal levels of overall capabilities, but different scores in the freedom to choose and in the achievement of valuable functionings. Such frameworks allow us to take into account three different scenarios of capability deprivation (or lack of capabilities) with different consequences on SWB, which lead to the four scenarios we mentioned earlier.

Full capabilities deprivation: Individuals face a restricted set of choices, and cannot achieve the choice they have been constrained to choose. Such deprivation at each step of the capability building process will negatively affect individuals' well-being.

Adaptive preferences: In this scenario, analysed by Sen (2001) or Teschl and Comim (2005), individuals hold a reasonable level of capability to achieve, but only as a result of a restriction in the choices presented to them as socially achievable (low freedom to choose). We expect adaptive preferences to positively influence subjective responses on happiness or well-being, since individuals may be led to feel that they have "avoided the worst case scenario" or achieved "the best they could".

Frustration: People have a capability to make or pursue free choices, but fail to achieve them: they have both the freedom to choose and to achieve. This may lead them to feelings of frustration, injustice and grievance, and therefore negatively affects SWB.

These three scenario all contrast with situations of *full capabilities* (fourth case scenario), where individuals have the freedom to choose, and can attain the consequent capability to achieve. Analyses such as Ramos and Silber (2005) or Anand *et al.* (2005a) reflect scenarios of full capabilities and capabilities deprivation, i.e. positive relations between capabilities and SWB, but may also consider adaptive preferences as cases of full capabilities, and do not model situations of frustration. This is explained by conceptual issues: these analyses do not account for individuals' freedom of choice but rely on capabilities lists, i.e. a set of functionings assumed valuable according to universal criteria, but not necessary to the individuals themselves.

To conclude, the relationship between capabilities and SWB depends on where individuals stand in the process of capability building, and the four scenarios are summarised in Table 8.1.

Table 8.1 The four scenarios of capabilities and their relation to SWB

N	Scenario	Freedom to choose	Achievement of valuable functionings	SWB
1	Capabilities deprivation	No	No	No
2	Adaptive preferences	No	Yes	Yes
3	Frustrations	Yes	No	No
4	Full capabilities	Yes	Yes	Yes

Source: own source.

2.3 Gender inequalities in SWB and the four scenarios of capabilities

We believe that our framework helps understand the lack of consistent results on gender variables in SWB regressions. To correctly understand differences in SWB between men and women, they must first be positioned in each possible case scenario. In some instances, women have a lower freedom to choose and a lower capability to achieve than men (women in capabilities deprivation, i.e. scenario 1; men in full capabilities, i.e. scenario 4), which leads women to declare lower SWB than men.

In other instances, men hold full capabilities (scenario 4) but women are in situations of adaptive preferences (scenario 2), leading them to declare decent levels of SWB despite clear freedom deprivation: here, no significant differences in SWB should be found—both men and women are satisfied even if their reasons diverge. Lack of results of gender variables in SWB regression can also result from full capability deprivation (scenario 1) among women and frustrations (scenario 3) for men.

Finally, women may be in scenarios of adaptive preferences (scenario 2) while men are in the frustration (scenario 3): men's declared well-being will appear lower than women. This last scenario may help explain the surprising positive effect of gender variables on satisfaction levels found in some studies (Asadullah *et al.*, 2015; Di Tella and MacCulloch, 2005).

3 Context: Morocco, youth and gender

3.1 Social and economic challenges for the Moroccan youth

The Arab world is currently in a social and political turmoil that primarily affects youths and has brought them to the eyes of public policy and the international community (World Bank, 2012). Strong economic growth in Morocco (4.4 per cent in 2013) has not managed to create sufficient employment for all the newcomers in labour markets. Morocco, similarly to other Maghreb countries, faces an unprecedented demographic transition: the 15–34-year-olds represent more than half of the working age population, creating strong employment pressure. A large population of youth and rapid urbanisation creates potential conflicts of values between traditions and modernity and brings a number of socio-economic challenges. Data on the insertion of young Moroccans in the labour market show high unemployment rates and a lack of systematic correlation between education and employment: 24 per cent of youths holding a university degree are unemployed, compared with 4.4 per cent among the unqualified. Job deprivation and the discontent it creates among young Moroccans is one of the main challenges for the years to come (Serajuddin and Verme, 2015). Morocco also stands out for its poor performance in terms of literacy and education despite important progress in access to primary school.

Like most other Middle East and North African (MENA) countries, Morocco does not perform well in terms of gender inequalities (UNDP, 2014; Bekhouche *et al.*, 2013). In 2013, Morocco was ranked in 129th place among 136 countries in the Global Gender Gap Index (from the World Economic Forum). This poor performance results from social and economic discriminations (Davis, 1995).[3] Moroccan women have a lower access to education than men, especially in rural areas. According to the National Observatory for Human Development (ONDH, 2015), 41 per cent of Moroccan women have not completed primary education, compared with 25 per cent of men. In rural areas, the figures leap to nine out of ten women who have not completed primary education.

Women are also restricted in their access to the labour market (Assaad and, Zouari 2003): according to the *Haut Commissariat au Plan*, the activity rate for men was almost three times higher than for women: 74.7 per cent for men compared with 25.9 per cent for women. Despite this small rate of activity, women also face high unemployment rates: 9.6 per cent for women, 8.9 per cent for men. Finally, women's occupations are mainly in unpaid agricultural work on family farms—75 per cent of women—leading to huge wage inequalities (Muller and Nordman, 2014): the average wage for men is higher than for women, by 48 per cent in the agricultural sector, and 28 per cent in the industrial sector. The unemployment rate is 17.4 per cent for those aged 15–24 years, and falls respectively to 12.8 per cent for the 25–34 age group, and to 5.5 per cent for those aged 35–44 years (HCP, 2010).

Moroccan economic and social conditions are nonetheless changing rapidly, with recent progress in the legal protection of women and in education, especially for the new generation, which creates an increasing generation gap in social norms on women's role.

4 Empirical methodology

4.1 Mixed methods

We propose in this chapter to mix qualitative and quantitative methodologies to approach gender issues with SWB and the capabilities approach. Measuring the capabilities approach through the freedom to choose and to achieve implies a careful analysis of what freedom means in a particular context, and of which achievements individuals have reasons to value. How respondents understand questionnaire variables in a specific context may drive statistical results. Quantitative analysis allows statistical significance and detects adaptive preferences where lack of freedom is so well accepted that respondents do not self-report it in interviews. Qualitative methodologies give more ground to the interpretation of results and help embody the mechanisms underlying regression results, as well as the way actors legitimise and give meaning to their actions and opinions. Here, we use an embedded design of mixed methods (Creswell and Plano Clark, 2006) where qualitative data are given the secondary role and help the interpretation of quantitative results. Our quantitative results are analysed with the help of a case study among young Moroccans living in urban areas—Casablanca and Safi.

4.2 Data

4.2.1 The OCEMO survey

The data that we use in this study have been collected in the region of Marrakech-Tensift-Al Haouz in 2013 and survey the economic situation and aspirations of young Moroccans aged 15–34 years. Marrakech-Tensift-Al Haouz represents 10 per cent of the Moroccan population and includes both rural and urban areas. The questionnaire was established by a multidisciplinary expert committee mandated by the Office of Economic Cooperation for the Mediterranean and Middle East (OCEMO), in cooperation with the *Haut Commissariat au Plan* and the ONDH. The survey is complementary to the Morocco Household and Youth Survey (MHYS) implemented by the World Bank in 2009–2010, and provides additional information on youths' trajectories and opinions, although at a regional level.

The questionnaire was implemented with computer assistance and gathered information on personal and family situations, employment trajectories, education, opinions, living conditions and social environments. These themes are broken into eight sections and 457 variables. The random sampling methodology used to collect data and the high rate of responses (94 per cent) suggest data of a good quality.

Overall, 1,333 youths aged 15–34 years were surveyed, but we chose to restrict the sample to those older than 25 years of age (541 observations). A portion of the youths under 25 years old are still in the process of achieving their valuable functionings, which make them irrelevant for our research question and measurement methodology: for instance, youths aged 24 years may still be in education, which makes the evaluation of achievements more difficult.

We test the effect of gender on SWB and capabilities variables, i.e. freedom to choose, capability to achieve and aggregated capabilities indicators, with simple logistic regressions controlling a set of classic correlates.

4.2.2 Case study: interviews with urban youths

OCEMO data have been complemented with qualitative interviews, which were implemented in August 2015 in the areas of Safi and Casablanca, and targeted 15 urban youths—three females and 12 males—in three focus groups and four individual interviews.[4] The Moroccan youths are increasingly urban (41 per cent live in urban areas, and 45 per cent in semi-urban areas according to OCEMO data), with important consequences on how they value their lives, opportunities, and social change. Respondents were asked to present their personal and professional trajectories, self-assess their satisfaction and freedom, define the meaning of those concepts for them and for the Moroccan youth in general; define the life they would have had reasons to value, the compromises they feel they have had to make, and their view on gender inequality and women's roles in Moroccan society. The interviews were conducted in Arabic.

4.3 Measuring SWB and capabilities

SWB measurement methodologies have witnessed considerable developments in recent years (Zeidan, 2012; Teschl and Comim, 2005; Kahneman and Krueger, 2006), but the multidimensional or experimental data suggested are not widely available—due to heavy experimental designs or big questionnaire spaces. OCEMO data only provides for a global assessment of respondents' life satisfaction, such as that classically found in much SWB empirical literature. To measure SWB, we therefore look at the answer to the question "Are you satisfied with your life?" If respondents are very or quite satisfied, then the dummy obtained is equal to 1.

Our measure of capabilities diverges from the dominant operationalisation through a list of capabilities. As discussed earlier, we prefer a processual approach that takes into account the freedom to choose and the ability to achieve, and relies on functionings that youth have reason to value. The ability to achieve valuable functionings has, to a certain extent, been measured in the literature through indicators of factor/resources conversion, or input/output efficiency analysis (Ramos and Silber, 2005). We supplement these methodologies with the consideration that the achievement of valuable functionings works as a capability indicator only if the valuable functionings have been freely chosen by individuals.

Our capabilities indicator therefore results from two indicators. The first asks about the freedom to choose through the following question: "Would you say that you are free to decide your life?" We note that such a question asked in the Moroccan context may lead different individuals to understand the notion of "freedom" differently. In qualitative interviews, we therefore asked respondents how they would define the freedom to decide. For some, it was a mix between the freedom to choose and the freedom to achieve.[5] For others, and women especially, "being free to decide your life" is a matter of choices. To describe freedom deprivation, one respondent answers: "There is no choice to make because there is no choice", "I do not have the choice although this doesn't prevent me from thinking about it" or "you have no choice, you have to make compromise". Another concern relates to the conditions in which questions were asked: 56 per cent of respondents were surveyed in the presence of an external observer—parent or husband—and in 25 per cent of cases this potentially influenced the quality of responses. To cope with this issue, we rescale our variable as binary, equal to 1 if the respondent is very or quite free, 0 otherwise.[6]

The second capability variable measures the achievements of valuable functionings. We propose to measure it with an innovative variable that matches respondents' declared life projects with their actual situations. Youths were asked for their main life project and could choose between having a successful professional life, earning a lot of money/becoming rich, starting a family, being free, working for the public good/commit to a cause, or others. We compare each of the life projects with the actual achievements at the time of interview, and create a binary indicator equal to 1 if the youth have completed their projects, 0 otherwise.

Finally, we create a capability indicator that simply aggregates the freedom to choose and the achievement of valuable functionings, taking a value from 0 (no capability) to 2 (free to choose and achieved valuable functionings). The value of 1 indicates that the individual has one of the two dimensions of the capability to choose, being either free to choose or to achieve functionings.

The scant amount of SWB and gender literature has indicated correlates to explain the lack of significance of gender in life satisfaction (Posel and Casale, 2015). We therefore add a set of control variables.

5 Results

5.1 Descriptive statistics

We now come to the main descriptive statistics of our OCEMO data. The youths in our sample are 29 years old on average, with 54 per cent being female. Of the young Moroccans in the 25–35 age group, 38 per cent live in an urban area, and 33 per cent hold a qualification from middle school or higher.

Generally speaking, females are more subject to inactivity and unemployment than males, and can be said to be excluded from the labour market, even for precarious employment, which is—to the same extent as stable employment—men's prerogative. Females hold lower degrees as well: only 24 per cent hold a secondary education qualification or higher, a number that almost doubles for men. It is finally worth noting that only 23 per cent of the sampled women are single, a number that jumps to 54 per cent for men. This confirms the widespread feeling that men have of strong pressure to get married, and they often struggle to find a spouse. Qualitative evidences confirm that marriage is high on young men's agendas; and it is contingent on access to employment and a stable financial situation that many fail to meet (on this issue see Assaad and Krafft, 2014).

Basic descriptive statistics give a first glimpse of the gender and SWB puzzle. Young women are on average more satisfied than young men (82 per cent of women declare themselves satisfied with their lives, against 73 per cent of men). Despite the positive relationship between income and SWB found in the literature, women here report more worrisome financial situations than men.

If women are more satisfied with their lives than men but with a more deteriorated financial situation, how do they score in terms of capabilities?

As Tables 8.2 and 8.3 show, young women's main life project is to start a family (for 61 per cent of them), a project that does not seem to be the hardest to implement, since 57 per cent of them were married and/or had children at the time of the survey. Men seem to have a harder time achieving their own choices, which mainly concern professional success and earning money and, albeit to a lesser extent, starting a family. As qualitative evidence suggests in Section 6, access to stable employment is a difficult road, and a precondition to achieving marriage. With respect to "achievements", men therefore seem to have a harder time than women: only 34 per cent had completed their life project at the time of

Table 8.2 Main declared life project, by gender

Life project	Men (%)	Women (%)	Total (%)
Have a successful professional life	*72.32*	*27.68*	*100*
	52.46	16.90	33.15
Start a family	*28.51*	*71.49*	*100*
	29.10	61.38	46.63
Earn a lot of money, become rich	*53.33*	*46.67*	*100*
	13.11	9.66	11.24
Be free	*27.50*	*72.50*	*100*
	4.51	10.00	7.49
Work for the public good, commit to a cause	*50.00*	*50.00*	*100*
	0.41	0.34	0.37
Other	*16.67*	*83.33*	*100*
	0.41	1.72	1.12
Total	*45.69*	*54.31*	*100**
	100	100	100

Note
* Sample size: 534. Italicised percentages measure row relative frequencies.

Table 8.3 Completion of life project, by gender

Life project status	Men (%)	Women (%)	Total (%)
Not completed	*56.69*	*43.31*	*100*
	66.26	43.16	53.79
Completed	*33.61*	*66.39*	*100*
	33.74	56.84	46.21
Total	*46.02*	*53.98*	*100**
	100	100	100

Note
* Sample size: 528. Italicised percentages measure row relative frequencies.

the survey, against 57 per cent of women. An alternative explanation is that men's projects take longer to accomplish than women's.

The capability to achieve seems to result from the selection of valuable life-styles by individuals, i.e. the freedom to make choices. Women's performance in freedom to make choices is poorer than men: almost half of the young women sampled declared themselves as "not free", against 10 per cent of men (see Table 8.4). We note that reports of a lack of freedom by the surveyed women may have been biased by the presence of external observers—generally the father, husband or brother—during interviews.[7]

Table 8.4 Freedom to choose one's life, by gender

Freedom	Men (%)	Women (%)	Total (%)
Not free	*13.95*	*86.05*	*100*
	9.76	50.17	31.79
Free	*60.16*	*39.84*	*100*
	90.24	49.83	68.21
Total	*45.47*	*54.53*	*100**
	100	100	100

Note
* Sample size: 541. Italicised percentages measure row relative frequencies.

5.2 Results from the quantitative analysis

Regression results show that women are more satisfied with their lives than men, even after controlling for education, living location, marital and family situation, health, social mobility trajectories, unemployment, family income or the perceived financial situation (Table 8.5). Table 8.6 shows that this greater satisfaction among women is paired with greater achievements—or completion of the main life project—but a lower freedom to choose a lifestyle. Women are indeed almost twice less likely than men to feel free in choosing their lives, but also almost twice as likely to achieve their choices. As we will discuss in the next section, this seems to indicate an issue of adaptive preferences for women vs a frustration due to lack of achievements for men. Overall, women's capability levels are lower (Table 8.6, specification 3).

Further significant results of these regressions concern the coefficients of the capability indicators introduced in the satisfaction regression as explanatory variables. Overall, the aggregated capability indicator is positively correlated with life satisfaction, a result coherent with the literature (see Section 1). Yet, if we decompose this indicator between the two different moments of the capability building process—the freedom to choose and the achievement of aspirations—we find that achievements seem to matter more for SWB, as the coefficient of the freedom to choose is not significant. Yet, the results do not hold after introducing all control variables, especially the dummy for being married, suggesting an issue of collinearity—see Table 8.5, specifications 1 and 3.[8]

The results do not purport to show causal relationships. Still, the three main conclusions that we would like to draw from these regressions is: first, SWB indicators are biased due to adaptive preferences—since they reflect achievement, rather than the freedom to choose. Second, SWB is a particularly unfit measure of gender inequalities in Morocco, where social and cultural norms confine women's position in society and limit their aspirations to a few attainable choices, while men's social role in a globalising economy has generated a wide range of aspirations for young men, although they lack the opportunities to implement them. Finally, the positive effect of gender on satisfaction can

Table 8.5 Logit regressions on satisfaction, odds ratio

Dependent variable: SATISFACTION	(1)	(2)	(3)	(4)
Completion of life project	1.95***		1.45	
Freedom	1.35		1.83*	
Capability indicator		1.46***		1.61**
Female	*1.56**	*1.59****	*1.90***	*1.77***
Control variables:				
Education			1.06	1.07
Age			1.00	1.00
Married			0.67	0.65
Live with parents			0.96	0.96
Have children			2.45	2.39
Unemployment			1.01	1.04
Subjective health			1.44*	1.45*
Upward social mobility			1.90**	1.90**
Schooling of father			0.94	0.95
Subjective financial situation			1.53**	1.52**
Income per consumption unit			1.00	1.00
Live in urban areas			1.17	1.19
Ethnic group: Berbers			2.27**	2.24**
Control classic Arabic			0.72	0.72
Control French language			1.96	1.91
No. siblings			1.08	1.08
Rank among siblings			0.92	0.92
No. unpaid family members in household			1.17	1.10
No. civil servants in household			1.01	1.03
No. unemployed in household			0.84	0.84
Observations	528	528	518	518

Notes
*   90 per cent confidence level;
**   95 per cent confidence level;
*** 99 per cent confidence level.
Figures for the main explanatory variable in model are italicised.

sometimes be considered a "false positive", as it seems to result from a combination of adaptive preferences among women with lack of freedom to choose leading to a high rate of achievement; and frustration among young men, where freedom to aspire without achievements leads to dissatisfaction.

6 Interpretation of results

We now come to the second step of the mixed method analysis: we embed a qualitative component within the quantitative analysis.

Where SWB leads to ambiguous analyses of gender inequalities and some counterintuitive trends—young women are more satisfied than young men, even if they are in a country with evidently large gender inequalities—the processual capabilities approach clearly reflects the complexity of gender inequalities in

Table 8.6 Logistic regression: capabilities

Dependent variable	Freedom (1)	Completion of life project (2)	Capability indicator (3)
Completion of life project			
Freedom			
Capability indicator			
Female	*0.05****	*2.40****	*0.45****
Control variables:			
Education	1.21	1.19	1.23*
Age	0.97	0.97	0.98
Married	2.55*	10.91***	9.53***
Live with parents	1.21	1.14	1.21
Have children	0.34**	0.77	0.55
Unemployment	1.24	0.34**	0.50
Subjective health	1.25	0.84	1.12
Upward social mobility	0.79	1.25	0.95
Schooling of father	0.98	1.01	0.99
Subjective financial situation	0.91	1.66***	1.41**
Income per consumption unit	1.00*	1.00	1.00
Live in urban areas	2.57**	0.51**	1.14
Ethnic group: Berbers	0.94	1.07	0.97
Control classic Arabic	1.85	1.62	1.85*
Control French language	0.25*	1.00	0.61
No. siblings	0.93	1.19**	1.11
Rank among siblings	1.01	0.84**	0.86**
No. family aid in household	0.59***	0.77*	0.65***
No. civil servants in household	2.94	0.71	1.33
No. unemployed in household	1.15	0.95	0.95
Observations	528	518	518

Notes
* 90 per cent confidence level;
** 95 per cent confidence level;
*** 99 per cent confidence level.
Figures for the main explanatory variable in model are italicised.

achieved valuable functionings and in the freedom of choice. These two dimensions are fundamental in the capabilities approach: achieved valuable functionings represent an individual's *achievements* and freedom of choice refers to *freedom to achieve* (and thus to the "opportunity space"). Both are needed to enhance capabilities: having a large degree of freedom without really reaching our valuable functionings means formal, but not real, freedom; whereas achievement only, without the freedom to choose, means a lack of capabilities to aspire.

Our research shows how gender inequalities among young people can be reflected in each of these dimensions. In our data, young women seem to be more satisfied than young men, which can be explained by a greater achievement of valuable functionings, i.e. getting married and starting a family. On the other hand, they are less likely to feel free than men in choosing their lives. One can interpret this result as adaptive preferences. Indeed, a woman in a deprived situation "knew that this was how things were and would be … she didn't even waste mental energy getting upset, since these things couldn't be changed" (Nussbaum, 2000: 113). The qualitative data that we have gathered illustrates this fact well.

Many of the young women interviewed express their overall satisfaction when asked, but do not feel free to choose their lives out of the weight or pressure exercised by the family's judgments—parents and brothers—and the society. We find expressions such as: "On the condition that I inform my father and my brothers"; "The problem is that of the street, the society and their judgments". Interviews also reveal how, with more or less self-awareness, young women admit to an adaptation away from their first life ambitions. The case of Loubna is very eloquent. During the first part of the interview, she tells of her great satisfaction and how she has achieved her goals. A few questions later, she reports that she can be called free, although not in all her choices. At the end of the interview, she confides that she is not really free because of her mother's judgment, which has diverted her away from her true project: "I am willing to make it [this project], to begin tomorrow if needed, but my mother opposes this project, I cannot contradict her, she is my mother" (interview with Loubna, 2015).

The weight of family and society value judgments is mentioned both by women and men: "For women, to be and live independently, is taking the risk of feeding the rumours of bad behaviour" (interview with Fadwa, 2015), or:

> For today's women in Morocco, it is difficult to be independent, an independent woman in our society arouses suspicions, she will be subject to rumours of the worst kind. Being a grown-up in Morocco today means having a job, but being independent means having a husband, as long as a woman is not married, she stays under the authority of her parents, whatever her age, it is my opinion.
>
> (Interview with Hind, 2015)

However, it does not mean that men have significantly higher capabilities. Qualitative and quantitative results show how the lack of capabilities affects different spaces for young men and women. Although the freedom of choice or opportunity space is larger for men, it is more difficult for them to achieve their valuable functionings: they have a larger freedom, but which remains mainly formal. Our interviews with young men help to understand the consequences of a lack of achievements on capabilities: despite having formal freedom, the poor employment records and lack of status create a strong sense of dissatisfaction among men. Young men's frustration with employment is given greater importance by the fact that it defines marriage opportunities. To get a stable job becomes the first inescapable step: "to me, I did not even reach the first goal to be able to aim towards others". Thus, constraints in the labour market and in personal spaces combine to build a growing feeling of frustration among men, which originates in the lack of employment opportunities and explains their contradictory scores in satisfaction and freedom. More generally, access to marriage in Moroccan society is seen as central to adulthood and social status, which creates a strong temporal pressure on youths. Various respondents felt that their life course had been decided before 30. Interviews from both young men and women reveal the pressure of time: "I am fighting against time … I am 30, so my life is over".

Our data are of course not sufficient to test such a hypothesis, but the combination of aspirations or freedom and a lack of achievement could become explosive and explain why, under the right political pre-conditions, youths from other MENA countries raised in the period of the Arab Spring: "The State also has to create jobs, it has the means to!"

Thanks to its multidimensional nature, the capabilities approach therefore allows to indicate a sort of "two-sided inequality" for young women and young men: a lack of capability to aspire for the former, and a lack of real opportunities to achieve for the latter.

As a concluding remark, the use of a mixed method seems particularly interesting for an operationalisation of the capabilities approach, and this is for two reasons. First, given the difficulty to operationalise the capabilities approach empirically and the lack of sufficiently precise data, qualitative analysis allows a multidimensional dimension where rough indicators are limited by the nature of secondary data. Qualitative data can allow a better understanding of respondents' perceptions of subjective concepts such as life satisfaction, feelings of freedom, or a life project. It seems more than obvious that young Moroccans may not define the idea of "freedom" in the same way as their elders, or youths from other countries. Men and women may also understand different things from the same word. When asked about how they define freedom, men refer to material constraints on achieving what they want: "I believe that what is really important for men is obtaining our own autonomy and material freedom"; while women have more difficulties explaining what being free means and refer more easily to the idea underlying the capability to aspire: "being free? I really don't know how to answer this question", or "being free means having good knowledge of the choices offered and available". As this section also illustrates, general assessments of freedom or satisfaction can be driven by specific aspects of life, such as the access to employment for men in Morocco and its relation to marriage. Second, some concepts embedded by the capabilities approach can hardly be proven with quantitative data or qualitative data alone. Adaptive preferences are a perfect example: quantitative results point towards this direction but adaptive preferences remain interpretative; while in qualitative data, approaching adaptive preferences demands great skills on the part of the interviewer and does not provide a greater picture of their significance. The case of Loubna clearly shows the difficulty of revealing adaptive preferences and the necessity to combine quantitative and qualitative methodologies.

7 Conclusion

We believe that our results can have significant consequences for the research on the link between the capabilities approach and SWB; on gender and SWB; and on the operationalisation of capabilities away from the traditional lists of capability dimensions. First, our study shows that the positive relationship between capabilities and SWB is far from automatic and depends on where individuals are positioned in the capabilities building process. Second, understanding capabilities as a process rather than an outcome helps in understanding how gender inequalities can be correctly or incorrectly reflected in SWB indicators. In the Moroccan case, the conjunction of young women with adaptive preferences and young men with frustrations through lack of achievements gives the astonishing results of a greater satisfaction among young women. Third, our research advocates for the use of mixed methods in the operationalisation of capabilities, and the use of a capability indicator that takes into account individuals' subjective perceptions on what can be considered a valuable achievement, their capability to make free choices from among them, and to achieve them. We believe measuring these dimensions will avoid adaptive preferences issues while reducing external value judgment or paternalistic approaches of capabilities. Our results also have implications for policy-making and evaluation, especially in the context of the Arab Spring where youths have been shown to be the main driver of the movement for political and social changes. In Morocco, young women primarily suffer from a deprivation in their capability to aspire, driven by social, cultural and family norms, which are hard to change through top-down policies. Increasing women's capability to achieve may not necessarily increase their overall capabilities levels, if the capability to aspire is not also targeted. It is also important to note that an increase in young women's freedom to choose or aspire could bring them closer to the situation of young Moroccan men, i.e. lower satisfaction levels: in a way, greater freedom to choose will mean a greater equality in capabilities, but also a decline in satisfaction. All in all, this proves that SWB indicators alone cannot serve as guides or evaluation tools in gender and youth policies in Morocco.

Notes

1 The informational basis represents: "the information on which the judgment is directly dependent and—no less importantly—asserts that the truth and falsehood of any other type of information cannot directly influence the correctness of the judgment" (Sen, 1985: 73).

2 Our approach can in some way be compared to Van Ootegem and Verhofstadt (2014), who decompose the effect of capabilities on SWB in actual realisations vs other aspects of the capability approach—personality in their case.

3 On the economic and social discriminations against Moroccan women, see Zerari, 2006; Skalli, 2001; or Sibley, 2013.

4 The interviewer was a man and encountered severe difficulties to sit an interview with female respondents alone, i.e. without the presence of a father or brother, who could

have biased the responses. It is not culturally accepted in Morocco for a man to meet a woman in person to interview.
5 A respondent defined freedom in Morocco as "the fact to do everything you want to do with no constraints", a notion that according to him goes against the "fundamentals in the notion of freedom".
6 We believe that extreme answers (very free, or not free at all) are the most sensitive ones to influence external observers.
7 Women may not have been feeling free to report lack of freedom, or a great freedom, in the presence of their father or husband, as such a context puts strong social pressure on women.
8 Being married and having achieved the life project are highly correlated as a number of control variables are used in the regression.

References

Anand, P., Hunter, G. and Smith, R. (2005a). Capabilities and well-being: evidence based on the Sen–Nussbaum approach to welfare. *Social Indicators Research*, 74(1), 9–55.

Anand, P., Hunter, G., Carter, I., Dowding, K., Guala, F. and van Hees, M. (2005b). *The development of capability indicators and their relation to life satisfaction*, Milton Keynes: Economics Department, The Open University.

Anand, P., Krishnakumar, J. and Tran, N. B. (2011). Measuring welfare: latent variable models for happiness and capabilities in the presence of unobservable heterogeneity. *Journal of Public Economics*, 95(3), 205–215.

Appadurai, A. (2004). Culture and the terms of recognition: the capacity to aspire. *Culture and Public Action.* California: Stanford University Press.

Asadullah, M. N., Xiao, S. and Yeoh, E. (2015). Subjective well-being in China, 2005–2010: the role of relative income, gender and location. *China Economic Review.* https://doi.org/10.1016/j.chieco.2015.12.010.

Assaad, R. and Krafft, C. (2014). The economics of marriage in North Africa. (No. 2014/067). WIDER Working paper.

Assaad, R. and Zouari, S. (2003). Estimating the impact of marriage and fertility on the female labor force participation when decisions are interrelated: evidence from urban Morocco. *Topics in Middle Eastern and North African Economies*, 5, 1–37.

Bekhouche, Y., Hausmann, R., Tyson, L. D. and Zahidi, S. (2013, September). The global gender gap report 2013. Geneva, Switzerland. World Economic Forum 2013. Online, available at: www.popline.org/node/578350.

Bonvin, J. M. and Thelen, L. (2003). Deliberative democracy and capabilities: the impact and significance of capability for voice. In: *Third Conference on Capability Approach.* Italy: University of Pavia.

CESE. (2013). Rapport annuel 2013 (pp. 1–121). Conseil Economique, Social et Environnemental du Royaume du Maroc. Online, available at: www.cese.ma/Pages/Rapports%20annuels/rapport-annuel-2013.aspx.

Clark, A. E. and Oswald, A. J. (1994). Unhappiness and unemployment. *Economic Journal*, 104(424), 648–659.

Creswell, J. W. and Plano Clark, V. L. (2006). *Designing and Conducting Mixed Methods Research.* Los Angeles: Sage Publications, Inc.

Davis, D. A. (1995). Modernizing the sexes: changing gender relations in a Moroccan town. *Ethos*, 23(1), 69–78.

Di Tella, R. and MacCulloch, R. (2005). Partisan social happiness. *Review of Economic Studies*, 72(2), 367–393.

Dolan, P., Peasgood, T. and White, M. (2008). Do we really know what makes us happy? A review of the economic literature on the factors associated with subjective well-being. *Journal of Economic Psychology*, 29(1), 94–122.

Fujita, F., Diener, E. and Sandvik, E. (1991). Gender differences in negative affect and well-being: the case for emotional intensity. *Journal of Personality and Social Psychology*, 61(3), 427–434.

Graham, C. and Nikolova, M. (2015). Bentham or Aristotle in the development process? An empirical investigation of capabilities and subjective well-being. *World Development*, 68, 163–179.

HCP. (2010). Activité, emploi et chômage: Premiers résultats. P 64. Haut Commissariat au Plan. Division des enquêtes sur l'emploi. Direction de la statistique. Online, available at: www.hcp.ma/downloads/Activite-emploi-et-chomage-premiers-resultats-annuel_t13036.html.

Humpert, S. (2013). Gender differences in life satisfaction and social participation. *International Journal of Economic Sciences and Applied Research*, 6(3), 123–142.

Kahneman, D. and Krueger, A. B. (2006). Developments in the measurement of subjective well-being. *Journal of Economic Perspectives*, 20(1), 3–24.

Keleher, L. (2014). Sen and Nussbaum: agency and capability-expansion, *Ethics and Economics*, 11(2), 54–70.

Kingdon, G. G. and Knight, J. (2006). Subjective well-being poverty vs income poverty and capabilities poverty? *Journal of Development Studies*, 42(7), 1199–1224.

Kroll, C. (2011). Different things make different people happy: examining social capital and subjective well-being by gender and parental status. *Social Indicators Research*, 104(1), 157–177.

Louis, V. V. and Zhao, S. (2002). Effects of family structure, family SES and adulthood experiences on life satisfaction. *Journal of Family Issues*, 23(8), 986–1005.

Meara, J. G., Leather, A. J., Hagander, L., Alkire, B. C., Alonso, N., Ameh, E. A. and Mérisier, E. D. (2015). Global Surgery 2030: evidence and solutions for achieving health, welfare and economic development. *Lancet*, 386(9993), 569–624.

Muller, C. and Nordman, C. J. (2014). Task organization, human capital and wages in Moroccan exporting firms. *Middle East Development Journal*, 6(2), 175–198.

Nussbaum, M. (2000). Women's capabilities and social justice. *Journal of Human Development*, 1(2), 219–247.

ONDH. (2015). Rapport des premiers résultats de l'enquête Panel de ménages 2012 (pp. 1–134). Observatoire National du Développement Humain. Online, available at: www.ondh.ma/fr/evenements/rapport-premiers-resultats-lenquete-panel-menages-2012.

Picchio, A. (ed.). (2005). *Unpaid Work and the Economy: A Gender Analysis of the Standards of Living*. London: Routledge.

Posel, D. and Casale, D. (2015). Differences in subjective well-being within households: an analysis of married and cohabiting couples in South Africa. *African Review of Economics and Finance*, 7(1), 32–52.

Ramos, X. and Silber, J. (2005). On the application of efficiency analysis to the study of the dimensions of human development. *Review of Income and Wealth*, 51(2), 285–309.

Robeyns, I. (2000). An unworkable idea or a promising alternative? Sen's capability approach re-examined. CES discussion paper 00.30, Katholleke Universiteit, Leuven.

Robeyns, I. (2003). Sen's capability approach and gender inequality: selecting relevant capabilities. *Feminist Economics*, 9(2–3), 61–92.

Robeyns, I. (2006). The capability approach in practice. *Journal of Political Philosophy*, 14(3), 351–376.

Schwarz, N. and Strack, F. (1991). Evaluating one's life: a judgment model of subjective well-being. In F. Strack, M. Argyle and N. Schwarz, *Subjective well-being: an inter-disciplinary perspective* (pp. 27–48). Oxford: Pergamon.

Sen, A. (1985). *Commodities and capabilities.* Amsterdam and New York: Elsevier Science Pub. Co.

Sen, A. (1992). *Inequality reexamined.* New York: Clarendon Press.

Sen, A. (2001). *Development as freedom.* Oxford: Oxford University Press.

Sen, A. (2008). The economics of happiness and capability. In: Bruni, Luigino and Comim, Flavio and Pugno, Maurizio (eds), *Capabilities and happiness.* Oxford: Oxford University Press.

Serajuddin, U. and Verme, P. (2015). Who is deprived? Who feels deprived? Labor Deprivation, Youth and Gender in Morocco. *Review of Income and Wealth,* 61(1), 140–163.

Sibley, S. (2013). Women's empowerment and the feminization of poverty among female-headed households in rural Morocco: challenging stigma in an unequal society. Queen Mary University of London, MA Globalization and Development Working Papers, series No. 1. Online, available at: www.geog.qmul.ac.uk/docs/research/87689.pdf.

Skalli, L-H. (2001). Women and poverty in Morocco: the many faces of social exclusion. *Feminist Review,* 69, 73–89.

Suppa, N. (2015). Capability deprivation and life satisfaction: evidence from German panel data. *Journal of Human Development and Capabilities,* 16(2), 173–199.

Teschl, M. and Comim, F. (2005). Adaptive preferences and capabilities: some preliminary conceptual explorations. *Review of Social Economy,* 63(2), 229–247.

Tesch-Römer, C., Motel-Klingebiel, A. and Tomasik, M. J. (2008). Gender differences in subjective well-being: comparing societies with respect to gender equality. *Social Indicators Research,* 85(2), 329–349.

United Nations Development Programme (UNDP). (2014). Sustaining human progress: reducing vulnerabilities and building resilience (pp. 1–227). United Nations Development Programme. Online, available at: http://hdr.undp.org/en/content/human-development-report-2014.

Van Ootegem, L. and Verhofstadt, E. (2015). Perceived capabilities as an aggregated indicator for well-being. *Applied Research in Quality of Life,* 10(4), 615–629.

World Bank. (2012). Morocco—Promoting youth opportunities and participation (No. 68731) (pp. 1–163). Washington, DC: World Bank. Online, available at: http://documents.worldbank.org/curated/en/507941468109463283/Morocco-Promoting-youth-opportunities-and-participation.

Zeidan, J. (2012). Les différentes mesures du bien-être subjectif. *Revue française d'économie,* 27(3), 35–70.

Zerari, H. (2006). Femmes au Maroc. Entre Hier et aujourd'hui: quels changements? *Recherches Internationales,* 77(3), 65–80.

9 Agency, forced migration and social capital

The case of young Syrian refugee women in Turkey

Zeynep Balcioglu

Introduction

According to the UNHCR, more than two-thirds of all refugees in the world live outside of camps. Most refugees prefer to reside in cities because urban life brings hope for integration, due to the wide spectrum of opportunities it provides. Urban refugees generally do not have the necessary legal documents that allow them to move within and around the host country. Therefore, very often they strive to be invisible to survive, using coping strategies to become integrated into their new life in the host country (UNHCR). Hence, while non-camp refugees enjoy empowerment and freedom compared to their counterparts who reside in refugee camps, they deal with increased vulnerability and marginalisation at the same time. Besides the humanitarian perspective that dominates the majority of the literature, an increasing number of urban refugees call for a development approach to the issue that would move the focus from resettlement to local integration.

Half of the 2.7 million Syrian refugees in Turkey are women. Of these, 90 per cent live out of the camps, mostly belonging to the urban poor in the cities (UNHCR 2016). For most of the refugee women, the moving process from Syria to Turkey comes with brand new challenges that require them to develop new strategies. Non-camp refugee women are generally deprived of economic capital; consequently, they are highly reliant on their social capital to survive. Therefore, the relationships and the ties they have with each other, with the host community, and with the people in decision-making positions at both the local and central level have the most significant role in their process of integration, because their social capital bolsters the refugees' control over their life decisions.

Contrary to the works that discuss the impact migration has on women, this chapter looks into what women can make of migration by giving a gender-sensitive and contextual analysis of social capital and agency. In a migration context, opportunities and constraints exist simultaneously, depending on the types of strategies that agents employ. Despite their uneven positions in social, political and economic structures, young refugee women are not incapable of exercising their agencies in the host country. Indeed, on many occasions, they can transform constraints into opportunities by altering the meanings attached to the norms and values that discriminate against them. Throughout their journey, young refugee women generate resilience that both emanates from and develops into social capital. The capability approach provides the framework that could enable young refugee women to control their own environments and make effective choices about what they value in life.

Key capability asset: social capital

Social capital emerges as an essential aspect in refugees' decision-making processes at many stages of migration. As noted by many researches, refugees generally move to places where their fellow citizens—or more specifically, their townsmen—have already settled (Jacobsen 2006). In addition, refugees in urban spaces not only utilise their pre-existing social capital, but also form new relationships with other minorities, with the neighbours and shopkeepers from the host population and with institutions. Therefore, social capital is not only the preliminary determinant of the moving destination; it is also an important tool in refugees' integration into the host country. It plays a significant role in determining information channels, patterns of inclusion and exclusion, and trust networks within the migrant community and between the host and migrant communities.[1]

According to Lin (2002: 24) "social capital can be defined operationally as the resources embedded in the social networks accessed and used by actors for actions". As Lin argues, it is crucial to acknowledge that all forms of social capital are highly enclosed within the social structure and networks that are made up of many power positions. Thus, each and every individual has differential forms of access to the resources, while making her way through multiple social networks. Lin's emphasis on the embeddedness of social capital makes it possible to build a bridge between the social capital approach and the capability approach. In a similar way to Lin's approach, which differentiates between resources, structure and action, Sen (1992) also identifies the distinctions between the resources available to individuals (means), what an individual is and does (functionings), the external factors that affect an individual's ability to transform means into functionings (conversion factors), and the combination of beings and doings that the individual has the real freedom to achieve (capability sets). In addition, taking the discussion to a further level, Sen asserts that there is an ontological difference between well-being and agency. The over-emphasis on measuring outcomes when evaluating well-being has its own limitations, because it rejects the independent role of agency in well-being.

Sen (1999: xii) defines agency as a highly interdependent status of not being under any form of coercion when making choices about things people value in their lives. Social capital can be integrated into this equation as a resource, or a "means" in Sen's words, that improves the refugees' livelihood in the host countries. Therefore, I argue, when analysing the causality between agency, social capital and structural factors in refugee settings, the capability perspective allows us to re-conceptualise refugees as active agents in their integration process, as opposed to passive recipients. Furthermore, the approach can also work as a guide to developing practical tools in assessing refugee well-being in relation to social arrangements, social policies and proposals for social change in a given setting. In the context of refugee assessment, "development as freedom" can be interpreted as "full integration as freedom", where full integration can be seen as the ultimate end or functioning, in which each individual refugee can enjoy their effective freedoms (Landau and Duponchel 2011). Finally, recent studies on social capital also show that social capital alone is not effective on the development performance at all times, but the combination of social capital and agency gives the best results (Krishna 2001). Although this is beyond the scope of this chapter, it is possible to say that from the capability perspective, with a distinct focus on refugees, the combination of agency and social capital might have a similar impact on the integration process.

Methodology

Doing research with refugees is not easy due to many ethical and practical limitations. However, particularly insufficient attention is given to urban refugees and urban refugee well-being and livelihoods, both by practitioners and academics. For a researcher, an urban environment is harder to control compared to camps. In addition, reaching out to urban refugees for interviews or conducting a survey with them is not easy either, since they are usually hiding among the urban poor and striving to be invisible. Therefore, it becomes highly difficult to assess their level of integration.

The dataset used in this chapter was collected during the fieldwork conducted between May and August 2016 in Sultanbeyli, one of the districts with the highest population of refugees in Istanbul, Turkey. During my time in the field, I conducted 19 semi-structured interviews with 22 refugee women[2] between the ages of 16–38 and a focus group with the participation of 11 refugee women. All the interviewees had been residents of Sultanbeyli for minimum of four months, up to a maximum of three years. Their ages varied from 16–38, with an average age of 24.8 years. Among them, seven women were single. Only two of them were employed, and they earned 1,300 Turkish lire[3] per month on average, in addition there were three women who did unpaid voluntary work at a community centre. Only nine of the women did not have children, while the rest had at least one child, and seven at most. Just six women could speak or understand Turkish to a certain level. They generally lived in crowded apartments with an average of 8.2 people per apartment. Furthermore, thanks to the Red Crescent Sultanbeyli, a focus group was also conducted, with the participation of 11 refugee women. All the women in the focus group, whose ages varied between 23–55, participated in the free Turkish course at the community centre.

The interviews were made up of three parts in general. Interviewees were first asked about their demographic information, followed by questions about social capital and agency. To assess what types of social capital they possessed, the refugee women answered questions about the channels of information they used, levels of trust, and social coherence, including mechanisms of inclusion and exclusion. Measuring agency is more complex, since the concept is more fluid than that of social capital. Therefore, during the interviews, to be able to hear about the agency from multiple angles, the women were encouraged to talk about (1) their control over the family budget, (2) the obstacles that prevented them from socialising, (3) if they needed any permission before they could take an action, and finally (4) their future plans both in the short and long term.

Thanks to the availability of the cross-sectional survey data[4] collected with the initiative of the Sultanbeyli Municipality (2015), I obtained access to data on the demographics of the refugee population in Sultanbeyli. Although many of the survey questions addressed the broader experience of being a refugee in Sultanbeyli, questions about social life, satisfaction and future plans made it possible to acquire a broader picture of the level of social capital in Sultanbeyli. According to the individual level data ($N=10,281$) collected by the Sultanbeyli Municipality in 2015, the gender distribution among refugees in Sultanbeyli was 47 per cent women to 53 per cent men. Among these, 20 per cent were illiterate, 50 per cent graduated from primary school, 16 per cent from middle school, 4 per cent from high school and only 3 per cent had university degree or higher qualification. In total, 90 per cent of them were born in Aleppo and 95 per cent spoke Arabic as their native language. Only 38 per cent were employed, and earned an average of 858 Turkish lire per person.

Moreover, the household survey ($N=2,032$) provided more insightful information about the daily lives of the refugees in Sultanbeyli. The findings suggest that for a refugee family, the household income on average was 1,207 Turkish lire (€350). The majority lived in two- or three-bedroom apartments, with an average of 6.5 people per apartment. When asked why they chose Sultanbeyli as their final destination, 73.7 per cent said it was because they have family in Sultanbeyli, 13.7 per cent said a friend recommended it to them; and around 10 per cent declared affordable accommodation and job opportunities as their main priorities. As can be interpreted from these figures, social capital plays the most important role in the choice of migration destination.

When asked, 97.6 per cent of the families declared that they had no plans to move anywhere other than Sultanbeyli within a year. Among these, 13.7 per cent mentioned the positive attitude from neighbours and 7.2 per cent the proximity to their family as their primary reasons for staying in Sultanbeyli. In addition, 57 per cent of all families surveyed expressed that they were either "very content" or "content" with the neighbours, compared to 5 per cent who claimed to be discontent. The primary reason for contentment was being treated very well, while getting help from the neighbours also played a role in the refugees' satisfaction with the neighbourhood. Nevertheless, despite the high levels of satisfaction, most of the families expressed their willingness to go back to Syria when the war ends; 81 per cent of all the families and 75.5 per cent of those who claimed high levels of contentment had plans to return.

Finally, for the verification of the results, I obtained feedback both from scholars and practitioners who are active in the field. I had four non-directed meetings with nine practitioners who work in refugee assistance, mainly in Sultanbeyli. Before publishing, I presented the work in three different academic workshops and conferences in Istanbul, Amman and Boston, and received valuable feedback from many scholars working in the area.

Sultanbeyli: relentless sanctuary for refugees?

Sultanbeyli has been an interesting field for many scholars; with the opportunities it provides to study urban dynamics in Turkey (Tuğal 2006; Pinarcioğlu and Isik 2008). Due to the unprecedented growth it experienced, from being a village in the 1980s, Sultanbeyli became a powerful district municipality in the 1990s. Its population rocketed from 3,600 in 1980, to 175,000 in 2000, and to 309,000 in 2013 (see website, online, available at: sultanbeyli.istanbul, and migration inflow into the district played a significant role in this growth. As of March 2016, around 15,000 of the 39,500 Syrian refugees in Istanbul reside in Sultanbeyli. Approximately 5 per cent of the district's population consists of refugees. Indeed, the district is not new to the migrants. Between the 1940s and the 1950s Sultanbeyli had been the migration destination for those Turks who migrated from Bulgaria, and during the 1980s and the 1990s, it was among the top residential choices for seasonal workers moving into Istanbul. Since then, it has been a home to many communities from different ethnic and cultural backgrounds.

Sultanbeyli is also known for its support for right wing Islamist political parties. Pro-Islamists have won landslide victories in Sultanbeyli since the 1980s. According to Tuğal (2006), Islamic orientation plays a particular role in the everyday lives of the people in Sultanbeyli, particularly in shaping the networking relations among different migrant groups and community building processes. Pinarcioğlu and Isik (2008) expand on this by saying that besides the community's orientation around Islam, Sultanbeyli has served as a "survival project" for the urban poor for several decades. Despite the multiple identities and ethnic origins of the different migrant groups, there has never been a major conflict between the various groups in Sultanbeyli, since everybody has the same objective: upward mobility. Hierarchical networking relations based on trust have been the main source of mobility for decades, as Pinarcioğlu and Isik (2008: 1361) argue, because they substituted the inexistence of social services provided by the state. Today, Sultanbeyli is among the top five districts where the Syrian population in Istanbul settles (Kaya and Kirac 2016), and the new influx of migrants into the district makes Sultanbeyli an interesting target for studying social capital and migration once again.

Social capital is a complex phenomenon because of its highly interactive nature. Therefore, building social capital is accompanied by many aspects involving power relations, context dependency and agency. When analysing refugee women's capability to form social capital, it is important to take into account both micro- and macro-structures operating simultaneously and to acknowledge both the rigidity and the fluidity of the power relations in order to be able to see: (1) how and what migration does to women, and (2) what women can obtain from the process of migration. In their journey, besides facing many challenges, refugee women also develop resilience that both emanates from and develops into social capital.

Women instrumentalise different types of social capital at different parts of the journey. Putnam's original formulation (2001) regarding the different types of social capital—bonding, bridging and linking—works well for analysing social capital in refugees' capability formation, although Putnam's definition of social capital is highly contested by many scholars (Portes 2000). While refugees' relationships with co-nationals classifies as bonding, their interactions with the host community can be understood as bridging ties, and the connections between the refugee population and institutional structures can be considered as linking social capital. Likewise, Ager and Strang (2008) argue that such differentiation between the types of social capital matters, because each type is measured to have different levels of impact on "the quality of life" that refugees enjoy.

Bonding social capital plays an important role in deciding where to settle. Thus, it is assumed that the bonds they are accustomed to would provide women with a certain level of social support when fighting marginalisation and social exclusion in their destination country. Similarly, bridging social capital across different groups may improve women's sense of belonging by showing them common challenges that women from different groups experience. Finally, through linking they obtain access to the decision-makers in the new context that might even help them to overcome the structural injustices (Vissandjee *et al.* 2009: 192).

Refugee women in Sultanbeyli possess different types of social capital according to the different power positions they hold. Bonding social capital is among their primary resources that allow them to get by in the early days of arrival. When asked why they had come to Sultanbeyli, all the women, except two, had the same answer: they chose Sultanbeyli because their family had already settled there before they arrived. The way families migrate in general is by sending a young male member of the family ahead prior to the family's arrival, to rent an apartment and find a job, if he can. Thus, what usually happens can be described as a snowball effect in migration. Starting from one male member of the family, the whole extended family moves into the same district in a particular city within a certain amount of time, depending on their reasons for migration. Therefore, instead of having a brand new social life in the destination country, most families re-establish what they had in their hometown. When asked about their best friends, most of the interviewees named a female family member, such as a sister, a cousin or a sister-in-law. Habir, who is a 27-year-old single woman, said her family were her best friends, she had no other friends there. She only goes out to a park next to their apartment with her brothers. Similar to Habir, Leyla, 20 years old and married, said her in-laws are very conservative and they do not let her socialise with people they do not know, so she can only socialise with her family.

Family is not only a substitute for friends, it is also the main source of information. Women think of their family members as the most reliable source of information about daily life in Sultanbeyli. The information usually flows from the first person who arrived to the last. Hence, the experiences of getting by do not really vary for women of the same family immediately after arrival. Despite the economic hardships they are dealing with, nearly all the women have a smartphone and access to the Internet on their phones. Smartphones have two major functions. Besides being the last resort for keeping in touch with family members who are still in Syria; smartphones also work as a door to information on daily matters for women in Sultanbeyli. However, women also gather information from personal connections in cyberspace. Refugee women are active on many social media platforms, such as Facebook, WhatsApp, and Line. Instead of browsing the Internet, they think that it is more reliable to ask people they know about how to do something, via WhatsApp for example.

Symbolic use of bonding social capital matters, because it reflects one's social and cultural standing in life (Lin 2002: 44). Refugees maintain their sense of community and preserve their cultural identity, while at the same time, enjoying the solidarity network that bonding social capital provides. Nevertheless, while admitting its function upon first arrival, bonding social capital falls short of ensuring equitable access to resources in the host country. Access to resources is dependent on the individual's position of hierarchy in a given social, economic or political structure. Thus, when thinking about social capital, to be able to go back and forth between the micro- and macro-frameworks, "interactions should be analysed and understood not only as relationship patterns among individual actors and nodes, but much more importantly, as resource patterns linked in interaction patterns" (Lin 2002: 38).

Actors in high-ranking hierarchical positions in any community are those who are mostly likely to benefit from bonding social capital; since the community consensus, norms and values are in general parallel to their self-interest. People who hold the decision-making positions, therefore have the tendency to bolster the sense of belonging to a community and bonding social capital, because it serves them to maintain their positioning in the society. Young refugee women, however, mostly hold lower ranks in the community in terms of access to resources because of their gender and age. Except for three of the interviewees, all the women declared that they needed permission from either their husband or their father to go out to socialise. In addition, they are not only dependent on the will of the male head of the family, but also on the will of older women, particularly their in-laws if they are married. For example, Leyla said that her in-laws are very conservative, that is why she wants to leave to go to Germany, where her sister is, and have a separate life there. Gusan also said that she cannot socialise, because her in-laws do not give her any money to go out. Crowded households play an important role in oppressing young women's agency and blocking their access to bridging and linking social capital. Both Beyan and Imen, who are married and do not yet have children, dream of having their own houses with their husbands as the first objective in their future plans. Furthermore, during most of the interviews, it was not possible to remain alone with most of the interviewees, for two main reasons: first, the physical conditions where the interview was held were not very suitable; second, other family members, who wanted to hear both the questions and the answers, generally accompanied the interviewees. In many cases, either mothers, or mothers-in-law interrupted the interviews on multiple occasions.

Lin (2002: 32) argues, that to improve their structural positioning, people who have lower standings in their community can carry out two different strategies: (1) they either seize more of the valuable resources embedded in the social structure, or (2) alter the values assigned to the resources. Opportunities and constraints exist simultaneously in a given context depending on the type of strategies the agents come up with. Nevertheless, the opportunity-constraint scheme may not be clear during ordinary situations, since the actions are seen to be taken by the community's invisible hand to ensure the well-being of every member. Instead, it becomes clear in times of crisis, particularly when the community's survival is challenged (Lin 2002: 32). Indeed, the migration context constitutes a good example of this.

Among the refugee women in Sultanbeyli, the women with higher social status in the society were most likely to yearn for their lives back in Syria. For example, Ragat, who is 38 years old and has seven children, said her living conditions were much better in Syria. "I used to go anywhere I wanted during the day in Syria, here I am trapped in the house". She added that her sons want to go further, to Germany, but she is very against the idea. "I am sick of moving now", she said. She would prefer to go back to Syria despite the war, but now because she has to stay, she wants to stay in Turkey, because Turkey is closer to Syria both in terms of physical distance and cultural terms, so that her chances of returning when the war ends will not be ruined.

Of the 22 women who were interviewed, six stated that they would like to volunteer, but their families do not let them. They indicated a willingness to help the community as their primary reason for wanting to volunteer, but in addition, they admitted that they thought of volunteer work as an opportunity to socialise. In comparison, three women who were volunteering at the community centre said that they had to persuade their families before they started to work. Gofran, who is 23 and a volunteer at the Red Crescent, said her family does not like her spending her time at the centre every day, and that they think she is wasting her time there. "But in the end, it is my decision", she added. Similarly, Barna and Zehra, two sisters who are 16 and 24 years old respectively, said their family does not allow them to work. They did not work in Syria nor would they be allowed to work in Turkey, but their family do not mind that the girls do volunteer work at Red Crescent; because the centre is very close to their home, and they trust the people who work there. Another example is Leila, who got a job at a sweatshop, despite her very conservative in-laws. She said her in laws would not let her out to socialise, but she was able to persuade them to let her take a job, since they all need money.

In a similar way to volunteering, language is another chapter in the obstacle–opportunity scheme. Most of the interviewees indicated that language was the primary barrier to their social life. Learning Turkish is significant for many reasons: besides the fact that knowing the local language can improve women's weak ties, increase their access to information and therefore to public services and work opportunities; leaving the house for the language course is an opportunity in itself. The participants of the focus group, who were all attendees of the Turkish class at Red Crescent, stated that the class environment is the only place they can relax, not think about their daily problems and laugh together. "There is no sense of happiness at home, but we feel different here". They described the community centre as a great place to make friends and one added: "We did not know each other before coming here, but now we are like a second family". Although they have no time or financial resources to meet somewhere other than the centre, they keep in touch through WhatsApp. They have a WhatsApp group where they text and share photos with each other every day.

Briefly, improving one's hierarchical positioning by shifting the values assigned to specific acts requires more agency than preserving your position. In young refugee women's cases, it usually becomes evident in the way that they persuade their families to give them permission to do the activities they would not want—or be allowed—to do in Syria, such as attending a language course or volunteering at an NGO office. The context of migration is peculiar in terms of the obstacle–opportunity scheme it provides, because the norms and the values attributed to different acts can shift when communities move. Thus, for women, migration may lead to both capability expansion, and reduction in parallel to the strategies they develop and the policies that government and NGOs employ.

Nevertheless, despite its positive impact on the development level, social capital literature is also highly criticised for its Euro-centric focus that emphasises a static conception of social relations by prioritising Western forms of social conduct (Vissandjee *et al.* 2009: 196). Many argue that the mainstream accounts of social capital put too much stress on an improbable model of human agency and therefore have biased conclusions about an actor's capability to use social capital. In this sense, without the proper consideration of structural elements that has a defining power on social relations, social capital can be a tool to bypass the inequalities and structural constraints (Cleaver 2005: 894). Therefore, before using it in a refugee context for a gendered analysis, it is important to strip the concept of its apolitical stance and acknowledge that social relations are dynamic and organically bound to historical, political and economic conditions. Indeed, they mostly exist as the "manifestations of the power relations" (Vissandjee *et al.* 2009: 196). The social network account for social capital is useful in the way it addresses the power relations in a given society. It combines the elements of both *action* and *structure* when analysing social relations (Lin 2002). While emphasising the theoretical magnitude of choices, the account acknowledges the prevailing effects of structure and relations. As Lin argues (2002: xi), "Choices are made within structural opportunities and constraints, and choices interacting with structural opportunities and constraints can also alter or create structural opportunities and constraints".

Furthermore, a focus on agency in refugee assistance is significant in terms of understanding how actors constantly re-position themselves in response to the constraints and opportunities they deal with. Nevertheless, while acknowledging the refugee women's capability to transform their agency, it is crucial to take into account how much "room for manoeuvre" they have within the obstacle–opportunity structure described in the previous section. People with lower hierarchical standings are exposed to the negative sides of the vulnerability context more often. Thus, their "potential capacities are constantly, routinely and, indeed, systematically frustrated by the workings of inequitable social and economic structures and the institutions through which social norms and values are challenged" (Cleaver 2005: 895). In many cases, compared to the opportunities, the obstacles are so endemic in the social, economic and political structures that even when they take an action, young refugee women may be in a position to reproduce their uneven positions. Therefore, besides providing the preliminary means like language courses and job opportunities from the capability perspective, refugee assistance must supply refugees with an enabling environment where they can expand their agencies—meaning their ability to choose different ways of living. Instead of focusing on the welfarist treatments, using the capability approach in refugee assistance would aim to equip refugees with the capacity to control their own environments (Landau and Duponchel 2011: 3).

In Turkey, under the Law on Foreigners and International Protection (2013), the Regulation on Temporary Protection (2014) states that all refugees in Turkey have the right to public education and health services for free (UNHCR 2015). In Sultanbeyli particularly, the local government provides free and affordable housing for people with disabilities, unaccompanied children and widows (Sultanbeyli City Council 2015). In addition, three different community centres operate six days a week, providing psychosocial support, language courses, occupational training and many social activities that refugees can participate in. While acknowledging the vitality of the services provided, it is hard to assess if refugees can enjoy access to them in practice.

Young refugee women, as part of the urban poor, deal with many obstacles that prevent their access to public services. As well as the cultural restrictions they deal with, they suffer greatly from a lack of financial resources. The women in the focus group, who were all attendees of the Turkish language course at Kizilay, said that they walk for 20 minutes on average to come to the centre. It is not hard to walk a long way in summer, but they do not know what to do when winter hits. They cannot rely on public transportation either, because it is not free, and their budgets are too fragile to cover the expense. An excessive amount of housework is another burden on women's shoulders. Young women in particular are responsible for the crowded household's daily needs. A practitioner from the Blue Crescent Association explained that despite the wide variety of services they provide, women's attendance at the centre is very limited.

What refugee women experience is very similar to the conditions of the urban poor, but in a foreign environment. The state of permanent deprivation and poverty that young refugee women live in, undermines their agency both physically and cognitively. Most of the women interviewed stated that they did not have any future plans for themselves. Mulfide, 35 years old, said that she had no other plans than keeping her children's stomachs full. Many women focus on getting by day by day, instead of planning their future in Sultanbeyli. In a similar way to Mulfide, 27-year-old Ola said that she does not have any plans for herself, but that her husband wants to open a business in Turkey. When asked, these women generally had the tendency to talk about either plans for their children, or their husbands' opinions about the future.

Moreover, participants of the focus group expressed that the idea of getting a job is a challenge for them, because they have never worked before, and they never thought they would have to. Gusan, 24, said that she was working as a cleaner at an office in Istanbul, but then she felt sick, and left the job. She did not want to go back to work, even though her in-laws did not give her any money. Contrarily, eight of the women interviewed had a very precise picture of their career plans in their minds. Some examples are: Nubug, who is 27, who wants to get an MA degree in social sciences. Leila, 20, used to work as a caretaker in Syria, but she found a job at a sweatshop in Istanbul, and she worked there until she got pregnant. She knows that her in-laws will object, but she wants to get her job back after she gives birth. Cemile, 26, is a nurse at a health centre in Sultanbeyli, and she believes that she will be more successful in her job as she advances in her career. Betul, 26, is a widow with two children. She is staying at the guesthouse run by the local government. She used to work as an unskilled worker at a pharmaceutical plant in Syria and she thinks she can get a job in Istanbul as soon as she learns Turkish. In fact, while some women consider employment as an opportunity, for others it can be an obstacle.

Despite the similarity of the experiences they have in Sultanbeyli, each and every refugee woman values different things in their lives, as their future plans are immensely different from each other. The impoverished conditions may put them in such a position that they feel frustrated to make choices about their life, but that does not mean that they become incapable of exercising their agency. According to Landau and Duponchel (2011: 2) "the primary determinants of effective protection have considerably less to do with direct assistance than individual's choices and positions in social and institutional networks". In line with this view, instead of the mere provision of welfare services that regards the subjects as receivers, the capability approach calls for structural adjustments that would enable young refugee women to control their own environments and make effective choices about what they value in life. Only then would women's endeavours and abilities allow them to achieve their objectives. Therefore, legal protection and primary services can only be the first step towards ensuring their de facto integration in the long term.

As stated before, agency is not a concept that exists inside a theoretical bubble that scholars try to apply to real people. Rather, it is highly shaped by social arrangements in any given society. Thus, for gendered and contextual analysis of social capital, it is significant to focus on the embeddedness of the concept by looking into how everyday interactions have an impact on institutional arrangements to see the role of agency in the workings of social capital and access to welfare provisions. Indeed, the three major concepts—agency, migration and social capital—evaluated in this chapter do not exist independently of each other. However, the humanitarian assistance programmes for refugees generally focus on social services, and rarely on social capital, when there is a need to frame it as an indicator of development. They emphasise the vulnerability contexts, define refugees as receivers and disregard the role of agency. However, for the young refugee women to alter structural constraints that prevent them using their social capital for increasing their access to resources, there is a need for policies that would enable women to exercise their agency freedom.

Conclusion

Social capital is an important tool in the integration of refugees into their host country, besides being the preliminary determinant of the moving destination. It has a vital function in shaping information channels, patterns of inclusion and exclusion and the trust networks that refugees employ, for many reasons. The literature on forced migration refers to social capital as a substitute for the loss of financial and human capital in the destination country. However, as the findings suggest, not all refugee women have access to all types of social capital per se to improve their livelihoods. In particular, young refugee women experience many constraints in their daily lives that may prevent their access to social capital. Added to the psychological trauma that comes with their journey from Syria to Turkey in war conditions, young refugee women in Sultanbeyli generally live in crowded households and deal with an immense number of chores, take care of all the children and the adults in their households, experience financial hardships and cultural restrictions. The findings suggest that the capability to utilise social capital is very much dependent on the level of agency freedom that young refugee women enjoy. Although, social and psychosocial support services, language courses and volunteering opportunities improve their lives perceptibly, refugee women's access to even most basic services is in correlation with the agency freedom they enjoy in the first place.

Before concluding, it is important to mention that this research has its theoretical and practical limitations. During the time I spent in the field, unfortunately I had no opportunity to make house visits and improve the randomisation of my sample. Most of the interviews were conducted either at the community centres, or at the health facility provided to refugees by the municipality. Thus, most of the women I had the chance to talk to were already involved in multiple social circles. As mentioned earlier in the chapter, carrying out fieldwork with refugee populations in urban environments is difficult for researchers for both ethical and practical reasons. However, the protracted nature of the forced migration requires greater attention to be devoted to the issue, and requires further qualitative and quantitative research.

Notes

1 Among many different schools explaining social capital, this chapter uses the network account pioneered by Granovetter (1973) and Lin (2008). For more information about social capital see the works by Putnam (2001), Coleman (1988) and Bourdieu (1986).
2 Six women were interviewed, in groups of two.
3 1,300 Turkish lire equated to approximately €390 in May 2016.
4 Both at individual and household levels.

References

Ager, A. and Strang, A. (2008). Understanding integration: a conceptual framework. *Journal of refugee studies*, 21(2), 166–191.

Bourdieu, P. (1986). The forms of capital. *Cultural theory: an anthology*, 81–93.

Cleaver, F. (2005). The inequality of social capital and the reproduction of chronic poverty. *World development*, 33(6), 893–906.

Coleman, J. S. (1988). Social capital in the creation of human capital. *American journal of sociology*, S95–S120.

Granovetter, M. S. (1973). The strength of weak ties. *American journal of sociology*, 1360–1380.

Granovetter, M. (1983). The strength of weak ties: a network theory revisited. *Sociological theory*, 1(1), 201–233.

Jacobsen, K. (2006). Refugees and asylum seekers in urban areas: a livelihoods perspective. *Journal of refugee studies*, 19(3), 273–286.

Kaya, A. Kirac, A. (2016). *Vulnerability assessment of Syrian refugees living in Istanbul*. Istanbul: Support to Life.

Krishna, A. (2001). Moving from the stock of social capital to the flow of benefits: the role of agency. *World development*, 29(6), 925–943.

Landau, L. B. and Duponchel, M. (2011). Laws, policies, or social position? Capabilities and the determinants of effective protection in four African cities. *Journal of refugee studies*, 24(1), 1–22.

Law on Foreigners and International Protection: Law No:6458. (2013). Official Gazette. Online, available at: www.mevzuat.gov.tr/MevzuatMetin/1.5.6458.pdf.

Lin, N. (2002). *Social capital: a theory of social structure and action* (vol. 19). Cambridge: Cambridge University Press.

Lin, N. (2008). A network theory of social capital. In D. Castiglion, J. W. van Deth and G. Wolleb (eds) *The handbook of social capital* (pp. 50–69). New York: Oxford University Press.

Pinarcioğlu, M. and Işik, O. (2008). Not only helpless but also hopeless: changing dynamics of urban poverty in Turkey, the case of Sultanbeyli, İstanbul. *European planning studies*, 16(10), 1353–1370.

Portes, A. (2000). The two meanings of social capital. *Sociological forum*, 15(1), 1–12.

Putnam, R. D. (2001). *Bowling alone: the collapse and revival of American community*. New York: Simon and Schuster.

Sen, A. (1992). *Inequality reexamined*. New York: Oxford University Press.

Sen, A. (1999). *Development as freedom*. New York: Anchor Books.

Sultanbeyli City Council. (2015). Survey Report.

Tuğal, C. Z. (2006). The appeal of Islamic politics: ritual and dialogue in a poor district of Turkey. *Sociological quarterly*, 47(2), 245–273.

UNHCR. (2016). Syria Regional Refugee Response. Online, available at: https://data. unhcr.org/syrianrefugees/settlement.php?id=59&country=224&region=38.

UNHCR. (2017). Urban Refugees. Online, available at: www.unhcr.org/urban-refugees. html.

Vissandjee, B., Apale, A. and Wieringa, S. (2009). Exploring social capital among women in the context of migration: engendering the public policy debate. In W. Agnew (ed.) *Racialized migrant women in Canada: essay on health, violence and equity* (pp. 187–203). Canada: University of Toronto Press.

10 Scrutinising the motivation of women

Stories of resistance to the 2016 coup d'état attempt in Turkey

Pinar Uyan-Semerci and Firdevs Melis Cin

1 Introduction

On the night of 15 July 2016, Turkey experienced a failed coup attempt to overthrow the elected government. The coup was led by a small group of soldiers within the army who are argued to be linked with an Islamic transnational religious movement and sect. The attempt was halted when people took to the streets to resist against the putschists. At least 246 people died and 2,100 were injured, but the coup was averted. The coup was attempted by the Gülen movement,[1] which was established in the early 1970s by a reclusive cleric, Fethullah Gülen, who is based in the United States. Upon experiencing such a critical event in the political history of Turkey during the writing and editorial process of this book, we thought it vital that we touch upon this issue and provide an analysis of the public resistance shown by people who poured into the streets to prevent the government being overthrown. Considering that we were working on the political participation of youth from a gender perspective in Turkey at the time, in this chapter, we decided to focus on women's participation in the protests held on the night of 15 July and its aftermath.

It is important to note that this resistance was different, as it was not focused against a political authority, but to defend and support the political authority. Thus, as revealed by the news coverage, many videos and the witnesses' statements, the violence that was shown towards civilians by a group of soldiers from the Turkish army makes this case extraordinary. The civilians stood up against the tanks, bullets and bombs, and, therefore, this is worthy of scrutiny in order to understand this courage and motivation. As Pearlman (2013) states, protest as a means to other ends and protest for the inherent benefit of voicing dissent are the two major arguments that explain individual action leading to protest. However, with evidence from the 2011 uprisings in Tunisia and Egypt and the absence of an uprising in Algeria, she argues that some emotions encourage the prioritisation of dignity and increase the willingness to engage in resistance, even when it jeopardises security (2013). Pearlman also underlines the importance of analysing the narrative data with an ethnographic sensibility in order to understand the meaning of the behaviour of the actors involved (2013: 388). Within the limits of this chapter, we want to question how, according to their own statements, the women who went out into the streets on 15 July 2016 explain their motivation, when their security—their fundamental physical security—was undoubtedly under serious threat.

With this in mind, one of the photos captured from the mass rally of that night is particularly relevant, as it took the attention of the public, the media, and the political leaders and elites. It was a photo of a veiled woman (wearing a hijab) driving a truck in a protest against the soldiers, accompanied by an unveiled woman sitting next to her. Another striking image was a sole woman (Safiye Bayat), whose head was covered, standing against the group of soldiers and tanks that blocked the Boğaziçi Bridge. Safiye left her two children at home with her mother-in-law and spearheaded the bridge resistance on the night of 15 July. The video of her challenging a dozen soldiers, some of whom are in tanks and some standing, has become a symbol of the failed coup.

The observations of the rallies and the memoirs/books/articles written on the public demonstrations taking place that night and afterwards, argued that it was predominantly a religious-conservative sector of society who went out and took to the streets (Çağlıyan-İçener 2016). In contrast to the general belief that conservative women rarely take part in the public and political spectrum of life in urban space,[2] these women established their presence in the squares from the very first hour of the attempted coup, and every night for a month, to show their support and belief in the elected government. In the last 20 years, women have been active in the conservative parties, first in the Refah (Welfare) Party (Arat 1999), and then in Adalet ve Kalkınma Partisi (Justice and Development Party) (Tür and Çıtak 2010; Acar and Altunok 2013; Doğan 2016). However, this active involvement did not necessarily signify a change in gender roles or taking an active role in higher positions (Doğan 2016).

This is rather an interesting story for Turkey, as political participation and activism of youth (especially of young women) is generally low (Erdoğan 2009, 2013, 2015) and there is a political unwillingness/inertia among young people, although this has to some extent been challenged recently by mass movements such as the Gezi event in 2013, and Kurdish, LGBT and feminist organisation movements (Lüküslü 2009; Erdoğan and Semerci 2016). However, the military interventions in the political history of Turkey—respectively, in 1960, 1971, 1980 and 1997—have especially contributed to the creation of apolitical youth whose political engagement is regarded as dangerous (Neyzi 2001). This was particularly true in 1968, when the communist movements made their appearance, in parallel with the social movements in Europe and Latin America, and the right-wing parties started to use Islam as a political tool to counter the communist threat. The fight between the secular left on the one hand, and the Islamist right on the other, soon escalated into a violent confrontation. Thus, the 1970s took their place in Turkish history as a period of bloodshed and hostility. This confrontation, and the bloodshed of the 1970s, is believed to have been caused by the engagement of youth in politics, which created chaos for the entire nation (Neyzi 2001). The political instability and violence brought about the military coup on 12 September 1980. The antidemocratic control of the 1982 constitution was accountable for widespread depoliticisation across the country and shaped a negative perception of politics among young people (Enneli 2011). Accordingly, in research (Lüküslü 2005) conducted on the political participation of youth, many young educated people therefore defined the political and public space in Turkey as corrupt and ossified. On the other hand, governments in Turkey have generally been repressive, aiming to create a political culture of passivity and a citizenry that is obedient and politically docile. For example, in the 1970s many activists were exposed to brutal police violence in general (Neyzi 2001). Regarding the political capabilities of young women, we could argue that repression against them may be more violent because they not only challenge the dominant political ideology, but also challenge the broader gender norms that place women's role in the home. One striking example that highlights this was when a 19-year-old pregnant university student was beaten and kicked by the police during a peaceful protest in 2010, and the violence of her ordeal led to her losing her baby (Erdoğan and Semerci 2016).

Despite examples and cases that show that the youth were subject to violent forms of suppression in the protests, regardless of their ideology (Milliyet 1998; Çağlayan 2007), many young people's political activism, particularly that of young women, remains restricted. To a large extent, this is due to structural and institutional challenges, but also because of familial, care work and economic restraints. Often, where women are concerned, almost all societies in the world show little interest in providing them with a minimum level of human functioning, including political functioning (Nussbaum 2000). Particularly in Turkey, the gender issues of domestic violence, poverty, crimes against women and the lack of schooling for girls often dominate over the problem issues of the political and civic participation of women (Şener 2014). The political, public and civic participation of disadvantaged, less-educated or lower-class women are often ignored and pushed to the margins of the agenda. Yet, a small amount of research on these women within Turkey (Alemdaroğlu 2015; Çelik and Lüküslü 2012) argue that for socio-economically disadvantaged, conservative and less-educated women, the impediments of a lack of physical mobility or failure of political participation are attributed to family/social culture, patriarchy and gender roles that force them to be primary care givers, domestic workers and biological producers of children. Therefore, we can consider the participation of young conservative women on the night of the coup attempt, in the following demonstrations and rallies, their physical visibility and mobility in squares, and their occupation of the streets every night for a month, as a case that requires scrutiny.

Moreover, as civil society in Turkey aspires to expand by widening the political space it occupies, a certain group of women, being care-providers and having limited capability sets, remain invisible as passive agents and onlookers. It is important to look into the experiences of these young and publicly invisible women, as research on youth studies in Turkey (Özerkmen and Kasapoğlu 2011; Konda 2014; Şener 2014) tends to focus on educated young people, university students for example, who have the necessary means to initiate a change and be social actors. However, more conservative or/and less-educated young women are not as extensively studied under the category of youth, and they form a disadvantaged group as they are trapped within a limited space and have restricted access to the public, and thus the political, sphere. This entrapment is mainly driven by the unpaid care and domestic labour women are compelled to undertake, or by the rise of neo-conservatism in Turkey, which further exacerbates their passive roles by ascribing greater value to the private sphere, focusing on traditional values foremost, and defining the familial sphere as the natural locus of women (Acar and Altunok 2013). This also determines who can participate in political life and social life, and to what extent.

Departing from this point of view, our aim in this chapter is to scrutinise women's political involvement on 15 July, and to reflect upon the stories of women who participated in 'democracy rallies and demonstrations' on that particular night, risking their lives, and to explore the factors that motivated women to go out into the streets and what conversion factors played a part in their enactment of political capabilities. Accordingly, in the next section, we briefly focus on the method and, in the third section, we analyse published interviews and memoirs of the women involved in order to understand how they were motivated to go out and navigate the traditional gendered structures in their decision to become politically involved. Lastly, in the conclusion, we question whether these women had a genuine political capability set and agency to perform, whether any other options were viable to them, and the remit of their political action.

2 Methods

Our starting point is to discuss and formulate the stories of women on their political participation. We built our analysis on the 14 publicly available interviews conducted with women who participated in democracy rallies. These interviews were conducted by journalists from the Turkish Radio and Television Corporation, also known as TRT (the national public broadcaster of Turkey). In addition, we used 12 published interviews, memoirs and stories of women who participated in the rallies and were open to the public. Thus, the data were systemically collected from open media resources (internet,[3] newspaper and TV documentaries) between 15 July 2016 and 15 January 2017, over the span of six months. The interviews in the study are not claimed to be representative. Yet, our aim in examining them is necessary to understand the dynamics of participation, that is to say, what framed women's participation in such a critical and historical event or how they made the choice to take part in these rallies, especially on that very night, despite the violence. We question how and why these women went out into the streets and how they narrated their experiences. We do not aspire to find concrete answers or to provide full explanations of the questions raised here with the limited narrations we have examined, but rather we aim to understand the motivation behind this action and to provide a starting point for further research. Based on this point of departure, our analysis and reformulation of their narrations from the home to the streets are presented under the two questions of 'how' and 'why'. Women did participate, but the whole event was violent masculinist in character (Gökarıksel 2017).

3 Home to streets: how?

At 10 p.m. on Friday 15 July 2016, the Boğaziçi and Fatih Sultan Mehmet Bridges, the two bridges linking Asia and Europe in Istanbul, were blocked by soldiers. At this same time, F16s began making low passes over Ankara. At 11 p.m., Prime Minister Binali Yildirim said an attempted coup was underway to overthrow the government, and called for calm. Meanwhile, a small group within the Turkish military said, in an emailed statement reported on TV channels, that it had taken over the country to protect democratic order. The coup plotters opened fire on citizens resisting the attempt in different parts of the country, and planes started bombing the Turkish Parliament. At midnight, President Erdoğan addressed the nation in a live video broadcast from a mobile phone and called for people to take to the streets:

> This [referring to coup attempt] was done from outside the chain of command. The lower officers had rebelled against senior officers. Those who are responsible, we will give them the necessary punishment. I call on our people to convene at public squares and airports. I never believed in a power higher than the power of the people.... Let them do what they will in the public squares and airports.

Upon receiving this call from President Erdoğan, citizens began flooding the streets in response and the coup plotters continued opening fire on civilians. Mosques began reciting the funeral prayer Salah, calling citizens to oppose the coup. Thus, one of the longest nights in Turkey's history began.

In memoirs and interviews, an overwhelming majority of women stated that they phoned their family members, relatives or close friends to find out how they were and to talk about what to do. This is important, as women went out in company, either with a husband, child, brother, friend or a neighbour, except Safiye who stood alone against the tanks. Many also stated that they performed an ablution and prayed. Depending on their situation on that particular night, either with or without their families (father/husband/brother/sister and, rarely, mother) and friends, they left their homes to take to the streets, which were literally full of life threatening risks. Those women who were mothers with small children left their children at home with grandmothers. As one mother stated, my son could live without a mother but could not live without a homeland. So, many women took their sons and daughters with them to the streets if they were old enough.

When they went out, the performance of the experience itself created a new reality. Similarly to other protest movements, 'being there', witnessing and experiencing differing degrees of violence in different localities, the solidarity and the collective resistance made them stay. The group dynamic flourished and the call for resistance began among the people. They even called to others by shouting while they walked, they also phoned friends and family members to share the experience, the historical moment. This collective action and the group dynamic, that your neighbour, your colleague, your relative was there and was calling for you, had an effect on the decision to go out. This group action/conformity with the group is an important element to study further, in order to understand how people go out into the streets and, furthermore, how they continue to stay there when their security, their life, is at serious risk.

4 Why? *Reis*'s call

Although there were a few women who went out before President Erdoğan made the call, in most cases women highlighted that their main motivation to go out to gather in the streets, squares or airports on the night of 15 July was the call from Erdoğan—made via FaceTime and broadcast on the television—for people to take to the streets against the military coup. Jale Usta (45), who was injured by bullet on that night, states:

> On that night, I said that men will go out to stop the putschists and we, as women, will stay at home and pray, but then I saw the call from *Reis*[4] on TV. He was calling us to the streets to resist to the death.

Şerife Boz (50) became the symbol of anti-coup protests when she jumped inside her truck, wearing a burka, and drove as many people as possible to the squares across Istanbul to protest against the violent putsch. She said she would 'go anywhere with her truck if only President Recep Tayyip Erdoğan [president] and Mr. Binali Yildirim [prime-minister] asked her'. Likewise, Mümine Bingöl explained her presence in the squares as follows: 'We, as women, are on the streets because the commander in-chief [referring to Erdoğan] ordered us to be here and we will continue our democracy watch [rally] until he tells us to go home!'. 'I am a university student' says Süheyla S. and adds:

> We saw that there was an attempted coup on TV and then the we heard the Salah from the mosques. The Imam was making an announcement and telling everyone to go out. We were silent and confused as to what to do. Then we heard that the commander-in-chief [referring to President Erdoğan] was calling us into the streets to express our national will, and we went out.

While Ayşenur C., who is in her late twenties, says

> I have parents who experienced the coup d'état in the 1980s and I spent my childhood listening to their stories.… As I was watching what was happening on TV, our president's call to the streets on TV, and his firm and calm stance strengthened us. The persistent stance and determination of the people brought a victory to this country.

All these stories and quotes, and many others that we have not included above, were very powerful in the sense that women, no matter what their age, did not hesitate to respond to the call for help of a leader figure, even when this involved standing up against other male figures, such as father and husband at home. In the women's stories, there was a transference of a leader figure to a father figure who holds more power and authority than the other male members within the house. This is because Erdoğan addresses the Turkish infatuation with his charisma and, rarely indecisive, passionate attitudes. Thus he becomes the ultimate alpha male; the father figure capturing souls and spirits. Driven by this father figure, we could argue that these women's political capability of establishing their visibility in the public sphere and participating in protests was both spontaneous and extraordinary. They displayed a direct and unconventional political participation with the consent of the 'idealised father figure'. The father figure displayed by Erdoğan had such a powerful standing in women's lives and narratives that it stood for 'a father of a father', meaning he was even more influential than, and held more power than, the 'father' in their natal families—who did not let them go out—that many women, particularly young women, challenged. It was only after Erdoğan's call that young women, as daughters, were allowed to go out by their fathers. 'For the first time, I did not listen to my father, he did not let me go out, but I went out in the middle of the night because our leader called us' (Ayşegül Tolon).

> I was asking my father to let me go out that night, I was trying to persuade him. And the long-expected call came from our commander-in-chief (referring to Erdoğan), thank god he urged us to go out, and we got into the car to go to the city centre.
>
> (Melike G.)

Furthermore, as Süheyla S. states, some fathers instructed their daughters to go out. Süheyla's father asked his daughter 'If she was not going out that particular night, when would she? If she would not die that particular night, when would she?'. Young single women associated Erdoğan with the father figure, whereas for the young married women, the call from the president was a legitimate way to challenge the male figures (husbands, sons) at home as he was an 'alpha male' whose authority cannot be questioned by other males within the family. For instance, Derya Ovacıklı, who was injured on the night of 15 July, recounts her son telling her not to go out: 'I am going out no matter what, you can join me later on', she replied to her son, leaving him alone at home.

Şerife Boz, who did not even have a driving licence, upon hearing the call, took her husband's truck and drove to Taksim square, despite his objections:

> Upon the call of Erdoğan, first my husband left for the streets and he told me to stay at home, but soon after he left, I did not listen to him and took the truck and drove to the square to protect our country and to help Erdoğan.

Another woman, Tuğba Kaplan C., says:

> When we first heard what was happening, we went to a friend's house in Karagümrük and there my spouse and my friend's spouses told us that they would go out and that we should stay at home. We were not so sure about what was happening and *Reis* had not yet called for us to go out, but I was worried about him … I even wondered if he was alive … my friend and I thought that our spouses cannot expect us to stay at home…. A friend of ours came to pick us up and we went to the headquarters of the AKP in Istanbul.

In the same way, Hacer Bulut, one of the women who participated in the democracy rallies, said she refused to 'go back home until President Erdoğan tells us to do so'.

It is important to decipher this participation, and how women framed their experiences, in order to understand their unconventional actions. This is because many women across the nations, including Turkey, have a nominal right of political participation and they do not truly have this right in the sense of it being a capability for the reasons of gender and moral codes that dictate for them to stay away from public space, or fear of violence should they leave the home. Yet, these women's narratives and stories challenge the arguments of studies on the political participation of conservative women, which stress that there are negative relationships between the strength of traditional gender norms in society and the level of women's political representation (Paxton and Kunovich 2003; Inglehart and Norris 2003), or their participation in civic organisations (Inglehart and Norris 2003), as they uphold traditional gender norms hindering women's political participation. The accounts above, in particular, show that by responding to the call from Erdoğan, these women dismantled the traditional gender norms, which prescribe the primary roles of women as mothers, daughters and wives in the home and, therefore, hinder women's political participation. Some, at the same time, challenged family hierarchy where men exert power and social monitoring. This shows how Erdoğan's call to oppose the putschists opened a space to deconstruct male authority in the family, as legitimate consent coming from him was a true opportunity for them to enact their right to go out into the streets. In this sense, they also betrayed their commitment to traditional roles at home as mothers and wives and contradicted their feminine duties.

Women's agency was not only triggered by a legitimate consent and a call but also by an appropriate political social climate that would ease the process of converting their capability to protest against the putschists, and their show of support for the government into a functioning. Such an atmosphere is not a usual scenario in Turkey, as protests, assemblies and the right to speak up or express oneself often face police violence and the suppression of the political capabilities of citizens, despite the fact that the right to assembly is guaranteed under the constitution,[5] even for non-political and rights-based matters, such as women's rights. These women apparently had an other-regarding motivation, driven not by their self-interests, but also engaged in social change by being a part of a bigger movement to prevent the elected government from being overthrown. In so doing, some women sacrificed their achievement of well-being and went out knowing that they could be injured. For instance, Adeviye Gül, who is only 14 and was shot on that night, stated that she was determined to go out, no matter what the consequences were:

> Soldiers were making a coup d'état and I thought we should prevent this. Upon the call from the president, I told my family that we should go out, no matter what.… When were out, we saw that soldiers were shooting people with the aim of killing and hurting them.… We were not scared and we kept on walking towards the soldiers … I got shot … I would do it [go out] again … I cannot go out now to the rallies as I am injured, but when I get better, I will go out again.

From these women's stories, we can deduce that they devoted themselves to the call and cause coming from a leader or a father; looking beyond their own welfare, they went into the streets knowing that there would be risks. Thus, the information they first had may not have included its severity, that they could be injured, shot or killed. The brutality they witnessed, of the soldiers towards the civilians, were reflected by some as being beyond their imagination. For some, being on the street and witnessing and experiencing that night changed their attitude and 'fear turned to anger and excitement'. They were afraid, but also excited to experience something that they could die for. As Rümeysa said: 'In contrast to all the men who stayed at their homes, I am out'. This is also a point that is raised by Pearlman (2013: 395). She stated that, in the Tunisian case, the killings created an emotional climate of righteous anger, beyond fear. Similarly to Pearlman's observations, the narratives highlight feelings of fear that, through the experience itself, turned to anger and excitement.

Although we can say that these women had other-regarding agency in showing a political protest, to what extent we can name this as 'agency freedom' for all is a question. Agency freedom stands for an effective power that a person has, and these women's agency was ultimately and primarily triggered by 'a father' who asked them to show their support in alliance with the government. The question one needs to ask here is whether women would still opt for such a freedom by their own will, or would they even be aware of such an opportunity or alternative if there were not such a call.

By and large, it is important to stress that their political activism was mainly triggered by the call from Erdoğan, who urged them to not give up on the resistance for the country, land and flag and the women's presence in the squares pledged support for him. Erdoğan was a victim of, and suffered under, the suppression of political Islam in the 1990s, and his rise to power involved a promise that he would be the voice of the oppressed. For many people, this gave justification to his call for help. However, it is still unforeseen whether these women going out into the streets will be triggered to challenge their gender role. They continued to go out every night until the president said, 'It is over'. Therefore, we cannot speculate if these women would have gone out without the call. The debate around the call leads us to a further question: 'Was it just a call that took these women to the streets?'

5 Why? Islam, homeland and martyrdom

One of the most common themes that we heard when we listened to how women narrated their experiences of 15 July is martyrdom, combined with language describing dying for the homeland. In their own narratives, they state that Allah grants the reward of martyrdom to those who die for the Cause of Allah. A martyr sacrifices her life as it is of less value than striving for the Cause of Allah, and most of the women's narratives are full of references to this sacrifice: 'May my God honour me with martyrdom'; 'If we had died, we would have been martyrs *insallah*'; 'Bullets did not make it'; 'We would have been martyrs for the homeland'; ''Rather than my homeland, let it happen to me'; Love of homeland is *iman*'. Being driven by prayer calls from mosques calling people to the streets and women's reference to Islam in explaining patriotism, seeking consolation and power in faith and prayer, indicate that one of the most important motivations was Islam. It would be wrong to argue that the women participating in the protests were only conservatives, as people of different race, status, faith or social and economic class were also an important ally of the movement against the failed coup. However, Konda's research (2016) shows us that 84 per cent of the participants were AKP voters, whereas 48 per cent of them defined themselves as traditionally conservative and 25 per cent were devout. This was also evident in women's narratives, especially those women who became symbols of 15 July. For example, Jale Sita defined Erdoğan's call as 'a jihad'; Safiye Bayat (34) argued that Allah gave the people courage and power to stand against the putschists. Duygu Çetinkaya (30) states 'We are a Muslim society, the crescent on our flag represents Islam and the star stands for the five pillars of Islam, so we have to fight for this country'.

Other researches (SETA 2016; Miş 2016) likewise echoed in their findings that, in addition to calls from a conservative leader whose political view has its roots in Islam, the Salahs, coming from the mosques, were equally important in encouraging people to go out (SETA 2016; Miş 2016). By focusing particularly on women's accounts in this research, we could see that their identity as Muslims came before their identity as women, and they had group conformity in the sense that their individual capabilities of political participation depended on a collective action that occurred through the identity of conservatism, a sense of belonging to AKP, and having a genuine Islamic faith. Accordingly, conservatism as a group identity was instrumentally valuable in enhancing women's participation, which was not an available option in their everyday life, and encouraging them to be a part of a historical moment and event. This collective of conservative identity was indeed a strong and a dominant individual-social structure forming shared and collective intentions with respect to social groups.

It was, therefore, a stronger identity than being a woman or any ethnic identity. This also touches on the argument that a conservative vision is not always helpful in making processes dedicated to a substantive representation of women and only aims to better women's lives, freedoms and capabilities in traditional terms, not in feminist terms (Celis and Childs 2014), and uses them as symbolic pawns for nationalism or interests of the nation that cannot be contested, as in the case of the early Republican Period of Turkey (nation-building era).

The emphasis of being morally right and superior is more dominant in the narratives of the women than those of the men who were on the streets on the night of 15 July. Safiye stated: 'As Prophet Ali stated: *Jihad* is to stand up against the cruel and state that they have done wrong'. This is also something that needs to be further researched, as in the publicly available statements from women, interestingly, this sacrifice and/or martyrdom has been a very dominant discourse. Although we do not have detailed information as to what extent these women had been active in the AKP's women's branches, it is important to note that, in Doğan's research, she argues women who are active in women's branches of the AKP express altruism, rather than self-interest, and emphasise voluntariness (2016: 225–238). This discourse, that we ourselves are not important, but the homeland, the party, *Reis*, Erdoğan are important, is note-worthy and deserving of further research.

6 Conclusion

By analysing the publicly available narratives of the women who went out into the streets on the night of 15 July 2016, we tried to reflect how they did so and what their main motivations were. This is a limited attempt, as we need to know more about each individual case and related past experience. Nevertheless, the narratives highlight important issues that need to be further researched. Hence, whether young or not, the existence of women who stood up against the attempted coup is crucial in a context in which the capability to be on the streets at night, even without the tanks and the soldiers, is almost always very limited for the women. Therefore, despite the low political participation of young women in Turkey, we could see that being young or old did not have a massive impact on this particular participation, yet the nuanced differences can be tracked in the process of how they handled the patriarchal relationships at home upon hearing the call, as argued above.

As we emphasised, this stand was neither against the political authority nor a challenge to the existing dominant values and moral frameworks. As stated, standing up against the attempted coup was not only legitimate but also an action that was called for by *Reis*; approved by the family, neighbourhood and society. Although what *Reis*, the leader, stands for, is an important element to study, within the limits of this chapter, we have only focused on the way the women dealt with the call. Thus, the representation of 'we—the people', by one person, the charismatic leader is an important discussion point with respect to under-standing the relations between democracy and populism (Canovan 1999; Abts and Rummens 2007; Kriesi 2014), which, therefore, needs to be further studied through this lens. However, the important question is whether the experience itself and the subsequent rallies that followed may have led to an expansion of capabilities, individual and collective, for the women participating.

People in protests, demonstrations, do not only assemble to challenge a particular form of injustice, to protest or to voice their demands, but also take a relative position that could align with their collective groups (Jost and Kay 2010) and imply collective action, as they get together to make a demand about what they want, value and desire. The collective action that is formed via 'collective capabilities' plays an important role in expanding human freedom (Ibrahim 2006; Anand 2007; Murphy 2014). Collective capabilities in this respect can be defined as a freedom that is only exercised and owned by individual agents who work or stand together in association with others or within social groups (Ibrahim 2006). Although both Nussbaum and Sen (1993) argue the importance of individual political self-determination or having control over one's political environment, it should be noted that this individual capability is usually realised within a freely self-determining political community, as being able to exercise this individual capability is often largely under the control of some external authority (Murphy 2014).

Women's individual political capabilities are frequently drastically restricted around the world (Nussbaum 2000), but it may be possible to exercise this within a collective action. It is true that women and young people have a measure of individual political capability in the form of civil and political rights granted within an institutionalised system whose guiding principles are determined by others, but their freedom to be a part of an unconventional form of political participation is largely possible via collective identity. Thus, it became plausible that these women can indeed be a part of a greater struggle and social movement. However, in reading and interpreting this challenge, one may need to question what the limits of this challenge are, and whether there can be a genuine option for these women.

This is also a question that is valid for all the participants, leading us to the debates around populism, nationalism, conservatism and democracy, as the will of the people seems to be represented in the personality of the leader whose call to stand against the attempted coup legitimises 'being on the street' that night and the following nights. On the night of 15 July 2016, people stood up against the tanks, the bombs and the bullets and in the following rallies, they were in the squares. Whether this implies expanding their individual and collective political capabilities in the long run, is a subject requiring further research and observation.

Notes

1 The Gülen Movement is an Islamic transnational religious and social one with a focus on Islamic values. The activities of the movement involve a diverse range, from establishing school charters across the world to setting up media organisations, as well as

running charity and humanitarian aid organisations and professional associations, all of which serve to promote the cult's core values, protect its interests and influence Turkish politics from the outside. The Gülen movement is recognised as a terrorist organisation in Turkey under the name of Gülenist Terror Organisation or Parallel State Organisation. The movement is regarded to be running a 'parallel state' inside Turkey's state institutions by infiltrating their members to critical state institutions as civil servants, military and police officers to take control over the state and thus posing a threat to the government. The 15 July coup is read as a continuation of the movement's aim to take over the country and a threat to the democracy of the country (Mert 2016).

2 For some conservative women, this event was their first political participation. For instance, Zeynep, a young woman who participated in rallies with her mother shared a photo of her mother, who wears a black covering, and wrote: 'This is the first time my mother is appreciated for her appearance'. Here, Zeynep emphasizes that her mother was excluded for her dress code and this event was a particular one welcoming her presence in hijab.

3 The internet source data were mainly drawn from the following, online, available at: www.hakimiyetmilletindir.com. A digital archive of 15 July, is also used, online, available at: www.yenisafak.com/15temmuz/.

4 The word '*reis*' means the 'chief' and it has become a common title and frequent use for Erdoğan among his supporters to express his power and respectable status.

5 The thirty-fourth Article of the Turkish Constitution states that 'everyone has the right to hold unarmed and peaceful meetings and demonstration marches without prior permission'.

References

Abts, K. and Rummens, S. (2007). Populism versus democracy. *Political studies*, 55(2), 405–424.

Acar, F. and Altunok, G. (2013). The 'politics of intimate' at the intersection of neo-liberalism and neo-conservatism in contemporary Turkey. *Women's studies international forum*, 41, 14–23.

Alemdaroğlu, A. (2015). Escaping femininity, claiming respectability: culture, class and young women in Turkey. *Women's studies international forum*, 53, 53–62.

Anand, P. B. (2007). Capability, sustainability and collective action: an examination of a river water dispute. *Journal of human development*, 8(1), 109–132.

Arat, Y. (1999). Refah Partisi Hanım Komisyonları, *Bilanço 1923–1998*. (Cilt II) İstanbul: Tarih Vakfı Yayınları.

Çağlayan, H. (2007). *Analar, Yoldaşlar, Tanrıçalar: Kürt Hareketinde Kadınlar ve Kadın Kimliğinin Oluşumu*. İstanbul: İletişim.

Çağlıyan-İçener, Z. (2016). July 15: The siege of democracy in Turkey and the people's unprecedented resistance. *Bilig*, 79, 107–128.

Canovan, M. (1999). Trust the people! Populism and the two faces of democracy. *Political studies*, 47(1), 2–16.

Celis, K. and Childs, S. (2014). Introduction: the 'puzzle' of gender, conservatism and representation. In: *Gender, conservatism and political representation*, pp. 1–4. Colchester: ECPR Press.

Dalton, R. J. (2008). Citizenship norms and the expansion of political participation. *Political studies*, 56(1), 76–98.

Doğan, S. (2016). *Mahalledeki AKP: Parti İşleyişi, Taban Mobilizasyonu ve Siyasal Yabancılaşma*. İstanbul: İletişim.

Enneli, P. (2011). The Turkish young people as active citizens: equal participation or social exclusion? In: *Social peace and ideal citizenship for Turkey*, pp. 257–280. Lanham, MD: Lexington Books.

Erdoğan, E. (2009). Olasılıksızlığın kuramını aramak: Türk gençliği ve siyasal partilere katılım. In: *Gençler Tartışıyor: Siyasete Katılım, Sorunlar ve Çözüm Önerileri*, pp. 56–83. İstanbul: Türkiye Sosyal Ekonomik Siyasal Araştırmalar Vakfı.

Erdoğan, E. (2013). *Türkiye'de Gençlerin Siyasal ve Sivil Katılımı.* İstanbul: Sage.

Erdoğan, E. (2015). Türkiye'de gençlerin siyasal katılımı: Karşılaştırmalı bir perspektif. In: *Yeni Zamanlarda Genç Yurttaşların Katılımı Konferansı Bildiriler Kitabı*, pp. 37–52. Istanbul: İstanbul Bilgi Üniversitesi Yayınları Online, available at: http://stk.bilgi.edu.tr/media/uploads/2015/02/01/sebekekonferans.pdf.

Erdoğan, E. and Semerci, P. U. (2016). Understanding young citizens' political participation in Turkey: does 'being young' matter? *Southeast European and Black Sea studies*, 17(1), 57–75. Doi: 10.1080/14683857.2016.1235000.

Gökarıksel, B. (2017). Making gender dynamics visible in the 2016 coup attempt in Turkey. *Journal of Middle East women's studies*, 13(1), 173–174.

Ibrahim, S. (2006). From individual to collective capabilities: the capability approach as a conceptual framework for self-help. *Journal of human development*, 7(3), 397–416.

Inglehart, R. and Norris, P. (2003). *Rising tide: gender equality and cultural change around the world.* Cambridge: Cambridge University Press.

Jost, J. T. and Kay, A. C. (2010). Social justice: history, theory and research. In: *Handbook of social psychology*, pp. 1122–1166. Hoboken, NJ: Wiley.

Konda (2014). Türkiye'de gençlerin katılımı. Istanbul: Bilgi üniversitesi yayınları.

Konda (2016). Demokrasi nöbeti araştırması: meydanların profili. *Konda Araştırma ve Danışmanlık.* Online, available at: www.konda.com.tr/demokrasinobeti/

Kriesi, H. (2014). The populist challenge. *West European Politics*, 37(2), 361–378.

Lüküşlü, D. (2005). Constructors and constructed: youth as a political actor in modernising Turkey. In: Forbig, J. (ed.) *Revising youth political participation: challenges for research and democratic practice in Europe*, pp. 29–36. Strasbourg: Council of Europe Publishing.

Lüküşlü, D. (2009). *Türkiye'de 'Gençlik Miti'.* İstanbul: İletişim.

Mert, A. O. (2016). *15 July coup attempt and the parallel state structure.* Ankara: Cumhurbaşkanlığı Yayınları.

Milliyet (1998). 267 eylemci gözaltında. 13 Ekim 1998.

Miş, N. (2016). Measuring social perception of the July 15 coup attempt. *Insight Turkey*, 18(3), 169–204.

Murphy, M. (2014). Self-determination as a collective capability: the case of indigenous peoples. *Journal of human development and capabilities*, 15(4), 320–334.

Neyzi, L. (2001). Object or subject? The paradox of 'youth' in Turkey. *International journal of Middle East studies*, 33(3), 411–432.

Nussbaum, M. (2000). *Women and human development: the capabilities approach.* Cambridge: Cambridge University Press.

Özerkmen, N. and Kasapoğlu, A. (2011). Gender imbalance: the case of women's political participation in Turkey. *Journal of international women's studies*, 12(4), 97–107.

Paxton, P. M. and Kunovich, S. (2003). Women's political representation: the importance of ideology. *Social forces*, 82(1), 87–113.

Pearlman, W. (2013). Emotions and the microfoundations of the Arab uprisings. *Perspectives on politics*, 11(02), 387–409.

Sen, A. (1993). Capability and well-being. In: *The quality of life*, pp. 9–30. New York: Oxford University Press.

Şener, T. (2014). Civic and political participation of women and youth in Turkey: an examination of perspectives of public authorities and NGOs. *Journal of civil society*, 10(1), 69–81.

SETA. (2016). Demokrasi Nöbetleri Toplumsal Algıda 15 Temmuz Darbe Girşimi. Istanbul: SETA.

Tür, Ö. and Çıtak, Z. (2010). AKP ve Kadın: Teşkilatlanma, Muhafazakarlık veTürban. In: İlhan Uzgel and Bülent Duru (eds) *AKP Kitabı: Bir Dönüşümün Bilançosu*. Ankara: Phoenix.

Uyan Semerci, P. (2009). 'Gençlerle Beraber Siyasal Alanın Sınırlarını Düşünmek: Günlük Yaşam, Aileler ve 'Özgür'ce Karar Almak' in Cemil Boyraz (ed.) *Gençler Tartışıyor: Siyasete Katılım, Sorunlar ve Çözüm Önerileri*, pp. 163–189. İstanbul: TÜSES.

Index

For Product Safety Concerns and Information please contact our EU
representative GPSR@taylorandfrancis.com
Taylor & Francis Verlag GmbH, Kaufingerstraße 24, 80331 München, Germany